T0385151

ALL SECURE

ALL SECURE

A SPECIAL OPERATIONS SOLDIER'S FIGHT
TO SURVIVE ON THE BATTLEFIELD
AND THE HOMEFRONT

TOM SATTERLY
AND STEVE JACKSON

CENTER
STREET

New York   Nashville

Center Street
Hachette Book Group
1290 Avenue of the Americas, New York, NY 10104
centerstreet.com
twitter.com/centerstreet

First Edition: November 2019

Center Street is a division of Hachette Book Group, Inc. The Center Street name and logo are trademarks of Hachette Book Group, Inc.

The publisher is not responsible for websites (or their content) that are not owned by the publisher.

The Hachette Speakers Bureau provides a wide range of authors for speaking events. To find out more, go to www.HachetteSpeakersBureau.com or call (866) 376-6591.

Library of Congress Cataloging-in-Publication Data has been applied for.

ISBNs: 978-1-5460-7657-5 (hardcover), 978-1-5460-7656-8 (ebook)

Printed in the United States of America

LSC-C

Printing 5, 2024

For my father, Stephen C. Satterly, who loved fiercely and provided me the tools to be the man I am today.
Save me a seat on that bench. I love and miss you.
June 25, 1943–December 17, 2018

Some of the names and details in this book have been altered for privacy and/or secrecy considerations. In the case of soldiers who served in the Unit, first names and last initials have been used; in a few cases where the soldier is deceased, his full last name was used to honor his sacrifice. Every soldier sees war through their own lenses. *All Secure* is Tom Satterly's journey and is not meant to represent the experiences or thoughts of anyone else.

ALL SECURE

October 2013
St. Louis, Missouri

THEY'D BEEN STROLLING around the Clayton financial district for a couple of hours when Jen suggested they stop for a drink at a little bar with sidewalk seating. It was one of those pleasant fall afternoons in the Midwest, wedged between the sweltering summer months and the gray misery of winter. She was in no hurry to end what had been a perfect day.

In a few hours, they'd have to get ready for Tom's last night in the city. In the morning, he was flying to Fayetteville, North Carolina, for the twentieth annual reunion of the Unit "operators" who'd been in the Battle of Mogadishu.

Wanting to understand more about Tom, Jen had watched the movie *Black Hawk Down* to learn about the battle. She still couldn't wrap her mind around what it had taken to fight for eighteen hours against such incredible odds while thousands of Somalis tried to kill him and the other trapped American soldiers.

Although curious about his role in the fight, she'd hesitated to ask him about it, unsure if the topic would be taboo or the question inappropriate. She knew only that he carried many scars, both external and internal, and she didn't want to tear them open if he wasn't ready.

However, on this nice afternoon in downtown St. Louis, Tom seemed relaxed—as much as he ever was, anyway—and that weekend they'd already shared stories that were the most personal of their budding relationship. She felt he might be open to talking about what happened twenty years earlier that first week in October of 1993 in Somalia. She sensed that it could be good for him. The right moment, she thought, might arrive while relaxing with drinks at an outside table watching the world go by.

As the hostess guided them through the restaurant to the outdoor seating area, Jen noted Tom's eyes darting around, and that he kept turning his head slightly to glance back over his shoulder. She knew that while she was thinking about what cocktail to order, he was assessing the demeanor of other customers and the staff. As she checked out the art on the walls, she could tell he was memorizing the layout of the restaurant, looking for escape routes in case one was needed.

Outside at the table, Tom sat down with his back to the building, facing the street so that he could watch for potential danger. She was sure he'd already determined what weapons were available if necessary. A fork. The butter knife. A glass or bottle to break, which could then be used to stab an assailant. Continually looking for a place to take cover from gunfire, such as a brick wall or parked car.

Tom's habit of "pulling security" on their dates didn't bother Jen. It came with the territory when going out with a retired command sergeant major from the Unit, the most elite and secretive special operations force in the US military. Thinking that visiting some rougher area of St. Louis might trigger a more aggressive mindset, Jen had chosen the gentrified Clayton district precisely because it was a "safe" enclave, largely free of crime and unsavory characters.

It wasn't so much that Tom was expecting an imminent terrorist attack on Bemison Street. Intellectually, he told her, he knew that the danger was minimal for people living in the States. However, he hadn't spent twenty years as an operator with the Special Forces Operational Detachment known as "the Unit," without developing ingrained survival habits. Most of the time he didn't even realize he was doing it until she waved a hand in front of his face and insisted that he actually make eye contact while she was talking.

Jen thought of the hypervigilance and constant threat assessment as a type of muscle memory—not unlike his heralded ability to move and shoot with uncanny accuracy, or to act calmly and deliberately no matter how chaotic the situation. These were traits instilled in him by countless hours of relentless training. Those hours had then been reinforced on thousands of actual missions he'd participated in, and usually led, most of them Close Quarters Battle, or CQB, in Iraq and other hotspots around the world. Street to street, house to house, room to room—where the hardest lessons were written in blood and not soon forgotten.

Jen understood that this constant wariness is what had kept Tom and his men alive on the danger-filled streets from Mogadishu to Baghdad and a lot of places in between. But those same qualities had also undermined the stability of his previous three marriages and, sadly, made him a stranger to his son, his family, and all too many former friends.

Some of the influences from his life as a warrior were subtle. Trained to carry out missions at night, Tom's attempts at "normal" sleep patterns were ineffective, and what sleep he did get was tormented by nightmares. In the daytime, loud noises made him duck. A car parked innocently on the side of a street might be viewed as a potential roadside bomb and avoided. Someone approaching too quickly could make him switch from a relaxed state to high alert in the blink of an eye.

In addition to Tom's mental baggage, his neck and back ached from the times he'd been blown up as well as the surgeries to patch him back together. Sometimes he just hurt in ways that were hard to explain or diagnose, but the pain was severe, and it was unrelenting.

On that pleasant afternoon in St. Louis, Tom had been out of the Unit for three years. He was making a living working for a company that contracted with the military to prepare a new generation of special ops commandos for war, as well as a more demeaning entertainment enterprise that trained civilian "commandos" to "kill zombies" with paintball guns. But he was still living with a vicious cycle of booze, pain pills, sleeping pills, and antidepressants that had been part of his life in the military, and that the Veterans Administration now handed out to him like Halloween candy to dull the physical pain—and cloud the memories of the things he'd seen and done.

Tom and Jen had met several months earlier, when the film and photography company she co-owned with her husband was hired by Tom's company to produce military training videos as well as an advertising movie trailer.

This past May, Jen had driven from St. Louis to Indiana to meet the owner of Tom's company, and to become acquainted with some of the people she'd be working with. One of them was Tom Satterly, who was described to her as a "special operations legend"—not just in the Unit, but in the competitive and ego-driven world of commandos.

Whatever she was expecting, she wasn't impressed at first sight. Tom was five-feet-ten-inches tall, and overweight, with a gut; his wide face was ruddy and bloated by alcohol and hard living. He was far from the "super soldier" she had imagined based on the little she knew about the Unit. When they met, Tom had hardly acknowledged her, just a few grunted words before leaving the meeting as soon as he could excuse himself.

It didn't take long after their work began, however, for Jen to realize her first impression of Tom had been deceiving. While he rarely said anything to her, she noticed how he commanded instant attention from everyone, including the other former operators working for him on the filming project. He didn't raise his voice or make demands; when he said something, people listened, and tasks were completed immediately. If someone was carrying on a side conversation while he was talking, a glance was enough to shut it down.

Sitting at the bar in St. Louis, Jen liked knowing that the man across from her sipping a vodka soda could handle pretty much any dangerous situation. A real-life Jason Bourne. While Jen could understand the environment and experiences that had created this unusual man, she wasn't fond of the macho posturing, especially around other special ops veterans who too often acted like a bunch of immature frat boys—particularly when drinking. There were crude remarks about women and disturbing references about the cultures in the places where they had fought. She was annoyed by the casual references to violence as the best way to deal with situations, even when those references were intended to be "funny."

Nor was Jen comfortable around Tom when he was angry. Small things, at least small to her, could trigger him: someone who messed up because they didn't follow his instructions to a tee; people who showed up late or didn't take proper care of equipment; poor service at a bar or restaurant; loud, rude people. Any of these could leave him seething. Or worse.

When angry, Tom could be frightening. The lines around his eyes and across his forehead got deeper and harder; his cobalt blue eyes darkened until they seemed black and filled with such malevolence that they reminded her of a shark's eyes. These physical changes helped her to comprehend the terrible violence he was capable of inflicting. Most of all, it helped her to understand that there were indelible horrors buried in his psyche.

If that had been the only Tom she knew, she wouldn't have been sitting at a St. Louis bar with him. But as they had gotten to know each other working on the training films, he let his guard down. Someone would tell a funny story, and his eyes would light up with merriment. A practical joker by nature, he'd start some bit of mischief with a fun-loving grin and then laugh like a kid.

Occasionally, as their friendship grew, he would open up and talk to her about his insecurities, fears, and regrets, especially his frayed relationship with his son, Thomas. In those moments, the hard, intense exterior would soften and reveal a kind, big-hearted—even sweet—side to him.

That's when Jen could glimpse what she liked about this man—a good-natured kid who'd grown up in a small town in Middle America, where celebrating the Fourth of July was a bigger deal than Christmas and fishing with his dad as they floated down the Blue River was an ideal summer day. Back when he was young enough that war was just a game to be played in the woods with his buddies. Back when the biggest threat he faced was getting kicked in the nuts by the town bully.

As a self-professed "liberal hippy chick," Jen had even learned to appreciate his view of the military. She liked the way he talked about the Unit as a family and the immense love and respect he had for his brothers-in-arms—his tribe, as he called them. He was passionate about having been part of something bigger than himself, something he had been willing to lay down his life to defend. He believed that he and those like him were out there beyond the walls, protecting Americans from evil, knights in battle fatigues standing against the darkness on the other side.

Looking back, it was hard for Jen to tell when their professional relationship morphed into friendship, and then into something more. It could have been the afternoon in August, after filming, when they pulled into the parking garage of the hotel in Akron, Ohio, where they and the crew were staying. It was unusual when Tom told everyone in the car to go on ahead without him. He said he had some things to do and would meet them later in the hotel bar.

WHEN HE DIDN'T SHOW up a little later, as expected, Jen was concerned. She texted Tom and asked where he was. Normally he answered her immediately; when he didn't, she tried again. "Are you okay? . . . We're waiting for you." This time he replied and said he was on his way. Jen could not precisely explain why, but that small interaction seemed to be a pivotal point. Their relationship began to grow into a courtship, mostly long distance and conducted in flurries of daily texts and long phone calls.

Now, relaxing over drinks in St. Louis, Jen felt it was finally okay to ask him about Mogadishu. She'd been told that the battle had been the longest sustained firefight in US military history since the Vietnam War. It also had been Tom's first mission with the Unit. "What can you tell me about Black Hawk Down?" she asked during a lull in their conversation.

Tom hesitated, but then seemed okay with the question. He began talking about the sights, smells, and sounds, the fury and the fear. A friend of his had died, shot in the face, at the beginning of the fight . . . and then his voice began to drift. She noticed him shift uneasily in his chair; he looked off, his gaze growing distant.

"It's okay," she said. "We can stop."

He shook his head. She was surprised to see his eyes grow wet as he tried to say something funny—always his way when a conversation turned uncomfortable. Then he apologized for "being weak."

She grabbed his hand. "It's not weak to cry."

Tom fought to control his emotions. It had been almost twenty years since someone—his first wife—had asked him what it had been like on that awful night. He reacted now the same way he did then.

He wept.

CHAPTER ONE

Summer 1977
Edinburgh, Indiana

OH GREAT! How'd they find us this time?" At ten years old, the objects of my dismay had just appeared in the woods where my best friend, Robby, and I were playing. The two older boys were now stalking toward us with wicked grins and clenched fists.

I felt helpless. Robby and I weren't even supposed to be in "the woods"—a circular, overgrown, and fenced-off lot the size of a football field. The property was at the end of my street, near the edge of town. It was overgrown with dense brush, grass, and scrub trees; crisscrossed by dirt trails; and a dumping ground for abandoned appliances and cars. There was also a small pond, which made the enclosure far too much of a temptation for a couple of adventurous boys like us to ignore.

The woods were the perfect place to play Army, reenacting the fighting we'd seen on television documentaries and newscasts about the Vietnam War, hunting through the undergrowth and discarded machinery for "gooks" to ambush and kill. Up until now, the woods also had been a good place to avoid the two bullies but, apparently, that was no longer the case.

"Well, look who we have here!" sneered one, a fat farm kid who was always in the company of his tall, skinny friend.

I groaned. I knew what was coming next, starting with a few choice slurs. *You little faggot. You're a pussy. Your dad's so dumb he has to work at the grocery store. We steal whatever we want and he's too stupid to catch us.* Then the fat kid would punch me in the face, laughing and continuing with the name-calling while I cried. It would end with the skinny bully kicking me in the balls. After that they'd turn on Robby and rough him up, though never as much as they did me.

It always went the same way. Insults. Face punch. A kick in the balls. Crying—partly from the pain, but mostly from the shame, believing that I couldn't do anything about it. My adversaries were two years older, and a lot bigger. Worst of all, I was afraid of them.

For some reason, I seemed to attract bullies. I didn't know if it was because I was small for my age, or because I had allergies that would make my eyes water and appear like I was crying. Even the girls picked on me. But these two older boys were the worst.

At the age of ten, I was just a small, skinny kid who practiced violin, was somewhat fussy about keeping my room neat, and hung out with Robby during the stiflingly humid days of summer in small-town Indiana. The two of us played Little League baseball and fought battles with our green plastic toy soldiers or with imaginary enemies in the woods. Then, often as not, we walked across town to cool off at the public swimming pool. About the only damper on my summer was trying to steer clear of my two antagonists. But they seemed to show up everywhere, stalking us like great white sharks circling baby seals before moving in for the kill. Insults. Stand there and take it. Face punch. Kick in the balls. Cry.

I never told my parents about the bullying. They would have just told me to turn the other cheek. "Don't stoop to their level. Try to reason with them. Take the high road." I did confide to my older brother, but he didn't seem interested in helping me, instead advising me to fight back. But I didn't really believe I was capable.

I was the last of three children born to Steve and Martha Satterly. My brother, Steve Jr., was two years older. My sister, Shelly, was four when I joined the Satterly household—and none too happy about it. In fact, she asked our parents to return me to wherever they'd found me. When they declined, she went on a hunger strike until the family doctor threw her under the bus by assuring our parents that she'd resume eating again "when she [got] hungry enough."

However, Shelly's feelings for me eventually changed. The sweet, good-natured little guy was her baby. Sure, I could be a nuisance. By the time I was five, I followed Shelly and her friends everywhere; they'd ditch me, of course, and she'd complain to our parents about her miniature shadow. But God help anybody else who picked on me.

We were a middle-class family, living middle-class lives in Middle America. The Fourth of July, with its flags and firecrackers, was as big a holiday as Christmas, and we children were brought up knowing that compared to most people around the world, we had it good.

My father worked a variety of jobs—from a tool and die maker in Seymour, Indiana, where I was born, to managing the local IGA grocery in Edinburgh. However, it wasn't his fault that he kept having to change jobs. My mother was a nurse, and her obsession for more education, ostensibly to get a better job somewhere else, meant that our family had to pick up and move more often than others.

Most of my own nurturing came from my father. He was a musician and played the guitar, harmonica, and the banjo, sometimes on stage. Bluegrass music was his favorite, but country music was a close second: Boxcar Willie, Waylon Jennings, Willie Nelson, and anyone who'd ever appeared on the television show *Hee Haw*.

But there was nothing my dad enjoyed more than spending time with his children. He taught us how to pick and cook dandelions and to find persimmons, showing us how to tell which were good and which were too bitter to eat. He took us on excursions to gather blackberries and laughed at our efforts to ward off chiggers.

Best of all was fishing with my dad on the dock or floating down the Blue River from Edinburgh to Columbus in our flat-bottomed boat, camping out at night, telling stories around the campfire. I always felt safe with my dad and, while I didn't know it as a child, these were the memories that would sustain me when all else was dark, violent, and full of fear.

I was born on January 28, 1967, a portentous year considering the path my life would take. That was the year of the "long hot summer of '67," marred by more than a 150 race riots in cities throughout the East and Midwest that claimed nearly a hundred lives and reduced many millions of dollars of property to rubble.

Meanwhile, on the other side of the world, the war in Vietnam was raging. As US casualties mounted—more than 9,000 dead that year alone—the American public began questioning what the United States was doing by propping up a corrupt South Vietnamese government. Antiwar demonstrations rocked college campuses. Six years later, the longest war in America's history was over—a war the United States had suffered at the cost of 58,200 dead and more than 300,000 wounded, some whose scars were not visible on the outside, as the nation came to understand.

I knew that my mother's brother, Terry, had served with the Marines in Vietnam. He had been awarded the Silver Star for his heroism when his unit was ambushed. However, Terry, who had become a minister after returning from Vietnam, never talked about his experiences. It was only after I'd been through my own hell that I learned he, too, was haunted by what he'd been through. He had wrestled his own demons as best he could and fought the tough battle with alcoholism.

But when I was a child, Uncle Terry always took time to talk to me and encourage whatever my interests. He even took to calling me "Snake Eyes" for the way my blue eyes glittered and narrowed to slits when I was angry. I liked that. It made me feel tougher to have such a dangerous-sounding nickname.

Make-believe war was a game I played with my friends. We were always the "good guys," who acted heroically while vanquishing the "bad guys." And even if my friends and I "died" on our imaginary battlefields, we could always get back up and live to fight—a privilege denied in the real life that would come later.

"Well, if it isn't the little faggot," the fat bully said while his buddy laughed. "You're a pussy."

I briefly considered trying to run away. I was fast and probably could have escaped. But the bigger boys would have caught Robby, who wasn't as swift, and I couldn't leave my friend behind, especially knowing that he would have to take the brutality intended for me.

So, already aware of the tears welling in my eyes, I readied myself for the blow. Only this time, it never came. Just before my adversary began his assault, my brother, Steve, and one of his friends emerged from the woods and walked over to the four of us.

"What's going on?" Steve asked calmly.

Still smirking, the fat bully acted as if nothing was happening. He leaned over and picked a leaf from a plant. "Think this is pot?" he quipped sarcastically.

"It's ragweed," my brother replied evenly. He was taller than the fat kid, but skinny and unimposing. I had never known him to get into fights—or raise his voice, for that matter—except as older brothers will with their younger siblings.

Apparently, the bully wasn't impressed either. He made a half-hearted feint at Steve, as if to try to intimidate him, too.

Quick as a snake, Steve's right hand lashed out and caught the bully square on the jaw. The bully went down hard, but Steve wasn't finished with him. He jumped on the boy and pummeled him in the face until he started crying.

"Get the fuck out of here," Steve snarled as he stood up, "and don't touch my brother again."

Both bullies scurried off, but Steve and his friend waited to make sure they didn't return. They then walked Robby and me back to the street.

My opinion of my brother shifted that day. What used to be sibling rivalry, and at times dislike, turned into love and respect for the way he had defended my friend and me. But something else changed in me that afternoon—something that may have been a critical turning point in my life.

It became evident three weeks later when Robby and I were on our way across town to the pool, and we were again accosted by our two tormentors. "What are you gonna do without your brother to protect you, pussy?" the fat bully hissed as he and his friend walked up to me.

Prior to my brother's intercession, I would not have answered, and would have just stood there and taken the insults, the inevitable punch, and the kick in the balls. But not this time. I had seen the enemy on his back, crying and defeated.

Something snapped. Instead of fear, I felt only rage and hatred as I launched myself at the other boy. Every bit of stored up shame, and fear exploded in a flurry of fists that caught my antagonist by surprise.

The older boy again went down, and then it was me who jumped on top of him, pummeling the bully's face until he was bloodied and shrieking in terror and pain. Lost in the heat of battle, I might have kept at it, but Robby pulled me off. The bully got up and ran away with his friend.

Later in the pool bathhouse, I washed the other boy's blood from my hands at the sink and tried to remove the red stains from my T-shirt and swim trunks. Seeing the pink swirl of the blood mixed with water as it went down the drain, I knew something had changed in me and with that came a sense of guilt. I hoped I had done the right thing, but it was not what my parents had always taught me. *Turn the other cheek. Take the high road.*

But, of course, I reveled in my victory over an enemy. Again and again, I relived the moment—in technicolor! I was proud that I'd stood up to the bully and protected myself and my friend. From that day forward, I knew that I would never run from another fight.

CHAPTER TWO

August 1990
Camp Mackall, North Carolina

THE TALL BLOND MAN materialized out of the dark on the rough dirt road I was walking down. He seemed to come from nowhere, and he startled me.

"Don't you think we should get off the road and move tactically through the woods?" he growled as he fell in alongside me.

It took a moment as I peered through my night-vision goggles, but I recognized him. His name was John M., a tough-looking, hard-built man who quite frankly made me nervous with his intensity. I'd noticed him and his companion, Mike Rampey, as I'd worked my way through the Special Forces Qualification, or "Q," course, the last phase of training before I became a Green Beret at twenty-three.

Neither of the other two was physically imposing. Mike was also tall and blond, but like his constant companion John, he was more fit-looking than big. In their mid-thirties, they were a bit older, more mature, than all but the oldest Special Forces instructors. Even around the instructors they seemed to exude a whole other level of competence and professionalism.

They kept mostly to themselves and I had little contact, though

I'd noticed small differences in their personalities. Mike was soft-spoken and seemed friendly. John, on the other hand, hardly talked at all. Asking me whether I thought we should be walking down the road or "tactically through the woods" were more words than he'd said to me in the five months we'd been at Camp Mackall.

That night I had been placed in charge of fifty other candidates during an ambush training mission. We'd just completed a four-mile hike through the woods over rugged and swampy terrain on a moonless night, when one of the instructors told me to move my men down the road back to the trucks that would return us to our barracks at Camp Mackall.

Having been given only those instructions, I was left on my own to decide how to implement them. I deemed that with the mission over, there was no reason to move tactically by approaching the trucks stealthily through the woods. So I'd told my men to just walk down the road to the waiting vehicles.

Now this strange, severe man, John, had just questioned—or more accurately commented on—my decision. I didn't take it well; I felt he was inferring that I was doing something wrong. So I explained to him my rationale for walking down the road. I was sticking to my plan, too, I added.

John, with his lower lip bulging out from dip, cocked his head and gritted his teeth, which caused his jaw muscles to bulge, and said, "You know I've killed a lot of people." With that, he walked off into the darkness, leaving me behind to wonder what he meant.

Here at Camp Mackall in North Carolina, I was going through the agonizing training to become a Green Beret. But my sojourn as a soldier had started in the fall of 1985 when a high school friend who was home on leave from basic training talked me into enlisting. Of all things, this happened as we were driving to a John Cougar Mellencamp concert in Indianapolis, rolling down Interstate 65, tossing beer cans into the backseat with Mellencamp blasting on the stereo. *"The Army is fucking great!"* my buddy exclaimed as he rubbed a hand across the stubble on his head. *"I don't even mind the haircut!"*

At the time, I was a normal, if unremarkable, young American, rocking a mullet and living in Columbus, Indiana, where my family had moved when I was twelve. I'd participated in sports in high school and seemed to have a knack for being the guy my friends and teammates rallied around.

Right out of high school, I had started working construction, which I liked a lot, and was thinking about starting my own company. I also smoked a lot of pot, drank too much beer, hung out with my buddies, and was seeing a pretty, petite brunette named Debbie.

But I knew I was not on a fast track to where I wanted to be, and not even sure where that was. Cold beer, chasing girls, and rockin' out were certainly fun, but they really didn't get you very far. The military had always interested me, so I listened to what my friend had to say.

I had eagerly watched war movies like *The Green Berets*, *Rambo*, and even older films like *Sands of Iwo Jima*. I preferred their unabashed patriotism and the heroics of the soldiers they portrayed to "serious" films that showed the darker sides of war and the gory details of actual battle, like *Platoon* and *Full Metal Jacket*. War seemed heroic, even if sometimes the good guys died; it involved parades, and adoring women and neighbors waiting for the warriors' return with big "Welcome Home" signs.

I didn't connect what I was seeing in the movies to the homeless Vietnam vets I'd see when I visited the "big city" of Indianapolis with their long stringy hair, bloodshot, desperate eyes, bushy beards, and filthy field jackets, standing on street corners begging for money. I couldn't help but think they should be doing more to help themselves, instead of looking like bums, smelling of alcohol, and lowering themselves to plead for spare change. They made me nervous, and I wanted nothing to do with them.

In February 1986, I enlisted and was sent to Fort Leonard Wood in

Missouri for basic training, or boot camp as it was called. I enjoyed the basic training and especially liked learning to shoot. And I was really good at it. My range instructor said I was the perfect student because I'd never handled anything more than a BB gun. I could learn fresh without the baggage of bad firearms habits.

I appreciated that the Army was demanding and required discipline. If you were out of shape, they got you into shape. I had no problem there and sailed through the physical fitness requirements. On the other hand, if you were a smart-ass, like me, they quickly knocked it out of you. I seemed to get my fair share of that, including being given the nickname "Shit," as in *"You're in a world of shit, Shit."*

I figured that the verbal abuse was to make recruits mentally tough and build a sense of "us against the world"—our world, in this instance, being that of the drill sergeants. Nobody escaped the berating, the ridicule, or the physical abuse. Everybody was treated equally.

The Army wanted to break us down to human clay so we could be remolded into its image of a soldier. It was about taking individuals and merging them into a whole unit, who did what they were told to do, when they were told to do it. The emphasis was on building a belief that we were stronger together than apart.

We marched together. Ran together. We stood at attention for hours in the hot sun together. We ate together. We exercised together. We went to the bathroom together in a long line of toilet bowls openly displayed along a wall with no dividers or stalls. We went to bed at the same time as one another and got up together. They even cut everybody's hair off so that we all looked the same. And if someone messed up, we suffered the consequences together. What better way to turn two hundred strangers into two hundred soldiers who belong to a fraternity and call each other "brother" than to put them all through the same hardships?

As boot camp progressed, I felt I was becoming a part of something larger than myself and the small-town world I'd grown up in—that the path I was on now had a purpose. Protect America. Protect my home and family. Protect those who could not protect themselves. Save innocent lives. Kill bad guys.

After basic I was assigned to the US Army base in Wildflecken, Germany. Nervous about going overseas and into my new life with the Army, I married Debbie so I wouldn't have to go alone. Not exactly the best reason to get hitched, but I was like a lot of other newly minted soldiers off to see the world for the first time.

Arriving at Wildflecken, I was assigned to the 54th Engineer Battalion as the driver of an M113, a fully tracked armored personnel carrier. The battalion's job was to prepare to halt the Russian horde crossing into the Fulda Gap, a primary invasion corridor into Western Europe for Soviet and Warsaw Pact tanks. If war broke out, my unit's mission would be to slow down the onslaught long enough for NATO and the US military to respond.

My job was fun at first. Not everybody gets to drive what is essentially a small tank, minus the gun turret. Another facet of Army life, especially for a young married couple, was drinking a lot of beer and schnapps. Go to work, train, get drunk, go to bed, and do it all over the next day. It was beginning to seem a lot like home.

As I grew tired of the monotony of regular Army routine, I began hearing about the Green Berets, a part of the revered Special Forces. I'd met a Green Beret while training for my specialty after basic and been impressed with his professionalism and how he carried himself. He was obviously a cut above the other soldiers I'd met, including my drill sergeants. An Army buddy of mine, Kevin, had a photograph of his dad, who'd been a Green Beret in Vietnam, holding him as a baby wearing his father's green beret. Kevin dreamed of following in his father's footsteps. I didn't tell Kevin, but looking at that photograph, I adopted his dream as my own. The thought of being one of "America's best" appealed to that part of me that was always trying to prove that I was strong enough and good enough to make a difference.

Another great influence on my future path were a couple of my platoon sergeants who encouraged me to attend commando training courses run by special operations units in France and Germany. The courses were physically and psychologically demanding—designed to weed out the weak.

One of the toughest of the commando courses, Platoon Confidence Training, or PCT, was put together by Green Beret sergeants. They had a motto: "Pain is only weakness leaving the body."

It was the sort of challenge that appealed to me. When other soldiers quit the courses, it made me more determined to finish, and finish first if I could. I took pride in being one of the few still standing at the end.

I got into every specialized course I could, including one with German special operations in which I had to compete against a thousand other guys in the battalion. I took extra classes offered by the Army and in 1987 was named the battalion's Soldier of the Year. This honor was all I needed to whet my appetite for going as far as I could in special operations.

There was one other event that would change the course of my life. It started when I attended a recruiting and informational briefing for a "special missions' unit," which was in fact the Unit.

I HAD NEVER HEARD of the Unit and was wondering how it might be different than any other special operations forces. Then a map of the world flashed onto the screen. "This is our training area," the lecturer, a man dressed in a cheap suit with longish hair who had been introduced simply as "Mr. Smith," said.

Standing at the back of the auditorium, listening and looking at that map of the whole world, I found myself thinking: *This must be the way the real pros do it. No borders. No restraints. Just doing*

what needed to be done, wherever it needed to be done. This was why I
signed up for the Army.

I knew I couldn't get into the Unit right away. I didn't have the
rank and, apparently, they only took the best from those who were
already in a special operations unit, like the Green Berets or US
Army Rangers. This was a dream that was a long way off.

By late 1988, with one more year left on my enlistment, I considered what to do about the future. I didn't want to stay in if it
meant being in the regular Army. I decided I'd try to get into Special
Forces. I knew that the Green Berets were tasked with five missions:
unconventional warfare, foreign internal defense, special reconnaissance, direct action, and counterterrorism. But the primary
mission since Vietnam was to train local defense forces, or guerilla
units, in occupied nations.

It all sounded exciting and meaningful, however, it was the Special
Forces motto—*De Oppresso Liber*, to "liberate the oppressed"—that
particularly appealed to me. Due in part to my experience of having been bullied while I was growing up, I believed I knew what it
felt like to feel helpless against a more powerful enemy. Conversely,
I also knew how good it felt when I'd stood up for myself and my
friend.

The idea of teaching others how to defend themselves from
tyrants and terrorists was a powerful draw. I hadn't been to war and
had no idea what it could do to a man. It still sounded like the great
adventure they sold in movies, on TV, and in parades where the soldiers were the heroes.

After deciding I wanted to be a Green Beret, I immediately ran
into a roadblock. One of the basic requirements for the Green Berets
was a course that would not be offered for another six months.
Rather than wait around, I decided to volunteer for jump school at
Fort Benning, Georgia, which was required for Special Forces anyway. If I made it, I'd be assigned to an airborne unit at Fort Bragg,
the massive Army base in North Carolina, which also happened to

be the home of special operations. That way I would be that much closer to my dream, and Debbie would be closer to home, which I hoped would make her happier.

Working to advance my Army career meant a lot of time training in the field, often several days a week without going home, as well as the specialized courses that could run for weeks. Meanwhile, Debbie didn't have much to do except wait for me. Sometimes it didn't feel like we even lived together, and there'd be an emotional distance we had to overcome when I did return.

As a result, we fought a lot. Over money. Over the amount of time I spent in the field. Over nothing, except the fact that we were growing apart. I hoped that being back in the States would help with that, but first I had to get through jump school, which meant more time away.

In August 1989, with jump school under my belt, I was accepted to the Special Forces Assessment and Selection (SFAS) program at Fort Bragg. As opposed to jump school, and even other commando courses, the twenty-eight-day SFAS process was a nightmare. It began with the recruits having to pass a physical fitness test by meeting or exceeding minimum requirements.

I prided myself on always exceeding minimums. I showed up and crushed the test by pumping out as many situps and pushups as I could before running the two miles like I was in a race.

Passing the fitness test was only to establish that a recruit was in good enough shape to take on the grueling physical requirements of SFAS. As with the European commando schools, there were long marches carrying heavy loads and weapons, as well as land navigation tests to master. However, Special Forces emphasized teamwork—after all their main mission was getting locals to form their own units for defense—which included obstacle course runs as a team event that might include carrying long telephone poles, or finding ways to work together to push an old truck that was missing a wheel eight miles while still carrying all their own personal gear and weapons.

During the team events, candidates could not encourage, or pressure, other candidates. They had to struggle on their own, which meant the team struggled. It was okay, however, for leaders to step forward and, without speaking, take up the slack.

I was one such leader. When others were down, I prided myself on getting stronger. I helped any way I could, even if it meant putting an extra sandbag on top of my rucksack and carrying two or three more in my arms to take the load off of others on my team. Whatever it took.

The events brought out the best and the worst in candidates, sometimes leading to arguments and scraps as men broke down. Personalities changed, like on a reality show where the participants start out as friends but, when push comes to shove, are at each other's throats. But I remained even-tempered, with most of the personality clashes rolling off my back, as I focused on completing the selection process.

As the days passed, candidates started dropping out. It was like a virus: one guy would quit, and then it would spread to others. Once someone voluntarily withdrew (VW), word spread quickly, and others would get on the truck to be taken back to the barracks to gather their gear and out-process for their home station.

Quitting ended a candidate's chances of ever becoming a Special Forces Green Beret, and that was not on my agenda. I was never quitting, not even at the end when I faced storming through the final timed thirty-two-mile road march that had to be completed while carrying a forty-five-pound load.

After completing the SFAS program, my next stop would be the Q course where I would train for my specialty as a Special Forces engineer. In the meantime, I went back to my airborne unit at Fort Bragg.

Although I was excited about having made it through the SFAS process, there was one drawback. It meant that I missed Operation Just Cause, the US invasion of Panama on December 20, 1989, to overthrow dictator Manuel Noriega, who the United States accused of drug trafficking, as well as endangering US citizens in the country.

Debbie and I were home in Indiana visiting our families for the Christmas holiday during the invasion. My airborne unit wasn't part of the invasion force, but it still sucked watching it happen on TV.

Missing the deployment weighed heavily on me. I wanted to know what combat was like. I *had* to know what it was like. I'd played soldier as a young boy and watched war movies sitting on the edge of my seat as a teen, thrilled as the heroic American warriors overcame impossible odds and defeated evil men.

Now that I was trained for combat, I was at home decorating Christmas trees, visiting old high school buddies, and drinking my woes away. I wondered what my friends in Panama were doing, even who they were killing. I wasn't exactly in the Christmas frame of mind.

A few months later, I was back in full swing and working hard on all of the Special Forces training requirements. Then, in September of 1990, my first big goal was achieved—completion of my training and graduation.

DEBBIE AND MY FAMILY showed up. My sister, Shelly, in particular, was proud of me; she saw a striking difference between the common soldier who drank too much and fought with his wife and the young Green Beret who now stood before her. I was glowing with pride, and she was happy for me.

Debbie was happier, too. I'd told her that when I was a Green Beret, I'd be done with all the schools and be gone less often. My father was especially proud. He wanted to know everything I had been through and what was next for my career.

After graduation, as with all Green Beret candidates, I began a four-month language school course at Fort Bragg.

About a month into the language program, I was approached by two men, Mike and John, the guy who'd questioned my tactics and ended the conversation with "I've killed a lot of people." They asked if I knew about the Unit and whether I would be interested in going through the selection process. They said they had noticed me during training and thought I had what it took to at least try out.

"Sure...um...well, it sounds great," I replied. "Yeah, I'd like to try. When do I start?"

Actually, I didn't know much at all about the Unit, as it was known around the base. Just that they were secretive, dressed like civilians, had long hair and beards, wore Oakley sunglasses, and carried pagers. Although there were the usual jealousies with other special operations groups, most seemed to have a lot of respect for the Unit, which drew most of its members from Rangers, Special Forces, and even the occasional Navy SEAL or marine.

I did know that the Unit worked all over the world in small teams—rescuing hostages, killing terrorists, and even breaking up drug cartels. Word was that they had an "unlimited budget" for their operations—an unheard-of extravagance in the US military—but they avoided any kind of publicity. Their missions rarely made the news and if they did, the Army usually attributed them to some other group.

I liked the whole mystique and secrecy surrounding the Unit and was elated that I had been noticed and invited to try out. It was supposed to be the best of the best and that appealed to me. I'd get better gear, be working with the best of the best, travel the world, take out the bad guys, and protect my country. I didn't give any thought to what it might mean to me, or my family and friends, on a personal level.

ONE OF THE MEN, Mike, explained the selection process for the Unit and slipped me a card with a number on it. "Call them *now*," he said.

There was something in the way Mike said "*now*" that I realized meant do it right then instead of waiting until the end of the day. After the two guys walked away, I did exactly that. I was surprised that the person who answered already seemed to know about me and was waiting for my call. They had all the necessary paperwork ready to send to me. It was my first taste of the efficiency level at which the Unit operated.

The phone call caused me to be late for my language class. It didn't matter. I was now aiming for a higher goal, and that was all I could think about.

CHAPTER THREE

March 1991
West Virginia

SOAKED TO THE BONE and covered with mud and plant debris, my eyes rimmed in red from a lack of sleep, I emerged from the woods onto the dirt road and staggered toward the intersection, hoping to see an Army truck waiting. If I did, I was getting on it, and getting the hell out.

I'd been hiking for eighteen hours, moving constantly through some of the toughest terrain in all of mountainous West Virginia, carrying a rucksack on my back loaded down with more than eighty pounds, and a dummy rifle that weighed another seven pounds. Add dehydration after several hours of diarrhea, followed by hunger, and I was drained to the point of collapse.

More than that, I was spiritually broken and ready to quit. Ready to give up becoming a Tier One special operator for the Unit, the most elite, secretive antiterrorism unit in the US military. I'd just go back to base camp, collect my gear, then get on the bus to the airport for the flight back to Fort Campbell with my tail between my legs. And I wasn't coming back for any do-overs. I was done.

It didn't matter to me anymore that the grueling cross-country forced march, known euphemistically as "The Long Walk," was the final physical hurdle in the demanding Unit selection process, and known to be longer than any other selection movement on the planet. I had to be getting close. How close I wasn't sure, but I no longer cared. For the first time since overcoming the childhood bully in Indiana, I was giving up.

"Probably wouldn't have made it anyway," I thought.

I'D KNOWN FROM THE beginning there was a good chance I wouldn't make it through the selection process, which was infamous for washing out even top soldiers, and I would wind up back with 5th Special Forces Group. Nonetheless, facing this reality was brutal.

The greatest disappointment was that only six months earlier, I was on top of the world over being asked to try out for the Unit. In preparation for the selection process, I had been told when and where I would be picked up, as well as what and what not to bring with me—no GPS devices, cell phones, or radios—and even specifically which type of boots were allowed. An instructor, known as a cadre, would meet me at an airport in West Virginia, where the selection process would occur. I was also informed that I would be told what I needed to know, when I needed to know it—nothing more, nothing less—which I would realize later would be the mantra throughout the selection process.

Upon our arrival in West Virginia, the other candidates and I wandered around the small airport looking for instructions on what to do or where to go. Soon, a van showed up; the gear was loaded, and we were off to the selection site in the nearby mountains.

There we were shown to our barracks and told to pick a bunk. At one end of the barracks, there was a chalkboard where, we were informed, everything we needed to know would be posted every morning. Nobody would be giving verbal instructions on what to do.

*   *   *

THE SELECTION PROCESS WAS divided into several phases: administrative, instructional, stress. None of it had anything to do with weapons or fighting skills. That would come later in the Operator Training Course for those who had made it through selection.

As I came to understand it, joining the Unit meant being constantly assessed from the day I called the recruiter to the day I retired or was killed. The Unit required perfection. Operating in small units—as small as two-man teams—every Unit operator had to be relied on to do not only his job but also tasks that in a regular Army unit would be assigned to several men.

Command loyalty was to the Unit as an entity, not to the men who comprised its ranks. If someone slipped up—physically or mentally—they'd be out. The only way to stave that off was to train constantly, and still be left wondering if it was good enough.

HOWEVER, IT WASN'T THE Unit's goal to wash out candidates during selection. The instructors taught what was necessary for every candidate and then gave them every opportunity to succeed.

But I quickly realized that the only person who cared if I made it was myself. The Unit didn't care—the candidate either had what it took, or he didn't. No one was going to offer encouragement, no one would be cheering me on. Nor would they be trying to discourage me. I had to do it on my own, or not at all.

The administrative phase began the first morning and was part physical fitness test and part psychiatric assessment. The fitness test began with timed pushups, timed situps, a "run, dodge, and jump" event, an inverted crawl, and a two-mile run in boots and camouflaged BDUs, or Battle Dress Uniforms. After what I'd put myself through leading up to the test, I sailed through.

We were then loaded up into trucks and taken to a pool where we had to pass a "drown-proofing test." The candidates had to tread water for several minutes with our uniforms on, then swim one hundred meters without touching the bottom or sides. The drown-proofing test was to make sure no one was unable to handle stream crossings during the stress phase.

After the physical fitness and swim tests, the other candidates and I spent the day completing more paperwork and psychological evaluations. All of this testing was designed to assess whether it was safe for the candidates to continue.

Those who quit or were pulled from the selection process weren't seen again by the other candidates. Their bags mysteriously disappeared, they ate at different times, and they were sent to another barracks to await out-processing and be flown back to their home base as soon as possible. Those in charge of running selection wanted to ensure that the men who either quit or were injured did not affect those still trying to make it through the course—the bad apple syndrome. The Unit wanted to make sure that if a candidate quit, he had no one to blame for it but himself.

In all of this, candidates were not referred to by their names or rank. Any insignia on our uniforms was removed. That meant that no one was in charge unless a candidate himself took charge in a situation. Although it would take time to sink in, a major difference between Special Forces selection, which emphasized teamwork, and Unit selection was that the latter focused on individual initiative and performance.

Instead of name and rank, each day candidates were given a different color and number, such as Blue Two. Each of us had to remember our assigned color and number, which, as selection went on and we grew more exhausted, became a chore. Some took to writing their color and number on their arms and hands; I chose to write it down on a piece of paper and place it in my map bag for quick reference.

After classroom instruction, candidates were put through the real physical event of the day. They'd drop weights into our rucksacks and drive us to a location where we would begin climbing up and down the mountainous terrain. The amount of weight required would be increased every other day. Scales were available to make sure our packs were properly weighted, taking into account that any food or water consumed would lessen the weight. There was no cheating—the packs were weighed before and after each march, as well as at random stations along the trail for surprise inspections. Woe to the candidate who showed up with a light pack. It meant getting written up by an instructor to go on his record, and a rock weighing more than the missing amount would be added to the rucksack until further notice.

We were shown ways to increase our efficiency as soldiers, such as how to drink water while continuing to walk. The instructor made his point by stopping the group so that we could have a drink, but meanwhile another instructor continued walking while drinking. After two minutes, the instructor who'd remained with the candidates pointed to the instructor who'd continued walking and noted the distance he had gained while we were stopped.

Another example was how to conserve energy while still covering a lot of ground. Run downhill, walk briskly on the flats, save energy for the uphill portions, but never stop moving toward the goal.

Everything the candidates were expected to do, we were told how, then shown, and allowed to practice before the cadre began keeping track. I got the point of the lessons and demonstrations. Every second counted. Keep moving until reaching the end. The importance of this would become more apparent as the selection process moved forward.

After three days of hiking with our instructors, we spent another eight days humping our rucksacks mile after mile through the mountains on our own. We were given a destination but not told how much time we had to reach it. To me, that meant going as hard as I could for as long as I could or risk not meeting the deadline. I was afraid of being put on the truck that parked at the "other" barracks—the one no one returned from.

As the days passed, the regular Army rules and regulations began to give way to the looser style of the Unit that had originally appealed to me. However, it became more and more incumbent on candidates to be where we needed to be and do what we needed to do without being told.

Sick call was conducted every morning. No one was pulled from the selection process unless their ailment was life-threatening. But candidates were given information about their physical condition and then allowed to choose whether to continue.

If someone was obviously dealing with a serious injury, he would be asked if he needed to see a medic. But if the candidate responded, "Will it count against my time?" the only answer would be a repeat of the question, "Do you wish to see a medic?" Behind the scenes, plans were made for the candidate's safety, but he had to start the conversation.

Every day during the instructional phase there were fewer candidates than the day before. Some were gone due to injury, but most simply quit by walking up to an instructor and announcing, "I want to VW."

The Unit had its own way of signaling the ever-dwindling numbers of candidates. Starting the first day, there were only as many chairs in the classroom as there were candidates. No more, no less. If someone asked to VW or was removed from selection because of injury or not completing a march in the required amount of time, they would be gone, and the next morning their chair removed from the room. There were only rumors about the washout rate. But Unit leaders never said anything about it, nor were they looking for a specific target percentage. A candidate made the Unit, or he didn't, based on his physical and mental toughness, his ability to achieve goals using a minimal amount of information, and his timely and professional performance in challenging and austere environments.

Looking around at the other guys I was with, they all seemed to be a cut above what I had seen everywhere else in the Army, even among the Green Berets in Special Forces. Some of them looked the part of supersoldiers—imposing brutes—but many were more like me, not particularly physically impressive, but fit.

In fact, it seemed that the two body types who had the most difficulty, and were the quickest to leave, were the large bodybuilders and the smallest of the candidates. These candidates were either carrying a lot of their own body weight along with their rucksacks up and down the mountains, or they were struggling with too much weight compared to their size.

I had watched some of the toughest men on the planet voluntarily withdraw and walk off in tears to return to their home bases. I knew they'd go back to their units still as superior soldiers, but the heartbreak of failing something so important to the heart of a warrior cut deep. Their chair would be missing from the classroom in the morning. I was determined that when selection was over, my chair would remain.

As THE INSTRUCTIONAL PHASE of the selection process ended, the physical challenges ramped up. This phase was designed to test everything we'd been taught, as well as our physical limits. Once again, we would be fighting our way up and down the mountains of West Virginia with weighted rucksacks, this time with the added strain of carrying a seven-pound, orange-painted rifle *without a sling*, while using our land navigational skills to make our way to a series of rendezvous points.

The difference between these marches and those we'd undertaken during the instructional phase was there'd be no more interaction, advice, or help from the instructors. Nor would we be returning to the barracks each night to take showers and sleep on bunks.

Instead, we spent the night on the mountain in whatever we brought to set up and sleep in. The only sign of civilization was a single-lane dirt road that circled up the mountain. Everything from tents to sleeping bags had to be brought in each evening after the hike, unpacked, and set up. Then, in the morning, the candidates had to pack it all back up and put it on the truck before being driven to the new starting point. The truck would arrive again at the base camp in the evening with only the bags of the remaining candidates.

I sailed through the physical challenge of the stress phase just as I had during the instructional phase. I attributed this to having the foresight to work out constantly prior to attending selection. To me, the key seemed to be to remain healthy. Any illness, pulled muscle, twisted ankle, or even blisters could end a candidate's chances. No amount of mental toughness would allow a candidate to traverse mountainous terrain day in and day out with his heels raw and bleeding from blisters.

One night in base camp, a friend of mine from the Special Forces Q course did ask me for help with the huge blisters on his heels. We knew we were getting near the end of the stress phase, but that meant something called "The Long Walk" was coming. And from what we knew about physical fitness and the body's ability to continue on, we all knew that this was responsible for more attrition than all other parts of the Unit's selection process combined.

Although he was swallowing Motrin like candy—the painkiller is practically a vitamin in the Army—to the point that he was rotting his stomach, my friend could no longer walk with his boots touching his raw and bloody sores. So, I cut the heels from his boots to give him a chance of making it.

Like everyone else, I was exhausted and spent a lot of time thinking about hot showers, pizza, and a soft bed. What I knew with absolute certainty was that I would never voluntarily withdraw; I had never wanted anything in my life as much as I wanted to be part of the Unit.

However, that was before The Long Walk through the toughest terrain West Virginia had to offer. Starting at night.

None of the candidates knew exactly when The Long Walk would start. But after a week of living outdoors in the mountains, we were driven back to the barracks and told we had an hour to shower, gather maps and fold them as instructed, and get back to the trucks.

We were then driven two hours to an unknown location in a national wilderness area where there were no roads for rescue vehicles. Once there, we were told to relax as best we could and wait for the start time around midnight. I stretched out in my shelter thinking about what lay ahead. I'd walked that far before, but never while I was as exhausted as I was then or carrying as much weight. I tried to get some sleep but decided I needed to put away as many calories as I could for the ordeal ahead. Candidates had energy bars, but many of the men didn't like them so I ate theirs as well. Only then did I fall asleep.

WHEN I WOKE UP around midnight, it was dark and cold. I was stiff from all the hiking we'd been doing. But worse was that, the overconsumption of energy bars had given me a severe case of diarrhea. Every few minutes I was having to run into the woods to relieve myself. My intestinal distress continued right up to when we were trucked to the starting point.

No more helping each other, no more talking. Travel cross-country, no going within two hundred meters of a road or trail unless instructed. The candidates then were sent off into the dark one at a time at approximately thirty-minute intervals.

When it was my turn, I received my instructions and was then asked if I had any questions. "No," I replied, though I had a million. I knew very little about The Long Walk except its length—and that one candidate had drowned when he tried to cross a swollen stream. I was then sent on my way in a light drizzle.

I walked about five hundred meters to be sure I was out of sight of the instructors at the starting point and sat down. I was still suffering from diarrhea and felt that, as a result, I was tiring too quickly.

I also felt light-headed and was having difficulty recalling what I'd been told. I knew this was not a good start and started to panic. The demons of doubt started raising questions.

What did the sergeant major say to do at this juncture? What were the instructions? But I forced myself to rally and I brushed off my qualms. *Fuck it, I'll just keep walking until I can't anymore.*

Soon I found myself confused at a junction in the trail. There were ChemLights heading up a trail over the mountain, and another set of the lights going off to the left. I couldn't remember what I'd been told about the ChemLights. *Do I follow them? Or do I ignore them? Why can't I remember?*

I decided that if the instructors didn't want me to follow the ChemLights, they wouldn't have placed them on the trail. So, I followed them up the mountain.

Then, as I was squatting off the trail, still trying to get over diarrhea, I saw a half dozen lights down the mountain. I quickly pulled up my pants and ran back to the trail.

After a quick, and unauthorized, discussion with the other candidates, I convinced them that they were headed in the wrong direction, which would route them back to the starting point. They started to follow me. However, after a little bit, they decided that they'd been on the correct course after all and, after another unauthorized discussion, changed back to the direction they'd been originally heading.

I thought about it and decided if so many others were convinced they were right, I had to be wrong. I concluded I must have gotten turned around when I stepped off the trail, so I decided to follow the other men. But I only made it five hundred yards before I stopped, told the others that I was sure I had been right previously, and turned around again. Alone.

Several kilometers later, I came to an intersection in the trail. I could either veer off to the left, or I could continue in the same direction. I dug around in the brush and found a sign that pointed toward the direction I was headed. The others, I thought, must have missed the sign and turned back toward the starting point—just as I'd thought when I originally saw them. I beat back the brush so that others would see the sign and then continued on my way.

I learned a valuable lesson: trust your judgment, even when everyone else thinks you're wrong. But as I continued on that night, I could only hope that the nagging voice in my head which had turned me around was truly right.

After much mental debate and confusion, I thought I was at last nearing the end. I headed toward the next checkpoint, on top of the mountain in front of me. There was a logging trail on the map that appeared to zigzag its way to the top, but there was another option, going straight up the mountain.

Concerned that I'd lost a lot of time with my false start, I went with the latter—straight up the mountain. I soon regretted my choice as I fought my way through thickets of mountain laurel with their tangled web of rubbery limbs that are too thick to cut and too soft and bouncy to walk on. It was a nightmare fighting my way through them as they grabbed at my legs and equipment.

Unable to walk, I finally resorted to throwing my rucksack ahead of me and then crawling after it while carrying the gun. The strategy backfired on me when I went to use my compass that had been tied to my equipment belt. It was missing, torn off its lanyard by the damned mountain laurel.

"Holy fuck," I screamed repeatedly. I would be lost without it and might as well quit; I'd never make it from RV point to RV point. Looking down the dark incline with all the tangle of vines, deadfall, and rocks I had climbed over and through to reach that point, I wanted to cry. *I'll never find it in that,* I thought.

I sat there for a few minutes thinking about quitting. But I had never quit anything and didn't want to start without at least trying to find the compass. Slipping and sliding, I started back down and fortunately didn't have to go far after all. The compass was just a few yards down the slope hidden under some leaves. It was pure luck I found it.

At last, I came to the stopping point and found an instructor who gave me water and, for the first time since I'd started, a few simple words of encouragement. However, the news wasn't good; I had more miles to go—at least to the top of another mountain.

Wet and covered with mud and debris, I struggled on, but I was drained. I could smell ammonia, the scent of muscles breaking down. My boots were waterlogged, and my feet were giving in to trench foot, an extremely painful condition caused by the wet boots. The diarrhea had abated for the most part but left me with little energy and a sense of being increasingly light-headed.

I began to doubt whether I had it in me to finish. Or, at that point, whether I even cared. I allowed myself to think about being warm, dry, and back home or in the barracks or a truck—anywhere but where I was. But I struggled on, willing myself to place one foot in front of the other.

After several more miles, I came to the intersection in the road. I was done—defeated physically, psychologically, and spiritually. I no longer even wanted to be in the Unit. Just give me a truck ride back to base, a shower, some sleep, and a return ticket to Fort Campbell.

Probably wouldn't have made it anyway, I thought.

My mind jumped to what a friend had told me just before the start of The Long Walk, that even if I got to the end, I might still be rejected. "You're young," he explained, maybe too young for the sort of person the Unit was looking for. Unlike other special ops units, such as the Navy SEALs or Army Rangers that recruited the young and gung-ho, the Unit preferred older, more mature soldiers.

My friend also assured me that getting turned down because of my age wouldn't be the end of my dream to make it into the Unit, pointing out that the selection process allowed for two tries. But I could not imagine not making it. The humiliation of trying out to become the "best of the best" and being rejected, then having to return to 5th Special Forces Group, even the vaunted Green Berets, would be too much. Still, that was before a miserable night and day of pushing my body and mind to the limit of endurance had broken my spirit.

In any case, the truck I had hoped would be sitting idling at the intersection was not there. I was alone.

After I took a few minutes to gather myself, disappointment gave way to thankfulness. A waiting truck would have made it easier to quit. Now I had no choice but to continue. I put my head down and pushed on.

Finally, late in the afternoon, I reached what I thought would be the last stopping point, only to learn that there was one more. It was almost too much. The words "I want to VW" began to form in my mouth, but I swallowed them. *Just keep walking until you're done.*

Hating life, I trudged up the trail that was actually more of a stream due to the rain that had been falling all night and day. I'd only gone about eight hundred yards and was just passing by a large boulder, looking down at my ruined, waterlogged boots and feeling sorry for myself, when I sensed someone and heard a voice coming from the boulder. I stopped and again heard the voice clearly and firmly call my name: "Sergeant Satterly."

I had not been referred to by anything but a color and a number since starting the selection process. At the start of The Long Walk, I was designated "Blood Two." So, I was momentarily confused when I heard my name and looked up to see two men sitting on the boulder. The first, a big but not particularly tall man with dark hair and a deep voice, said simply, "The stress phase is over."

I furrowed my brow. "What do you mean?" I asked in a daze.

The other man who was taller and clenched a cigar in his mouth rephrased his companion's statement. "Your selection has ended."

"Why? What do you mean?" I blurted out. I was suddenly terrified that these two men were telling me I'd failed, and that I wasn't going to be a member of the Unit.

The first man jumped down from the rock and tried to help me remove my rucksack. But I wouldn't let him. I hadn't come this far, suffered this much, to be told my dream was over.

After a brief struggle, I finally realized they weren't kicking me out. They were letting me know that I'd completed The Long Walk. I was done with the physical ordeal of selection.

Relieved, I allowed the two men—who I'd later learned were Dick D., a Unit command sergeant major, and Gen. Bill G., the legendary commander of the Unit—to lead me over to a fire pit. I was the only candidate there.

The rest of the day and evening was a fog. I sat around the fire pit wolfing down sandwiches and drinking German Glühwein, a spiced, mulled wine they'd been heating over the fire. When a van came, I got in, lay down on the floor, and passed out.

How many hours I was asleep, I didn't know. Bad weather prohibited the helicopter that was supposed to pick us up from flying, so we had to drive back in the van for several more hours. At last, one other candidate who'd completed the course, and I were dropped off at the "good" barracks. I found a plastic chair and dragged it into the shower where I sat for hours letting the warm water wash over me.

Of the approximately seventy men who started The Long Walk with me, only about twenty made it to the end. My friend whose boot heels I'd removed didn't; he'd ended up passing out on one of the last mountains when he stopped to rest his feet. They found him the next day when he failed to check in at the RV. As much as he wanted to make the Unit, his body had failed him.

Completing the walk, however, didn't mean that any of us had been accepted into the Unit. No one knew yet if they'd completed the course within the time limit, and they still had to get past the selection board and more psychological evaluations.

The remainder of the week was spent talking to a Unit psychologist and completing more questionnaires. The Unit left no stone unturned when choosing who would join its elite ranks. One question that was posed to me during the process that would stick with me over the years concerned a scenario in which I was the leader of a mission. If the mission failed, the war would be lost. However, on landing in enemy territory, one of my men was badly injured and couldn't go on.

"What would you do?" the psychologist asked.

I wondered if there was a right or wrong answer to such a question. How does one decide between the life of a soldier and the fate of so many others?

"I'd leave a security detail with him," I said. "Then take the minimum number necessary to complete the mission."

Other candidates said they'd shoot the soldier and bury him because the mission was more important. Still others said they'd scrap the mission to save the soldier.

I wondered whether I was mentally ready to make those sorts of calls. But the only thing I knew how to do was answer as best I could and not worry about whether I was correct.

Finally, I was called before the selection board: the Unit commander, Col. Peter S., and Unit Command Sgt. Maj. Dick D., the commanders and command sergeant majors from each of the three squadrons, the selection commander and command sergeant major, unit psychiatrists, and others I didn't know.

Needless to say, an intimidating panel to be tossing questions and assessing answers from a twenty-four-year-old. Flashing back to what others had told me, it seemed that a lot of their questions were aimed at determining if I had the maturity to join the Unit. I started to worry when they kept noting that I didn't have a lot of experience, none in combat and zero in special operations.

Following a flurry of rapid-fire questions and getting screamed at for my answers, I was on the verge of breaking down when I was asked to step from the room. I sat in the lobby pondering my next move. I figured it was over as far as the Unit was concerned, but I'd just reenlisted, so I couldn't get out of the Army. Visions of the bald sergeant major taunting me and making me paint signs and rocks with the group engineers for the next four years jumped into my mind. I was screwed.

After what seemed an eternity, but was probably no more than ten minutes, I was told to return to the room. When I was seated, Peter S., the commander, began. "Well, Sergeant Satterly, you're young..."

"Actually, very young," Dick added.

Great, they're going to tell me I'm not mature enough, but I can come back and try again, I thought. I felt like crying and bit my lip. *I'm never doing this shit again, I...*

"But we think you have what it takes," Peter said. "Welcome to the Unit."

In that instant, my world changed. I didn't know what I had just signed up for, or what it would do to the rest of my life and the people I loved, but I knew I was where I belonged.

CHAPTER FOUR

August 1991
Fort Bragg, North Carolina

WARRIORS OF THE WORLD

The Unit's headquarters and training areas were located in a remote expanse of the massive Fort Bragg complex that is also home to the 82nd Airborne and US Special Operations. The facility is surrounded by a forest, so I was surprised on my first visit when, coming through the trees, I saw a massive group of buildings that seemed to appear out of nowhere.

Originally located in the Army base's former stockade, the Unit's main building had once housed inmates and now contained class-rooms and administrative offices. The men had their team rooms on either side of a central area that was large enough to allow space for loading vehicles before missions.

There were state-of-the-art shooting ranges and an armory filled with ammunition on the grounds, as well as "shoot houses"—roofless or with cat walks so that the tactics of the "assaulters" could be observed from above. There were concrete-sided buildings with doors, hallways, and rooms where operators rehearsed Close Quarters Battle, known as CQB. Another site had a small town for urban warfare simulations.

In training, we were tasked with rescuing hostages and capturing or killing "high-value targets"—terrorists, insurgents, or drug lords. The Unit's ability at CQB—fighting from room to room while taking on defenders from a distance of only a few feet—was their combat hallmark.

The 1st Special Forces Operational Detachment, commonly known as the Unit, was established in 1977, after several well-publicized terrorist events had occurred earlier in the decade. The group's founder, Col. Charles "Charging Charlie" Beckwith, a Special Forces officer and Vietnam combat veteran, had been assigned as an exchange officer with the vaunted British Special Air Service commando unit that specialized in antiterrorism, hostage rescue, and pursuing high-value targets.

Impressed with the Brits' training and selection methods, Beckwith believed that there was a need for a similar "special missions" unit in the US military. After finally getting the go-ahead from the Department of Defense, he and Col. Thomas Henry created the Unit and modeled it after the British unit. Its "charter" primarily involved hostage rescue and counter terrorism, as well as direct action against and reconnaissance of high-value targets.

The Unit was placed under Joint Special Operations higher headquarters and is technically answerable only to the president of the United States. It was given a practically unlimited budget, including the right to pirate equipment from other military units, in order to perform their highly classified missions anywhere in the world.

It took two years for the first Unit team to become operational, just in time for the Iranian hostage crisis. On November 4, 1979, a group of fifty-three American diplomats and US citizens were taken hostage by Iranian militants and held in the US embassy in Tehran. The Unit was given the go-ahead to plan and execute Operation Eagle Claw to rescue and repatriate the hostages in April 1980. However, the mission was hampered from the beginning by the Unit's having to work with other military units, including Marine pilots flying Navy helicopters with no night-flying experience, which the mission required.

The mission seemed jinxed from the start as first a storm forced several of the helicopters, which had been transported via an aircraft carrier, to turn back. Then, after landing several hours late, another helicopter malfunctioned, leaving too few to complete the task. Beckwith, who was on the ground in Iran, decided it was too risky and aborted the mission. Then a collision between one of the helicopters and a ground-refueling tanker aircraft resulted in the death of eight personnel, including a number of Unit operators.

The failure of the mission was a huge embarrassment for the United States. The Islamic government of Iran was quick to capitalize on this failure, on the new Unit program as a whole, and on Beckwith personally. However, remedial efforts resulted in the 160th Special Operations Aviation Regiment (SOAR) being created to handle flying duties for special operations units, staffed by elite pilots and air crews who went through their own exhaustive selection process to identify the "best of the best" in their field. At the same time, SEAL Team 6 was created for maritime counterterrorism operations, though they would expand into ground operations as well.

At the main headquarters, deep in the forest at Fort Bragg, a black granite wall in a quiet courtyard serves as a reminder of just how deadly missions can be. Similar to the Vietnam Memorial in Washington, DC, the names of Unit warriors who had died while with the Unit, including those from the Iranian hostage mission, are etched into the shiny dark stone. The names of those killed from other special operations units while working with the Unit, such as the Rangers and Special Forces, are carved into other nearby memorials. The courtyard was designed so that sounds echoed, which has the effect of causing visitors to speak quietly in reverence for the fallen.

I knew that the public would never know most of the names on the Unit memorial, just like they had no idea about the "little wars" the Unit was constantly fighting all over the world against terrorists and criminals. The Unit operators prided themselves on being "quiet professionals" who went about their business without seeking publicity or the public's gratitude.

Most missions were highly classified and never made the newspapers or television reports. If a mission did make the news, the Pentagon, which did not publicly acknowledge the existence of the Unit, would ascribe the action to other Army units or even the military of other countries. The secrecy and aura of invulnerability were an important part of the Unit's culture, ingrained from the first day of Operators Training Course (OTC). We were taught that we could accomplish anything and practiced visualizing winning and never failing. If, for some reason, there was a chance we might fail, we visualized how to overcome the problem. We were invincible. No one could touch us.

MOST OPERATORS WERE MID-THIRTIES and older. The Unit was looking for mature warriors who could make snap decisions without a full body of information and in the most dynamic and dangerous environments in the world. Additionally, and unique even among other special operations groups, we had to be able to do it independently, without needing direction from higher ranks.

The Unit also wanted great battlefield warriors—physically superior and exceptionally well-trained killers—but also men who were strong leaders and instructors all rolled into one.

Although a squadron could deploy with as many as sixty men, including "heavy breachers," medics, and other specialists, the Unit normally operated in small teams. Depending on the mission, that could mean as few as one or two operators working in hostile territory with little or no backup or local operational support. Therefore, each operator had to be capable of planning and carrying out tasks that might be assigned to several people in another type of unit, a concept known as "force multiplication."

During the psychological evaluations, candidates were also assessed for their prowess in moral and ethical judgment. War tested a man's character like no other experience. Operating on their own, without supervision or even other witnesses, the Unit had to rely on its warriors to behave as if they were under a microscope, whether that meant complying with the rules of engagement or international law.

The psych evaluations weren't just to determine a potential operator's moral compass. They were also designed to determine who, among even elite soldiers, could perform the duties required of a Unit warrior.

One of those tasks was the ability to kill without hesitation. Various studies have shown that even in a pitched battle, the vast majority of combatants will not actually shoot at the enemy.* In battles where large numbers of soldiers are pitted against other large numbers, this phenomenon isn't as important from a military standpoint; there are still enough soldiers willing to kill.

However, with a small group—say a four-man team—entering a house where multiple terrorists lurk behind doors and in rooms, possibly in the presence of hostages, every man has to be relied on to make the kill-shot without wavering. Failure to do so could result in the death of not just the operator who froze, but his teammates and the hostages as well.

---

* In his book *ON KILLING: The Psychological Cost of Learning to Kill in War and Society* (New York: Back Bay Books, rev. ed., 2009), the preeminent analysis on the subject, author Lt. Col. David Grossman, a former Army Ranger and West Point instructor, cites studies indicating that only 15 to 20 percent of frontline soldiers will actually shoot at an enemy during a battle. The others have an "aversion to killing" even if it jeopardizes their own lives. This is not to say that they are cowards. As Grossman noted, they will usually remain on the battlefield reloading weapons for those who will shoot, or performing other duties, sometimes heroically, such as taking care of the wounded.

Sometimes this issue could be surmounted through training. But not every special operations warrior was psychologically prepared to kill, especially during CQB, the hallmark of Unit operations. And because it took a lot of resources to assess, equip, train, and support a Unit operator, it made sense for the Unit, and its psychologists, to try to determine who could handle the stress and the responsibility of such a fundamental decision.

One of the most basic skills for carrying out their missions was instinctive precise shooting. Unit operators were renowned for their lethal marksmanship with both rifles and pistols. Being able to correctly identify and kill an enemy combatant at close range, while also avoiding harming innocent people in close proximity, made it critical.

However, there was nothing magical about how Unit operators learned to shoot as well as they did. Part of it was practice, but mostly it was attention to doing the basics correctly time after time.

A plexiglass case inside the main building emphasized this: about two feet square and four feet tall, half of it was filled with .45 brass shell casings from the sort of semi-automatic pistol favored by Unit operators, the other half filled with 5.56 mm rifle shell casings. There were thousands of casings in the box which, I was told, represented the average amount of ammunition a candidate would shoot during his training.

We began on the very first day with basic rifle marksmanship (BRM), starting by relearning how to hold and shoot weapons by practicing dry firing—without live bullets—thousands of times from a variety of shooting positions. Standing. Kneeling. Sitting. Prone. We learned to place our hands on our weapons in exactly the same way every time, to hold our arms and place our elbows without deviation. We practiced proper breathing—letting out before pulling the trigger. Over and over again, we focused on sight alignment and trigger control, squeezing not yanking. And finally, how to recover after each shot, prepared to shoot again.

Only after perfecting the fundamentals did we go to the range and begin using live ammunition. Beginning with slow-aim-fire, we progressed to "controlled pairs," two shots fired in rapid succession using the front and rear sights. We then went on to "double taps," two shots fired in rapid succession but only using front sights, which was faster but harder to control.

After perfecting rifle technique, the candidates then followed the same process with pistols. We relearned, or in some cases learned, the basics and then dry fired thousands of rounds from all positions until we'd perfected the fundamentals. Only then did we progress to the firing range—slow-aim-fire, controlled pairs, double taps.

However, achieving a goal in the Unit didn't mean the candidate could relax. It meant advancing to the next challenge. Building off a stable platform, learned by dry firing, then moving on and perfecting the next technique, and continuing that process—all predicated on the basics—was what made Unit operators so lethal.

Of course, there was more to shooting than standing still at a firing range and shooting at a target. After that was perfected, with both rifle and pistol, efforts were made to re-create the physiological obstacles of a combat situation that could affect the shooter's proficiency.

During the stress of combat, a soldier will experience increased heart rate and heavier breathing. To mimic this, trainees had to run with cinder blocks in their hands to reach a target, drop the cinder blocks, pull their weapon and shoot, then pick up the cinder blocks and run to the next target. All while being timed.

The point of the repetition and adherence to the basics was to commit the act of shooting a weapon and hitting the target to pure muscle memory. At that point, there was no thought involved, just point and shoot—effortlessly killing the "bad guys," while allowing the operator to think about other tasks, such as being able to instantaneously assess that a person was not a threat and didn't need to be shot.

After meeting the requirements on the range, OTC candidates learned CQB: the ability to enter any unknown structure, without knowing the floor plan or the situation—such as the number of enemy combatants and possible hostages—and systematically clear the structure, room by room, in a hostage or counterterrorism scenario. The idea was to "flow" through the structure, smoothly, quickly, and efficiently. Each man on a team covered different sectors of a room, engaging threat targets, while avoiding hurting someone who was not a threat, or a high-value target who was wanted alive.

"Surprise, speed, and violence of action" are the characteristics of CQB, but not all special operations units do it the same way. The SEALs, the special operations group of the Navy, use what's called a "strong wall" method; entering through one point, whether it's through a door or by blowing a hole in a wall, and forming a wall of assaulters all with their weapons pointed in/toward the same basic direction.

On the other hand, Unit operators surround a structure and then attack from all sides through doors, windows, the roof—working toward the center. Because we are essentially shooting toward each other as we move to the middle, possibly with hostages present, there can be no mistakes A lethal ballet of sorts, CQB requires exquisite timing, nearly instantaneous life-or-death decision making, and perfect bullet placement. All of which, like learning to shoot, took thousands of hours of practice.

Unit candidates started with practicing CQB movements on the range that simulated the smooth, fluid transition into a building. However, after one short class on how to do CQB, including learning each operator's responsibilities, we were off to the shoot houses. After conducting dry runs at the shoot house without targets inside, our team was walked through a scenario in which the house contained several targets portraying realistic human "cartoons" of various sizes, genders, demeanors, and clothing.

We began by the instructors placing the targets in the rooms— first with one bad guy present, then with two, then three, and finally four. When we had demonstrated sufficient skill, "hostages" would be added to the mix. The key was the hands. Instead of focusing on the target's face or body, we were taught to look first at the hands— that's where the threat would be. If there was a weapon, shoot; if not, do not.

"Breaching" by blowing open doors with small shaped charges was added to the mix. As soon as the explosive opened the way in, the team would flow into the house going from room to room, killing bad guys and rescuing hostages.

Then, once everything was under control, the team would call in "All Secure," the signal that the mission had been accomplished and that, for the moment anyway, everybody could relax, knowing we'd done our job and were safe. On the battlefield, the All Secure call is relayed up the chain of command from the assault team, to the field commander, to the overall commander, until all leadership levels know that the target is secure, and the men are out of harm's way for the moment.

Shooting drills weren't limited to the shoot houses. Little towns were likewise set up so that the trainees learned to maneuver through an urban environment where a bad guy, or an innocent child, could suddenly pop up from any door, window, rooftop, or other hiding place. We also practiced night patrols in the woods, firing live rounds at targets that popped up from hidden bunkers in the woods in the dark.

Even then it wasn't just point and shoot. The operator had to see what was behind the target before firing, in case a hostage was behind the "terrorist." This was when the lesson I'd first heard in basic training, about being responsible for a bullet from the time it left my weapon until it stopped moving, truly sunk in.

On occasion, as Unit operators, we were told by the brass to demonstrate our abilities to members of Congress and other important visitors by simulating a response to an aircraft hijacking. The VIPs would be seated on a passenger jet fuselage that was suspended in one of the Unit's buildings; "hijackers"—paper targets covering steel "bullet traps"—were seated, or standing, next to the visitors who were told there would be a briefing before the demonstration began.

However, partway through the briefing, Unit operators stormed the plane and killed "the hijackers" in a matter of seconds. It still didn't dawn on the visitors that the Unit didn't kid around until, famously in Unit lore, one congressman put his finger in a bullet hole of the target's head next to him. "You were using real bullets?" he asked incredulously. "What if you missed?"

"We don't miss" was the answer. The Unit shooters during the demonstration were, of course, all experienced operators; trainees didn't participate in the shooting.

Practice at the firing range and CQB continued daily, with more obstacles and difficulties added as we continued our training. This constant training, to the point where we were so aware of our targets that we no longer consciously thought about what we were shooting, was one way that the Unit surmounted the issue of soldiers who would not shoot to kill an enemy.

The psychological evaluations had helped identify recruits who would practice so diligently that shooting a target was second nature. But the superlative training also took the emotional aspect of shooting another human being out of the equation. They were targets—threats to be identified and eliminated without thinking before quickly moving on.

Candidates also were expected to exercise daily to remain in top physical condition, whether by running, swimming, or lifting weights. At a hundred fifty pounds, without an ounce of fat on me, I handled this requirement with ease.

We practiced martial arts and hand-to-hand combat, including with knives and pistols, and learned how to make explosives, as well as how to breach a door or wall by setting explosive charges. We were taught the proper way to load onto helicopters with our legs dangling out of the doors, and how to "fast-rope" as far as ninety feet below, to the ground or a rooftop.

Although it usually took two years to transfer to the Unit's Sniper Troop, all trainees learned to shoot sniper rifles and set up positions around a house while the assaulters went in. We also practiced shooting all the heavy weapons in the US arsenal, including .50-caliber machine guns and rifle grenades, and how to operate foreign weapons, such as the ubiquitous AK-47.

We were taught and practiced "executive protection"—security measures taken to ensure the safety of military and civilian VIPs, particularly in foreign countries that were deemed to have an elevated risk. Originally advised by the other government agencies that conduct security at the highest levels, who had vast experience in these areas, the Unit course featured advanced driving and evasion tactics, as well as instruction in how to use vehicles as weapons, whether by ramming another vehicle or running attackers off the road. We were also taught how to dress and act to blend into the local population.

When the other new candidates and I were in our first week of classes in OTC, we were handed a book called *Dress for Success* by John T. Molloy. As Unit operators, we might be called upon to blend in anywhere in the world as businessmen, athletes, tourists, or even locals. So, if we weren't in battle gear, we'd be working in civilian clothes, even on base. The idea was to blend in whether our missions took us to South America, the Middle East, Asia, or Europe.

LIKEWISE, WHILE GROOMING STANDARDS were up to squadron commanders, they were generally more relaxed in the Unit than in the regular Army or even Special Forces. These were the days before the omnipresent "operator's beard," but many Unit operators sported neatly trimmed "porn star" moustaches and grew out their hair.

I couldn't grow a moustache that didn't look like it had mange but, thanks to my genes, I did have a thick head of dark brown hair parted on the side that I let grow over my ears. With my clean-shaven face, my look was best described as "fraternity boy."

When it came to teaching the candidates about blending in, Unit instructors didn't just discuss our physical appearance. They had to break their protégés of habits that would identify us, at least to the trained eye, as "military."

Even dressed in civilian clothes and sporting long hair and whiskers, there were still giveaways. For instance, when walking together down a sidewalk, soldiers tend to fall into step as we'd been taught to do since basic training. We'll also use military jargon whether saying "Roger that" for "I understand," telling the time—"We'll meet at 1700 hours" for 5 p.m.—or using the alphabet soup of acronyms that is practically another language for military personnel.

Candidates practiced everywhere we went. On base, if asked what we were doing wandering around in civilian clothes, we might respond that we were civilian contractors with the Department of Defense, or there to fix the plumbing. Some of that was due to the secrecy in which the Unit worked, including around other military personnel, but it was also to practice passing ourselves off as something other than what we were.

Traveling together, as a group of supremely confident and physically fit young men, we'd often get asked, especially by women, if we were athletes. We had a lot of fun with that one, such as claiming to be a foreign sports team or even an all-male dance revue.

The least popular aspect of OTC was learning how to handle being captured by the enemy. This included beatings, interrogations that could go on for hours, day after day, and even torture—such as being made to squat in a four-foot-square box for two days, deprived of sleep. Classes also included lessons about how to escape, using methods such as picking locks and hotwiring vehicles.

In spite of such torments, and the stress of having to be perfect at everything I did, I loved every minute of OTC. Even though I went home to Debbie most nights, when I wasn't out in the field practicing, I couldn't wait to get back to base the next day. I enjoyed not just the military training and the physical and mental challenges, but also the camaraderie of becoming an elite warrior with the other OTC recruits. I'd even been given the new nickname, "Nightcrawler," from the song of same name by heavy metal band Judas Priest.

Beware the beast in black, Nightcrawler.
You know he's coming back, Nightcrawler.

The OTC recruits were physical specimens in the prime of manhood, with a common mentality, who shared the bond of the brutal selection process. We were all overtly patriotic and "America First" in our thought processes, and I could not have been prouder to be one of them.

I finished OTC in September 1991. As with the selection process, not every recruit made it. Some simply weren't good enough on the firing range or in CQB, falling short by infractions such as too many "hostage shoots." Insufficient skills threatened the safety of their teammates, the hostages, and the mission's success. Others simply couldn't handle the stress and voluntarily withdrew.

But no one was criticized for not making the grade. They were all sent back to their original units with high praise for their abilities. They just weren't quite good enough for the Unit.

THE RECRUITS WHO SUCCESSFULLY completed the course went before a board to determine which squadron they would be assigned to join. I was assigned to C Squadron and the C-2-G team. I was proud of myself, and thought I'd made it as an elite Unit warrior, imagining the enthusiastic welcome I'd receive when I reported to my new team leader.

However, I was somewhat taken aback when I was introduced to my leader who was busy preparing to go on a mission. But he did take time for a quick one-pump handshake.

"Great," he said. "You've got a lot to learn."

Then he was gone. That was my welcome to the Unit.

CHAPTER FIVE

Bogota, Colombia
February 1993

THE BIG GUY in the suit with the bull neck and swarthy pockmarked face stood guard outside the hotel room in Bogotá, Colombia. He scowled at the three young gringos, obviously drunk, staggering toward him. The one in the middle, supported by the other two, was apparently sick to his stomach. He kept moaning and wiping at his mouth with a towel as they lurched down the hotel corridor.

"*Go!*" the man bellowed and then snarled something in Spanish.

The three of us, dressed in the usual *turista* shorts and colorful shirts, looked up as if surprised to see him standing there. "*Borracho, muy borracho,*" I pleaded, pointing to my slumped-over friend.

"*Go!*" the man yelled again and began to walk toward us, unbuttoning his jacket—the universal sign for: *I've got a gun. It's time for you to leave.*

We turned and stumbled back down the hallway and around a corner. Once we were out of sight, we straightened up and smiled at each other, sober as judges. We'd pushed the big man as far as we dared. Our training as Unit operators taught us to never cause a scene that might bring unwanted attention.

"Holy shit, that was a little scary," I said to my two older companions, one of whom laughed and dropped the towel he had been using to cover the video camera in his hand.

We were in Bogotá as a regional security team, assessing hotels, restaurants, and bars—anywhere Americans might end up as the prisoners of drug dealers, common criminals, or *Fuerzas Armadas Revolucionarias de Colombia* (FARC), the Revolutionary Armed Forces, the guerilla group that had been at war with the Colombian government since 1964. The objective was to familiarize ourselves with the city and take photographs and videos in case they were ever needed in a hostage rescue situation.

While filming the hallways, exits, and entrances of this hotel, we'd come across the *hombre muy malo*, who was probably a bodyguard for some drug cartel boss, and decided to return and film how he'd react if we approached. We'd come up with the "three drunks and a towel" plan on the fly.

As in this case, the Unit regularly sent out security assessment teams into risky places where Americans might find themselves in trouble. The United States wasn't currently in a war per se, but that didn't mean that the world was a safe place.

In addition to these training and surveillance forays around the world, we were constantly preparing and learning new skills.

One of my first assignments was being sent to Arizona for HALO training. "High Altitude Low Opening," meant learning to jump from an aircraft at 15,000 to 35,000 feet and plunging toward the ground at about 125 mph before opening the chute as low as 3,000 feet. Because of the altitude at which we jump, we carry oxygen.

After HALO, the other members of my selection class and I were sent to breaching school. While each team had members who specialized in breaching—blowing open doors or holes in walls with shaped charges—every operator still had to learn the skill and know how to do it effectively.

As my career progressed, the stress of having to constantly prove that I was good enough would have future ramifications on my mental health, as well as on the lives of my family and friends. But at this time, it also accomplished its goal of motivating me and my fellow Unit operators to hone our abilities to a razor's edge.

It was immediately clear that as Unit operators we were expected to train our bodies harder than anyone I'd ever met, and I dove right in. I was constantly in the gym getting stronger, running, swimming, or climbing. I also spent hours at the gun range and practicing CQB, five days a week.

Sometimes I trained alone or with a friend. But Unit operators also trained at team, troop, and squadron levels, which meant all three assault troops and the combat support troop working together.

After joining C Squadron and my assignment to the C-2-G team, I soon became friends with assistant team leader Rick L. and another experienced team member, Bill T. They made me the team breacher and proceeded to show me the ropes of daily life in the Unit.

While training was serious business, there were times that it resembled summer camp for big boys. An early trip was to Jackson Hole, Wyoming, in January 1992 to learn to ski, snowshoe, and drive snowmobiles, as well as to learn to complete missions in winter conditions. Upon arrival, we were handed over to ski instructors to teach us a certain level of proficiency on cross-country skis, but after that we were on our own.

One of our "missions" was spending several days and nights skiing over a mountain pass to reach a fictional downed helicopter and "rescue" the pilots. After the ordeal of sleeping in tents in subzero weather, the squadron commander treated us to a night in a hotel where we ate pizza and watched the Super Bowl between the Washington Redskins and the Buffalo Bills.

All new operators were required to take part in specialized training depending on which team we'd been assigned. Some took extra mobility classes, learning to drive many different kinds of vehicles in a variety of terrains. Others conducted missions involving skydiving.

My team specialized in mountain climbing. That included ascending 14,259-foot Longs Peak in Colorado, which required technical skills using ropes and, ensuring all team members could navigate the treacherous terrain.

As I learned my job, I understood where Unit operators' palpable self-confidence came from. They were the best, and knew it, because they trained to be the best. No other special operations unit trained as much, or as hard, as the Unit.

With our basically unlimited budget, we got a lot of training time that regular Army and other special operations groups did not. Even the best-trained Rangers and Special Forces units couldn't spend a fraction of the time practicing and training that Unit operators did.

THE CLOSEST SPECIAL OPS group to the Unit was SEAL Team 6, the nation's only other Tier One unit, which trained as much. But Team 6 was a group of the best of the SEALs, its members drawn from other SEAL teams. The three assault squadrons of the Unit came from one selection process and were all equally trained, equally motivated, and equally deadly.

One other important difference from other special operations groups was that the Unit was a bottom-up organization. Most of the men were senior non-commissioned officers—sergeants—highly experienced and exceptionally well trained, able to make decisions on the fly. Not waiting for officers' approval to make decisions enabled jobs to get done faster without wasting time.

The Unit's mission mandated constant training in preparation for precise, short-duration missions that didn't keep us in the field for extended periods of time. Our assault squadrons rotated every three months in and out of various stages of preparedness. We were either on call, including for deployment, or we were training to go on duty, including preparing for specific missions when it was our turn.

If a squadron was on call, they could be called to action at a moment's notice and would have to respond immediately. Our pagers were tuned to a secret Unit-only communications system. If my squadron was on call and my pager went off, I had one hour to report to the base. Then three hours later it was "wheels up" and we and our equipment, including vehicles, were on our way anywhere in the world. But a lot of advance preparation and work went into being able to meet such a tight timeline.

Some missions were planned months ahead of time and, while the exact day and time we'd have to report might be nebulous, we could at least prepare. However, a sudden crisis—such as a hostage situation—could arise at any hour of any day and require an immediate reaction. That meant that each man also had to maintain his personal equipment in order to be able to leave as soon as the pager summoned. We would not know if that crisis would be in a Central American jungle in sweltering heat or a European capital in winter. So, our "go bags" had to contain civilian clothing for any eventuality, as well as our BDUs. The go bags also contained our weapons—usually an M4 rifle, a .45-caliber pistol, and any personal preferences, such as shotguns—as well as Kevlar vests, medical equipment, and night-vision goggles.

Unit operators preferred skateboard helmets due to their light weight. A Kevlar helmet was safer and provided protection against bullets and shrapnel, but they were heavy and cumbersome. Besides, it wasn't like the Unit got into long engagements with the enemy; our tactics relied on getting in and getting out—or eliminating any threat—before the enemy could mount a counterattack.

After responding to the pager and arriving at Fort Bragg, each operator's personal gear was loaded onto vehicles. If specialized equipment was required, that had to be located and loaded as well. The vehicles then had to be weighed to make sure that the overall tonnage fit within the safety standards for the C-5 transport jets that would fly them to their initial overseas destination. In loading the waiting aircraft, everything had to be weighed by the loadmasters and strapped down so that the loads balanced, a separate skill unto itself. Ammunition and preloaded explosive charges also had to be loaded and stored. Then, within four hours of pagers going off, the aircraft lifted into the sky, bound for danger.

As with everything else the Unit did, we trained over and over again to go through this process to getting airborne. Usually it was just a dry run, but we wouldn't know until we were in the air and briefed by the commander.

In my first year and a half in the Unit there were no real deployments. We were called up for a couple of domestic airline hijackings but because we were in US territory—where the military is not allowed to operate—they were handled by the FBI's Hostage Rescue Team with our operators standing by to assist if needed.

Unit operators were expected to take the initiative. Sometimes teams would be assigned missions, but at other times operators would conceive a mission—usually by analyzing intelligence reports and identifying potential issues. For example, the missions my cohorts and I took to South America, as at the hotel in Bogotá, were for training purposes as well as to accomplish security assessments of places frequented by Americans. We then wrote up reports of our reconnaissance findings, which were cataloged in case of future need and provided to the US Department of State.

Sometimes our visits were "official." After arrival and check-in with the local US State Department officials, we were briefed about nefarious activity in the region, including which areas to avoid if we didn't want to be mugged or shot by drug dealers who were suspicious of our intentions. At times, we also let local authorities know we were there to assess security for American visitors. Of course, we didn't mention that we were Unit commandos and usually said we were working for the State Department.

On occasion, we just played the part of tourists, drinking, chasing girls, and sight-seeing. But whether on official business or as *turistas*, the trick was to stay in character and remember what we told the police and any other people we met.

Most of the time, even in the incident with the big man at the hotel, the danger—what we laughingly referred to as the "pucker factor"—was low. However, that changed near the end of that trip when we decided to venture to Barranquilla, a bustling seaport on the Magdalena River in Colombia.

We knew from observing as we drove in from the airport that the city was no place to mess around. There was clearly a lot of poverty, and everywhere rough-looking men walked around, openly displaying firearms.

An embassy employee briefed us, with only slight exaggeration, that the only people who lived in Barranquilla were men who either worked for the drug cartels or for the US Drug Enforcement Agency. Both sides, the employee said, were likely to suspect we worked for the other guys. And that could be dicey.

As we walked around the streets, it soon became obvious that we had been noticed by the rough-looking men who wondered why three young white *Americanos* were there. Barranquilla wasn't a usual tourist destination. Several times we were approached and questioned by pretty young women who had obviously been paid to do so. My teammates and I stuck with our stories and continued as if we were having the time of our lives.

One night my team decided to go to the beach. We were bored and reasoned it was something tourists would do, so we climbed in our rental car and headed out.

With me riding in the front passenger seat, we were driving down a dark road and getting close to the beach when we came upon a road-block manned by nervous-looking soldiers who ordered us to stop. While the driver fumbled for his US Embassy badge—what we referred to as our "get-out-of-jail-free card"—I rolled down my window.

A soldier carrying a large-caliber rifle approached my side of the car and put the barrel of the gun against my head.

Meanwhile, the driver couldn't find the embassy card and became more frantic in his search, which made the guards increasingly agitated. "Just slow down and don't make any sudden movements," I told the driver as calmly as I could while the soldier moved the gun from my temple to my cheek. Then, as if to convey the message to me that he didn't want me to speak anymore, the soldier put the gun in my mouth and kept it there.

Finally, the driver produced the embassy badge. As carefully and nonconfrontationally as possible, I reached up and moved the gun out of my mouth, sweating more than even a night on the sweltering equator called for. Later, back at our hotel and ensconced at the bar, I ordered a vodka soda to get rid of the taste of gunmetal in my mouth, I decided that the pucker factor had escalated from barely registering to off the charts.

But I didn't really know. I hadn't seen anything yet.

CHAPTER SIX

COUNTDOWN TO MOGADISHU

June 1993
Fort Bragg, North Carolina

SITTING BETWEEN TWO other operators in the doorway of the Black Hawk helicopter as it hovered over the pine trees below, I couldn't quite make out what the crew chief standing behind me was yelling. But it sounded a lot like "We're going to crash!"

We were waiting for several AH-6 Little Bird helicopters to stop the convoy of vehicles that was approaching the ambush site. Then we'd fast-rope to the ground from the Black Hawk, assault the convoy, and capture all the "bad guys" in the cars.

There was a particular purpose of this training. C Squadron, to which I was assigned, was practicing with the elite special operations helicopter squadron known as the "Night Stalkers" and Rangers for possible deployment to some place called Somalia over in Africa. Apparently, a warlord was attacking UN peacekeepers who were there to safeguard food shipments intended for starving people.

The mission wasn't a "go" yet, but we were preparing as if it was, with a lot of CQB and Military Operations in Urban Terrain (MOUT) training. Most of the operators disliked even the idea of working in an urban terrain.

Urban warfare had a lot of complicating factors, including the presence of many civilians. Fighting in a city negated advantages one side might have in armor, heavy artillery, and air support, especially if that side was concerned about civilian casualties. In a place like Mogadishu, it would be difficult to differentiate the militia from civilians because they dressed alike. The bad guys also had no compunction about using civilians as human shields, knowing that the United States would be reluctant from both moral and public relations standpoints to attack if civilians were in harm's way.

In the tight confines of a city, small groups of combatants had been known to destroy entire armored columns with anti-tank and other heavy weapons by concealing themselves until the last minute and then ambushing their enemies at close range. Buildings limited fields of view and fire, while the enemy would stay concealed inside, shooting from windows, doorways, and rooftops. And streets could be barricaded to limit the advantage of a mobile force.

Due to the way sound echoes around buildings, it could be difficult to determine where shots were coming from. Bullets also ricocheted off walls so that even if enemy fire was inaccurate, it could still be deadly.

In the US military, the regular Army is well suited for urban fighting because it has the numbers to go house to house. They can take terrain or blocks, set up security to hold that ground, and then push on. On the other hand, operating in small teams for specialized missions, the Unit wasn't designed to fight its way through a city against large numbers of combatants. Their entire strategy is to get in and get out as quickly as possible before the enemy has an opportunity to mount a counterattack.

Getting caught in such a scenario meant that something had gone wrong with the original plan. If there was a chance that it could happen, the Unit needed to train for it. So, we dusted off the old Army manuals on urban warfare and practiced.

On this particular day, we were training to interdict vehicles and kill or capture their occupants. And at the moment, I was more concerned about what the crew chief was saying than what was going on in Africa. I went from calmly waiting to do my thing with the other five operators in the Black Hawk to *oh shit!*

"What?" I yelled over the roar of the helicopter's engine.

Again, the crew chief said something with the word "crash" in it. I grabbed a rope and waited for word to descend, or to curl up in a ball on the floor of the aircraft and hope for the best.

The crew chief bellowed to me to throw the rope as the pilot flared the helicopter to stop its forward movement. That's when I smelled it: the pungent odor of burning pine needles familiar to anyone who'd been around Fort Bragg for any length of time during the summer. But there was something else...the stench of burning fuel.

Sliding down the rope to the ground, I turned to look back up. The crew chief was pointing to the woods. Looking in that direction, I saw a plume of dark smoke—the source of the smell. That's when I realized it was another helicopter that had crashed.

I took off running for the source of the smoke, followed by the rest of the team. Sprinting through the woods, we burst into a small clearing where two pilots were attempting to crawl away from what remained of a Little Bird.

The jet engines on the assault aircraft were still screaming with flames shooting out of them with blowtorch fury into the dry pine needles. A fire was spreading as we ran up and attempted to stop the engines by throwing dirt on them. Rick S., the team's second-in-command and a former helicopter crew chief, knew what to do. He rushed forward, located the helicopter's fire extinguisher, and shot it into the engines' intake, shutting them down.

As Rick worked, I switched to pulling the pilots away from the burning needles and engines to a safe spot. Medics arrived and soon had the pilots stabilized and ready for transport.

With the fire out and everyone safe, a platoon of Rangers was left to guard the site overnight. The All Secure was relayed back to command and the Unit operators returned to base to "hot wash" what had just happened—an After-Action Review (AAR) undertaken after every mission while all the details, good and bad, were still "hot" in our heads. While most special ops units conducted AARs, to my knowledge none were as thorough as ours in analyzing what went right and what went wrong, and looking for ways to improve, as well as to avoid making the same mistake twice.

According to the pilots, they'd been waiting below the tree line to interdict the convoy as it approached but caught a skid on one of the trees. There wasn't time to correct for the mistake, and they'd gone down. But other than two sore pilots and one less Little Bird, the day was chalked off to a learning experience. None of us could have known how the incident foreshadowed what was to come.

The next day, we were back to training for Mogadishu, which was increasingly looking like a real possibility for deployment.

Known to Somalis as Xamar or Hamar, Mogadishu is located on the Horn of Africa, nestled between the surrounding desert and the Arabian Sea. Extending hundreds of kilometers into the ocean, it has been an important seaport for more than a thousand years.

During the Middle Ages, the region fell under the governance of various Muslim sultanates. But like most of Africa, what is now called Somalia was subjected to European colonization—first by Portugal, and then in the late 1800s it became Italian Somaliland with Mogadiscio as the capital. A large Italian population moved in and set up several industries that helped create a prosperous city.

After World War II and the defeat of Italy, the British took over the country until 1960, when the Somali Republic was created. Known for its elegant colonial villas, as well as more modest but neat adobe-like homes, tree-lined streets, and public parks set against the lovely backdrop of a green-blue sea, the city was promoted as the "White Pearl of the Indian Ocean." If most of its streets were composed of hard-packed ocher-colored dirt, they were generally tidy and the inhabitants who strolled along them happy and well-off, at least by African standards.

However, by 1970, the political and economic situation had descended into bloody chaos and brutality. Resistance movements, sponsored and encouraged by Ethiopia, began fighting the government and each other, and by 1991 the country was fully embroiled in a civil war. In its aftermath, various clan-based militias fought for control of Somalia, particularly Mogadishu. Over a nearly two-year period, fifty thousand people were killed in Somalia's civil war.

Two warlords, Mohamed Farrah Aidid and Ali Mahdi Muhammad, and their militias clashed over who would rule, with Mogadishu as the main prize. The capital quickly went from a fairly modern, if sleepy, seaport to a bloody battleground where the clans fought vicious street battles to claim parts of the city, their territory sometimes delineated only by the width of a road.

Apartment buildings, businesses, hotels, and even hospitals were assaulted, with many reduced to rubble by bombs and rocket-propelled grenades (RPGs). Most homes were pockmarked by machine gun and semi-automatic rifle bullets; streets were pitted with shell holes and littered with rubble. Eventually, Aidid's forces gained not only the upper hand but also most of southern Mogadishu. The popular and expansive Bakaara Market became a place where, for very little money, anyone could buy an AK-47 or even an RPG. Armed men strolled through the streets with impunity.

At the same time that the civil war was raging, the Horn of Africa was undergoing a drought that resulted in massive famine, made worse by the breakdown in government and the rule of law. Beginning in 1991, more than three hundred thousand people, many of them children, died of starvation. Cruelly, the warlords, especially Aidid, sought to disrupt humanitarian relief efforts, using food as a weapon to control the population.

The UN Security Council declared Somalia a "failed state" and in December 1991 passed a resolution to provide a coalition of UN peacekeepers, led by the United States, to safeguard humanitarian efforts. On December 9, 1991, US Marines "stormed ashore" in Mogadishu, in a well-orchestrated, made-for-TV event called Operation Restore Hope. The media, which had been notified of the time and place, recorded the event to show the world.

With eighteen hundred Marines standing guard, humanitarian efforts began to have an impact. However, the militias, especially Aidid's, viewed the UN efforts as a threat to their supremacy. He encouraged his men—most of them hyped up on khat, a plant-derived stimulant native to the Horn of Africa that they chewed all day—to engage in running gun battles with the UN forces throughout 1992.

Then on June 5, 1993, a UN force composed of Pakistani soldiers was ambushed by Aidid's men. When it was over, twenty-four of the Pakistani soldiers had been massacred. The next day, the UN Security Council passed a resolution to "apprehend those responsible" for the attack, and on June 17, the UN commander in Somalia issued an arrest order for Aidid. Announcing the order was a mistake as it drove the warlord into hiding.

In the United States, the order was passed to Maj. Gen. William F. Garrison, the same man whose voice from the boulder had informed me that I'd successfully completed The Long Walk. He was now the commander of Higher Special Operations Headquarters, which oversaw the Unit.

Due to rotate into on duty status in July, my C Squadron was assigned the task of capturing Aidid and his top lieutenants. We immediately started "training up" to accomplish those goals.

Code-named Caustic Brimstone, the initial plan involved sending in a small force of fifty operators. But as the summer went on, and Aidid's Somali National Alliance militia continued to attack UN peacekeepers and hamper humanitarian efforts to deliver food and supplies to the population, the Unit plan increased in size.

Now code-named Gothic Serpent, the mission force included the entire C Squadron of about a hundred and thirty operators and all the necessary supporting elements, including a company from the 75th Ranger Regiment and sixteen helicopters from the 160th Special Operations Aviation Regiment (SOAR), the Night Stalkers.

The Unit had worked frequently with the 75th Ranger Regiment, a military group whose history went back to the French and Indian War. The Unit and the Rangers had fought together in Grenada and Panama; then again during the 1991 Gulf War when they were inserted into Iraq as small teams tasked with hunting for Scud missile launchers that were terrorizing Israel.

Lightly armed, but highly mobile, well trained and aggressive in combat, the Rangers' main objective, when working with the Unit in an urban environment such as Mogadishu, was to set up a perimeter while Unit operators assaulted the target building. They would shut down all ground approaches and block any attempt to hinder the Unit's operations.

The Night Stalkers were capable of flying at high speeds and low altitudes in tight urban environments, and to operate in the dark as the Unit preferred. When working with us, the Night Stalkers primarily used two types of helicopters, the workhorse UH-60 Black Hawk, named after the Native American war leader Black Hawk, and the AH-60 Little Bird.*

The Black Hawk had entered service with the US Army in 1979 as a tactical support helicopter. The four-bladed helicopter had a long, low profile so that it could be transported aboard C-130 Hercules and could be armed with 7.62 mm miniguns in the doors capable of spitting out thousands of rounds per minute at a sustained rate, as well as rockets.

As a combat transport, the "helo" was able to carry a dozen troops and all their equipment; both Unit operators and the Rangers generally rode sitting in the doorways on both sides facing outward, their legs dangling over the sides.

---

* The assault model preferred by SOAR as opposed to the standard MH-60.

If the Black Hawk was the workhorse, Little Birds were the angry hornets. Small, light, and highly maneuverable, they could operate in restrictive spaces, such as in cities. Outfitted so that commandos could sit on the pods that extended out from the helicopter—totally exposed—the Little Birds could be used for infil and exfil. But they were also used for reconnaissance and, with their rockets and 7.62 mm miniguns, were deadly when attacking.

As it became increasingly evident that we would be deployed to Africa, several new guys were brought aboard for the mission. One was Tim "Griz" Martin, a big man from Indiana who always seemed to have a smile on his face. He was an experienced operator who would also become a friend. Normally, Griz was the squadron's "master breacher" who made sure all of the teams were up-to-date on their breaching training and the latest technology. He was married and had three daughters with his wife, Linda. After nearly twenty years in active duty, he was thinking about retiring and starting a small business. But he had stayed on for the Somalia mission, and had been assigned to our group.

My best friend and teammate at the time was Jake L., a very tall blond guy as dedicated to the job as anybody in the Unit. He had arrived at the squadron six months after me and we'd hit it off immediately. The running joke was that we were so inseparable we were actually one entity, "Tom and Jake," to everybody else.

Matt Rierson was another friend. He was a great big guy from Iowa who was not part of the hard-partying culture that dominated the rest of the Unit. Instead, he was a dedicated family man who couldn't wait to get home after a day of training to his wife, Trish, and their two young boys. One of the best pistol shots in the squadron, Matt often invited me to accompany him to shooting competitions.

Our other friends—Earl Fillmore, Jon Hale, and Robin Rapp—were on another team. We'd met playing water polo and then hung out together after work at the bars.

In addition to the men who became my friends, the Unit certainly attracted its share of eccentric characters. One was Dan Busch, who had joined the team six months after me but had since moved on to the Sniper Troop. A quiet, religious man from the backwoods of Appalachia, he was a "creationist" who didn't believe in evolution and thought that the world was only a few thousand years old. His beliefs got him teased a lot, including by me, but he took the ribbing well.

As the summer wore on, there was a growing sense that the day was fast approaching when we'd be sent to Somalia. We all watched the news and read the intelligence reports on what was happening, and it wasn't good.

On July 12, 1993, a US-led raid attacked a compound in Mogadishu where it was believed that Aidid was hiding. US Cobra attack helicopters fired sixteen missiles and thousands of 20 mm cannon rounds into the compound.

The attack was a public relations disaster. Aidid was not present during the attack, but his interior minister claimed that seventy-three people were killed, including women and children. The United States placed the number at twenty, all men, while the International Committee of the Red Cross set the number at fifty-four. Four journalists were killed by an angry mob when they arrived to cover the incident. The civilian deaths would end up unifying the Somalis against the UN and US presence in Somalia.

On August 8, four US soldiers on patrol in Mogadishu were killed by an improvised explosive device (IED) detonated with a remote control by Aidid's militia. Two weeks later, another bomb injured seven more.

In response, President Bill Clinton, in his first year in office, ordered the four-hundred-man force, code-named Task Force Ranger, to Mogadishu to find, capture, or kill Aidid and his lieutenants.

BACK HOME AT FORT Bragg, the warriors of the Unit focused on our training and paid close attention to instructions from our leaders. The day our pagers went off and we reported to Fort Brag for a briefing, we were told that we would leave for Mogadishu in five days. We were given a list of things to accomplish prior to departing that included getting our wills updated, making arrangements for our families, and saying goodbye.

"And get your hair cut," we were told. The Pentagon had still never officially acknowledged the existence of the Unit, and the brass didn't want the media or anyone else, including Aidid, wondering about the guys with the long hair and whiskers accompanying the Rangers.

When I got home and told Debbie I would be leaving in a few days, I told her where I was going, but I didn't tell her about the mission, nor did she ask.

Her job at the post exchange (PX) kept her occupied while I focused on my career. I loved my job and that made me happier at home. We rarely fought or argued. But neither did we spend much time together, and intimacy was a rarity.

She had her friends and made frequent trips home to Indiana. I hung out with other Unit friends, a hard-charging, heavy-drinking crew who chased women and lived large. I wasn't fooling around on Debbie, at least not then, but I did my share of drinking and carousing.

On the appointed day, she drove me to Fort Bragg. We were quiet on the ride in. It was obvious I was excited; finally, I was going to test my mettle in combat. I'd trained for and dreamed of this moment for years. That we were going after a warlord who was starving people and attacking UN peacekeepers made it all the better. The kid who'd eventually stood up to bullies was only too happy, as a man, to go after one of them.

Pulling into the parking lot at work, I got out of the car. There was an awkward moment when I realized it was possible I might not be coming back.

Leaning in to grab my bag, I kissed Debbie on the cheek. "See you when I see you" was all I said.

She smiled slightly. "No news is good news," she replied.

As I turned to join my companions, Debbie pulled away to drive home. Neither of us knew it at the time, but our life together had just changed forever.

Three hours later and loaded up on six C-5 cargo jets, it was wheels up for Task Force Ranger. The more experienced operators, those who'd been to war, took it all in stride. They were ready to go, but not looking forward to it. They knew that killing went both ways.

The young guys like me were pumped up. This was no "security assessment" in South America, or even as part of a small team going after a terrorist in some far-flung part of Asia. We were going to war, where we'd be facing large numbers of enemy combatants while helping defenseless people get food and live peacefully out from under the shadow of a cruel warlord.

We had the best equipment and were the best trained warriors in the world. We could take on anything a ragtag bunch of Somali militias could throw at us.

THERE HAD BEEN A lot of excitement when we first took off for Africa, but then things quieted down. Some of the guys passed the hours with extended card games and Risk, the "world conquest" board game. But most seemed to withdraw into themselves and either tried to sleep or simply sat lost in thought.

CHAPTER SEVEN

August 1993
Mogadishu, Somalia

THE FLIGHT LASTED an interminable seventeen hours and by the time we set down at the Mogadishu airport, I was exhausted but amped about what was to come. Stepping off the plane, the oppressive heat and humidity hit me like a warm wet sponge, and I nearly gagged at the stench of rotting garbage emanating from the nearby beach.

The airport, which had been closed to all commercial flights due to safety precautions, was attached to the southern end of Mogadishu. On the east side it butted up against the coastline with a beautiful stretch of white sand beach juxtaposed with the azure sea—at least those parts not used to dump garbage. To the west was the desert, an inhospitable expanse of sand and rock.

Task Force Ranger troops were assigned to an old football-field-size hanger. Inside, row after row of cots were already set up on the concrete floor and each group was sent to their designated area. "Rangers over here. The Unit over there. Snipers in back."

August was rainy season in Somalia and the hangar's roof leaked like a sieve. The temperature also reached ninety degrees during the day, turning the hangar into a massive sauna.

Rain wasn't the only thing coming down on Task Force Ranger. Soon after we arrived, the locals started lobbing mortar rounds at the airfield, exploding with a "WHOOMP" when they struck the ground. The enemy wasn't particularly accurate, but on August 29, five servicemen were wounded when one landed near them.

The almost daily sound of mortar shells landing all around the airfield grew tiresome, especially after the Rangers discovered a way to turn it into a game. They had brought a freezer with them for ice cream, which when slammed shut made a similar sound to mortar rounds landing. That, of course, meant they'd wait until everybody else was settled in and then some smartass would slam the lid shut to make us all jump. Finally, someone grew tired of their game and took the freezer, and it was never seen again.

But we didn't come to Africa to eat ice cream or sit on our cots with the roof leaking and mortars thumping around us. Major General G., who had secretly left Fort Bragg several days ahead of Task Force Ranger in order to prepare for their arrival and missions, had a three-part plan to capture Aidid. Phase One was set to last four days to allow Task Force Ranger to set up operations and establish ties to other US forces already in Mogadishu under Maj. Gen. Thomas Montgomery, including the Marines and troops from the Army's 10th Mountain Division.

Phase Two would focus entirely on an effort to capture Aidid by relying on "current actionable intelligence" that would come from HUMINT, or "human intelligence," provided by CIA informants scattered throughout the city. If one of the informants spotted Aidid, he was to call in and Task Force Ranger would respond within an hour, either by helicopter or ground transportation. Upon arriving at the target, the Rangers would then set up a perimeter and the Unit would hit the target building; helicopters would hover overhead to provide firepower if needed and exfil the commandos with their prisoner.

If Aidid, who had not been spotted since mid-July, did not come out of hiding, Phase Three would expand the target list to include his six top aides. The idea was that capturing or killing them would force Aidid to expose himself to keep control of his militia and territory.

To jump-start Phase Two, Major General Garrison called UN headquarters in Mogadishu and asked for the best location Aidid had been known to frequent before he went into hiding. Armed with this information, at 3 a.m. on August 30, Task Force Ranger scrambled.

I was the first Unit operator to fast-rope to the roof of the target building. But I was almost immediately tangled up in antennae wires, a common feature on roofs in Mogadishu, that had been torn loose by the rotor wash of the Black Hawk. It was like fighting my way through a giant spiderweb as I made my way to the doorway leading down into the two-story building. Meanwhile, the rest of the team was backed up behind me.

On this night, I had decided to take a long Remington 1100 shotgun loaded with slugs that could be used to blow open the lock of a door, as well as kill. I'd just untangled myself from the wires when a man leaned out of a door on the right side of the hallway and looked at me.

"Freeze, motherfucker, or die!" But my command did not work. The man popped back into his room.

I yelled into my radio to my team that a "noncompliant" male had moved back into the room. I couldn't follow him because I had to hold security on a door across the hallway in case an attacker emerged from there. So, my team moved past me and into the room where the first man disappeared.

Disappointed not to be involved in clearing the room and not wanting to be left behind again, I took it upon myself to clear the next three rooms alone. Something that was completely against my training. I was about to clear another when my team leader grabbed me and ordered me to stop. "I love the motivation," he said. "But your tactics are fucked up."

In the end, the raid rounded up eight people who had been sleeping in the building. None of them were Aidid, or anyone else we were looking for. We did find cash, a large supply of khat, and stolen satellite equipment, all evidence of a black-market operation.

The house and its occupants turned out to be part of a UN Development Program and the takedown made headlines in the United States. Despite the evidence that criminal activity was going on, it was a public relations nightmare simply because we had failed to get our target.

The Americans at the airfield knew we were being watched from the city and some low-lying hills to the north, and that our every movement was reported by a loose network of hand-held radios. If we took off in the helicopters at night, the operators would see the spies blink the headlights of their vehicles as a signal to their comrades in the city.

So, to desensitize the enemy and lull them into a sense of complacency, we went for "signature flights" over the city. Twice a day we got into battle gear and went through the same routines we would if going on actual missions. That way the watchers wouldn't know what was rehearsal and what was real. Then we'd climb aboard the aircraft and take off.

Sometimes we'd head east out over the sea and then swing back to roar over the city. Or we'd head directly to the southern part of the city where Aidid's militia was in control, as if we knew exactly where we were going. Or we'd circle around and come in from another direction. But never the same way twice in a row.

From the air, I could tell that Mogadishu had once been a beautiful, if quaint, city with parks, neat rows of homes, high-rise hotels, and stadiums. Even the ocher-colored dirt streets looked pretty from a height. Like a giant spiderweb, they tended to run this way and that, changing direction or weaving around so that a road that began by heading north, might turn east, then north, then west, without much rhyme or reason. Little did I realize on these signature flights how that spiderweb could be turned into a trap.

But even from the air the effects of the civil war could be discerned in buildings and homes that had been reduced to rubble, much of it piled in the streets. Many of the larger buildings, like the hotels, appeared to have been abandoned and were now shells of what they had been.

The ocean was beautiful, too, but dangerous. Swimming was a risky proposition.

I'd heard stories of soldiers being attacked by sharks in the shallow waters near the shore. Apparently, the beasts had been lured in not just by the garbage, but by bodies and body parts that were victims of famine and war, which had been disposed of in the water.

Occasionally, the Unit operators and their Ranger companions would practice taking down a house, dropping down from the sky to infil, and then being met by Humvees to exfil back to the base. Or rolling in on the Humvees and exfilling by air.

Mogadishu looked even worse from the streets, and it was both more disquieting and more dangerous. In addition to the pockmarks on most of the buildings, gaping holes appeared in walls, apparently the work of RPGs and heavy weapons. Burned-out car frames littered the streets. There seemed to be an enormous number of tires lying around in intersections and next to sidewalks, something I noted but couldn't guess the reason for.

Driving through the winding streets, the operators never knew what to expect. Different parts of the city had been claimed by clans, some friendly to the United States and some not. Some people waved and smiled as they went past, others stared glumly, or even hostilely, as they chewed khat and watched the Americans go by.

We saw the evidence of mass starvation everywhere. People so thin they seemed to have no meat at all on their bones, and children with distended stomachs and big eyes set in gaunt faces. It was a shocking sight to a young man raised in the American heartland, where food was plentiful. Not even in my travels to South America had I seen such poverty and destruction, or such cruelty toward civilians, especially children. It was a good reminder for the men of why we were there.

When the Unit first started the signature flights, the watchers would signal frantically and the locals in the city would scatter and hide. The operators were sure that Aidid and his lieutenants were probably behaving the same way, wondering if their number was finally up. But as the Somalis got used to the flights, especially when nothing much seemed to come of them, they ignored the helicopters.

Occasionally someone would take a potshot at the birds. Most of the time, unless the helicopter was actually struck, and sometimes not even then, the guys being shot at didn't know it because of the roar of the helicopters. At night, they'd sometimes see tracer rounds arcing up harmlessly at them. But shooting at a helicopter was hazardous for the shooter. They traveled in groups and while the target helicopter might not even see who did the shooting, one of the others would and that would bring a swift and violent response.

When we weren't going out on signature flights, we worked to keep ourselves in top physical shape, running on the beach, playing sand volleyball, and lifting weights. Or we'd go to the beach and practice shooting at crabs. We even found an abandoned town for CQB and urban warfare training.

Otherwise we spent our free time reading intelligence reports, watching news reports from home on the television, or playing cards and board games. Our team played thousands of games of Risk, conquering the world one roll of the dice at a time.

On September 7, 1993, with Aidid still hiding, Major General G. implemented Phase Three broadening the hunt to include Aidid's lieutenants. The CIA's informants were proving to be less than adequate. For one thing, they would only work during the day. The city was too dangerous at night when the Unit liked to conduct missions, but by then the informants were all home safe in bed. It didn't help when one of the main informants accidentally killed himself playing Russian roulette.

The next mission involving the Unit didn't go any better than the first because of a case of mistaken identity. American troops had difficulty distinguishing one Somali from another. The "Skinnies," as they were called, were a tall, slender dark-skinned people known for their high cheekbones and broad foreheads. They tended to dress similarly as well.

Aware of Italy's colonial history in the region and the large ethnic Italian population that still lived in the city, the US command suspected them of sympathizing with Aidid's clan and even providing covert assistance to him.* As a result, Major General G. sent an intelligence officer to the Italian Embassy to smooth the waters.

While we were waiting, five Rangers sent as an escort for the intelligence officer saw a brown Land Rover pulling into the embassy compound. A Somali male got out of the car but when he saw the Americans, he jumped back in and sped off.

The excited Rangers thought the man looked like Aidid and reported that back to base. A reconnaissance helicopter was sent to follow the vehicle, which went to a house in northern Mogadishu. This should have been the first clue: Aidid controlled the southern part of the city.

Nevertheless, we scrambled and hit the building—a former police station—at 1 p.m. This time I wasn't in the assault party but remained with my team hovering overhead in a Black Hawk in case backup was needed.

Down below, our operators arrested the suspect who'd fled the Italian embassy, along with thirty-eight other individuals. The suspect turned out to be Ahmed Jilao, the former security chief for deposed dictator Siad Barre, considered by the UN to be an ally.

Once again, a Unit raid, through no fault of the operators, proved to be an embarrassment. And it, of course, made the news back in the United States.

---

* Ibid.

Always quick with a joke, I also added to the fun quite by accident during the next raid, a night hit on what had been an old Russian apartment complex. We'd already been in one building, going door to door and blowing the locks before hauling the surprised residents out of their beds, when we decided to try a building on the other side of the street. But as I stepped off the curb, I fell, breaking my night-vision goggles off my helmet and landing in a pile of urine and human feces.

Memories of my drill sergeant nicknaming me "Shit" flashed in my mind and I hoped it wouldn't stick again now. But after gaining access to another building where I took a knee with my teammates, someone asked, "Who shit?"

I didn't say a word. The question was asked again, but still I remained quiet. Then an angry voice demanded to know "Who the fuck shit their pants?"

"Um, I may or may not have fallen in a pile of shit," I admitted.

There was a moment of silence. Then someone chuckled, followed by someone else, and pretty soon everyone in the room was laughing at my expense.

Up to this point, the mission did not seem to be getting any closer to catching Aidid or his lieutenants. Nor had there been any firefights with the Somali militias. Other than the occasional potshot at the helicopters on their signature flights, no one had even tried to shoot at them. The raids were exciting—if I wasn't falling down in a pile of shit—but I was beginning to wonder if I'd ever find out what it was like to be in combat when we were sent on a mission to take down "Radio Mog."

Radio Mogadishu had existed since the days of Italian Somaliland, initially broadcasting the news in Italian and Somali. The Russians had updated the station after independence from the British in 1960 and it had continued broadcasting the news until the civil war.

The radio station had served as a propaganda platform for Aidid, who used it to broadcast messages to his militia, as well as stir up the population against the Americans. Broadcasts urged Somalis to fight. Worried that Radio Mogadishu was being used to communicate military plans and stir up resistance, the decision was made to go after them.

The problem was that the station operators moved their transmitter every other day to avoid detection. It took several weeks of tracking and then locating the signal in enough time to successfully launch a hit.

This time we went in at night on the ground, riding Humvees and five-ton trucks, with the Rangers in front to establish the perimeter and the Unit behind. Because the trucks weren't armored, the assault teams added sandbags and plywood before leaving to give them a little more protection.

The hit was going down in a "safe" part of town controlled by a clan friendly to the American forces. However, no place was considered truly safe in Mogadishu; there were no signs that said which side of the street belonged to a friendly clan and which belonged to the enemy. And sometimes they switched sides. The best strategy was to assume that they were all the enemy.

Arriving at the target, a walled compound with several small thatched-roof shacks inside, the Rangers moved out to set up the perimeter while our team assaulted the first shack. I blew open the lock with my shotgun, then stepped aside while the rest of the team flowed inside.

Pulling security to prevent anyone from surprising the team from behind, I walked into the shack and looked into one of the rooms that had already been cleared. A typewriter stood on a desk but otherwise there was nothing in the room.

Another commando appeared in the room. "You know you just shot a woman," he said. "Your round went through the door, skipped off the floor and hit her in the leg. Go take care of her."

I wasn't sure how to take the comment. Was he admonishing me or simply letting me know? His accusatory tone angered me. I didn't mean to shoot the woman; it was a ricochet. This was war and people got hurt, but now I had to attend to the woman as a "punishment."

I went into the room where a middle-aged woman was lying on her back wailing at the top of her lungs. There were several other operators in the room, and someone had tucked a pillow under her wounded leg, and it was soaked with blood.

Jake rolled her over so I could bandage her wound. I saw that she was lying on top of a knife. It could have gotten her shot if she'd picked it up when the operators first breached the door. But it was understandable that she kept one in her bed; this was Mogadishu, a lawless city where rape was a common occurrence.

We decided to transport the woman so that she could get medical attention. Jake and I were assigned to carry the stretcher. Leaving the building, we began to take fire from seemingly all directions. Red tracer rounds lit up the night, but it wasn't clear exactly where the shots were coming from—a lesson in the difficulty of fighting in a city where shots echo off walls and bullets are fired from hidden positions.

Jake and I took off running for the Humvees with our burden screaming every step of the way. As bullets traveling at supersonic speeds passed overhead, they sounded like tree branches snapping on a cold winter's day. I'd heard the sound before at Fort Bragg, but that was while safely crouched in a sniper pit, and I'd never heard so many at once.

The shooters weren't very accurate, and the bullets caromed off walls or cracked overhead and whizzed into the dark. But when Jake and I reached a point where we were going to have to run across the street to the waiting vehicles, we stopped and crouched down to see if we could determine where the shooting was coming from.

I looked at Jake who said, "If we start taking direct fire…"

"Yeah," I agreed and finished the sentence, "we're dropping her."

Reaching the Humvee, we loaded the stretcher onto the center bench in the back. There wasn't much room, so I had to sit on the woman's gurney. She was still screaming which added to the noise and chaos.

As we began to exfil, we began taking fire from an alley. I started pumping rounds of buckshot down the alley. Above me, the assaulter manning the .50-caliber machine gun on top of the vehicle opened up, blasting everything in sight. Apparently, that was too much for the woman, who stopped screaming and remained quiet for the rest of the trip.

Back at the airfield, we turned the woman over to the medics and met to go over the After Action Report. In summary, we'd arrived too late and didn't catch anyone operating Radio Mog or find the transmitter, just the typewriter that was probably being used to write radio dispatches.

I didn't think it was a complete loss. The cavalry rode in. Bullets flew. Just like in the movies. Except now I knew what it was like to get shot at. I was more excited than ever to do my job, and I soon got the chance.

One of the main Aidid lieutenants was a wealthy businessman named Osman Ali Atto. A former oil company executive, he was Aidid's money man, which meant he found ways to raise money from the less desirable characters working the black market, and then funneled the funds to his boss.

Aidid needed the constant flow of cash to pay his militiamen and to buy weapons and ammunition. If we could roll Atto up, he might give us his boss. If not, Aidid would run out of money and be forced to surface to raise money himself.

Unit command hatched a plan. Task force intelligence officers suspected that some Somalis worked for UN contractors during the day and for the bad guys at night. They began making electronic "imprints," as well as "voice imprints" of radio transmissions used to direct the mortar fire that badgered the airfield. This led to the arrest of twelve Somali contractors who were also working for the enemy. One of them gave up a location that he said would yield Osman Ali Atto.

This time the Unit operators decided to try a different approach. Instead of waiting for Atto to go into a house, we waited to catch him driving somewhere and interdicted the car, catching him in the open. We practiced in the desert away from prying eyes until we felt ready, then we went after him.

On September 21, we received information that Atto was going to attend a meeting that afternoon. It meant a daylight raid, which wasn't optimal, but this was too good an opportunity to pass up. The pagers went off and we scrambled to the helicopters where we were briefed on the mission. A few minutes later, we were in the air.

The operators hoped that Atto would drive somewhere away from the city. Nonetheless, when his driver remained in the city, the decision was made to go ahead.

The plan worked like a charm. A sniper in one of the helicopters took out the car's engine and, unknowingly, also hit the driver in the legs. Two men, one of them Atto, along with a younger man, jumped out of the vehicle. They dragged the driver out of the car and went into a walled compound around a two-story house with a small front porch.

A team of operators fast-roped to the ground and moved to take down the house where Atto had disappeared. Meanwhile, our team hovered above, ready to lend assistance if needed.

Unlike the Radio Mog hit, this neighborhood was in Aidid's territory and populated by his militia. Within minutes, the assaulters were coming under fire from multiple directions. Like most of Mogadishu, the neighborhood was composed of one- and two-story houses inside of six- to eight-foot walls, all of it providing cover for the enemy.

With the battle growing in ferocity, our team was called in. Jake and I roped down into the middle of the intersection near Atto's car and ran down an alley where most of the fire was coming from. A machine gun less than fifty yards away opened up on us. Chunks of dirt and concrete flew up as bullets struck the road and walls around us or cracked overhead.

Taking cover in the entranceways of compounds on opposite sides of the street, Jake and I returned fire. Our shooting was much more accurate than the machine gunner's, whose gun went quiet when he took a bullet.

Another man appeared, walking nonchalantly toward the machine gun. He obviously intended to use the weapon on us, but he was unarmed so we had to hold our fire. The Somalis knew that the Americans were hampered by our rules of engagement (ROE), which prohibited us from shooting an unarmed person.

As expected, the man dropped next to the machine gun and began shooting at us. We shot him, too. But another unarmed man strolled over and took his place.

This went on four or five times. Finally, I had enough. The Somalis were using the ROE against the Americans to feed their weapon. Sooner or later, either Jake or I was going to get hit. The next man who tried to reach the machine gun died before he ever got there. The rest stopped trying.

With the machine gun out of action, we continued to fight our way down the street. At one point we took cover, and it was obvious that the enemy couldn't see us.

Suddenly a tall woman in a black dress appeared in the road and walked toward us until she saw where we were positioned. She then pointed at us for the enemy gunmen.

I was stunned. She was obviously unarmed and a woman. I didn't know if she'd been ordered to risk her life to point us out or was doing it on her own. But she was clearly dangerous; bullets began skipping around our positions.

Loading bean bag rounds into my shotgun, I blasted the woman. The nonlethal round dropped her to the ground. But she got up and again pointed to where Jake and I were taking cover. I dropped her again and again until finally she'd had enough and fled.

A call came over our headsets from the team leader, Pete, telling us to return to the target house to pull guard duty on the detainees.

We left the street and returned to where the three prisoners were on the porch, two of them seated and the other lying on his side, all with their hands bound behind their backs with plastic ties.

One of the prisoners was Atto. Another was a young man who was obviously mentally disabled; he was smiling at us with his tongue hanging out of his mouth. The third was the driver, who lay on his side moaning.

Pissed off about having to stand guard duty while the battle raged around us, I approached Atto, who glared defiantly at me. I snatched his sunglasses off of his head.* I don't know why I did it other than I wanted Atto to know he was no longer in charge of anything.

At last we were ready to exfil by helicopter from the roof of the building. Word went out for everyone to collapse from the perimeter toward the building.

I went to make the driver stand up. I thought the man was faking his injuries and grabbed him by the ankles to force him up. That's when I discovered that the sniper's bullet had turned the bottom of his legs to jelly. He would have to be dragged up the stairs.

Most of the assault team raced for the roof. They took Atto and the driver with them but left the mentally disabled young man behind. I was told to hang back to provide covering fire from a window on the floor below.

If anything, the bad guys were showing up in greater numbers, shooting at the building from surrounding buildings. The sound of the battle was like a dozen maniacal, deafening popcorn poppers going off all around us, only with bullets striking the walls. The smell of gunpowder hung in the air, mixed with the aroma of the helicopter engine working overtime to hover on the lip of the roof so that the assaulters with their prisoners could get in.

---

* The sunglasses would end up in the US Army Airborne and Special Operations Museum at Fort Bragg.

Looking out, I saw a Somali in the window one floor above me in a building across the street. The man held an AK-47 and was aiming up at where I knew a helicopter was taking on operators.

I aimed at the man's head and squeezed the trigger as I let out my breath—just the way I'd practiced thousands of times before. I knew I hit the man by the way he suddenly disappeared from the window, his rifle clattering to the street below.

Excited about my first confirmed kill, I called out to Pete. "You see that?" I yelled, and explained what had happened.

"Good," Pete said and that was it. I'd done what I was trained to do and there was no need to go on about it.

I was the last operator to leave the roof. The helicopter was hovering just inches from the edge of the building and I had to climb up the tire to get in. Just as I thought I might fall, someone grabbed me by my pants and yanked me aboard.

On the way back, I thought about the firefight. That was the first time I'd actually seen people shooting at me from a distance. Shooting the enemy didn't bother me, even the guy in the window who'd been close enough for me to see his face. My training had taken over; they were just targets. But this battle had definitely been more intense than the Radio Mogadishu raid, and I wondered how much more severe it could get.

Arriving back at the base with our prizes, the mission was deemed a huge success. We'd captured one of Aidid's most important lieutenants and, amazingly, none of the Unit operators or Rangers had been hurt despite the fierce firefight.

The pucker factor had definitely soared to a thousand. But we'd all lived to laugh and joke about it as we recounted our adventures. A lot of sentences began, "Then I..." Others reflected a disassociation with the ethical questions surrounding killing. *Did you see the way that guy's head exploded?* It was as if it was all a game, like playing soldier with my friends as a kid, getting back up and dusting ourselves off to go home for dinner.

During the celebration, Pete showed up and took me aside to talk about Jake and me making our frontal assault on the enemy down the alley. "Again, your tactics are fucked up," he said. "But I'm thoroughly impressed with your balls."

I couldn't have been prouder. I was now part of the tribe of blooded warriors. What's more, I'd killed a man from nearly point-blank range who'd been about to shoot at my defenseless teammates as they were climbing on board the helicopter.

War was everything I'd imagined. The bad guys had been defeated. My friends and I had lived to fight another day.

We were invincible. We were immortal. We were the Unit.

CHAPTER EIGHT

October 3, 1993
Mogadishu, Somalia

FROM HELL: FIRE AND BRIMSTONE

It was a pleasant Sunday afternoon at the Task Force Ranger base. Guys were working out and relaxing. I was running around the airfield, trying to get in five miles beneath the blazing African sun.

Morale had gone up after the capture of Atto. We'd finally completed a successful mission that we hoped would lead to Aidid, but so far it had not resulted in rolling up the main man or any more of his lieutenants. And although the Unit continued making signature flights and forays into the city to practice CQB, we'd received no more intelligence that might lead us to our main targets.

There had been one disturbing event. A little more than a week earlier, on September 25, 1993, Aidid's militia used an RPG to shoot down a 10th Mountain Division Black Hawk. Three crew members were killed. Ominously, this was the first time a helicopter had been shot down in Mogadishu and the first US casualties since early August.

As a result, the command ordered "downed helicopter" practice; a scenario in which a Black Hawk went down, killing the pilots and leaving four others injured and in need of rescue. A lot was learned, including making necessary adjustments to our kits, especially that we needed to carry more medical equipment. But no one expected it to be a regular occurrence; Black Hawks were tough birds and the Somalis had gotten lucky.

However, when I left the hangar on that pleasant Sunday afternoon, I wasn't thinking about Black Hawks going down or any of us needing to be rescued. None of us were.

At the volleyball court, officers and NCOs were pitted against each other in a spirited game as only a bunch of young, testosterone-filled males could be. I'd smiled when I trotted past and saw that Major General G. and Lieutenant Colonel H. had been duct-taped to a couple of cots and propped up next to the court so that they could "participate."

In the hangar, guys were cleaning their weapons while the marathon games of cards and Risk continued. Some used the time to write letters home.

I had written to my parents that morning, in part a response to a letter I'd received from them complaining about everything from vacations that didn't turn out to be the way they wanted, to being tired, to my Dad wishing he had more courage to play his guitar onstage. Something about sitting in a giant sweltering metal shed far from home on the outskirts of a war-torn city in a country in which people were starving to death and killing each other over food and clean drinking water, while others were risking their lives to stop it, made me less than sympathetic to their gripes.

Although Task Force Ranger, as with any Unit mission, was classified, I began nicely enough by giving them a hint about where I was and what I was doing:

Well, if you watch the news at all, you know where I am and know what I'm doing and have probably seen footage of me doing it....I wanted the exciting life, dangerous, fast paced. Well, I got it.

I can actually enjoy the adrenaline rush after you get to your target, after you swallow your heart out of your throat, and get over the feeling of wanting to shit your pants when someone shoots at you.

Then I got to what was troubling me about their letter.

I want to tell you both something. You only get one life. One go-around at the game. One short section in eternity called "life" and that is it. So, do what you want to do now. Don't look back and say, "I wish I'd done that." Look back and say, "I'm glad I did that."

I thanked them for working so hard and giving up so much to raise my siblings and me. But now I wanted them to enjoy life.

Dad, get up on that stage and show everyone how well you play. And mom, sit your ass down.... You're the only one I know who can go on vacation to some beautiful island or take a cruise and when you tell me about it, you tell me how it rained, or you got sick. Well, it's all how you look at it. Rain is beautiful even on a beach. You're with Dad, the one you love, on a rainy beach in a tropical resort. That should make you happy.

I go to the most disease-infested shitholes in the world. You can't imagine how bad. And I always find a bar with beer and laugh with my friends.

I know I'm lecturing you two and you've got twice the amount of time on me. And I don't have a degree in any-ology. But I'll tell you something, I have lived and seen more places and people of all types and beliefs than you can put a label on.... I've seen life and I've seen death, and I have looked it in the eye and pissed on it because it all means nothing unless you can look back and say "I'm glad I did that" or at least, "I had fun doing it."

I closed out saying I hoped they would still go visit Debbie in North Carolina.

She is the most precious thing in my life, and I could never repay her for all the loneliness and worry she goes through because of me.

Hopefully I'll be home soon, then we can play guitar and listen to war stories. I don't want either of you to worry about me. I'm fine and I'll be fine. I love both of you. Watch the news...even though news people are assholes.

Love, Tom

When my pager went off, I looked at it and knew right away this was not going to be any signature flight. I was hot and sweaty and would have liked to get a shower and dry off before going on a hit. But I had just a few minutes to get back to the hangar, get my gear on—a ten-minute process in itself—grab my weapons and ammo, and get my butt on a helicopter. I took off sprinting for the hangar.

Unknown to me at the time, a couple of hours earlier one of the CIA informants had reported that two of Aidid's top lieutenants would be meeting that afternoon at a building near the white-washed, four-story Olympic Hotel, deep in the heart of enemy territory. There was even a possibility that Aidid himself might show up.

A reconnaissance helicopter had been dispatched to watch as the informant drove his car up to the curb outside a building where he parked. He exited his vehicle, lifted the hood, looked under it, then lowered it, got back in and left. That was the prearranged signal to indicate that the building was the location for the meeting.

Shortly before 3 p.m., Major General G. spoke to his counterpart in the city, Maj. Gen. Thomas "Bill" Montgomery, who commanded the other US troops in Mogadishu, and talked to him about the plan. "That's really Indian country," Montgomery warned him. "That's a bad place."[*]

Garrison was already aware of the danger. The Olympic Hotel was only a few blocks from the Bakaara Market, a virtual armed

---

[*] "The Raid That Went Wrong," by Rick Atkinson, *Washington Post*, January 30, 1994.

camp for Aidid's militia. In fact, in September, Garrison told his officers that if they had to go into the vicinity of the market, "there's no question we'll win the gunfight, but we might lose the war."

Making matters worse, this would be another daytime raid. The Unit liked working at night when the enemy was sleeping, or at least off guard.

Still, the chance to grab several of Aidid's lieutenants and even the man himself was too much to pass up. This would be a quick grab and go before the militia knew what was happening and, if we got lucky, Task Force Ranger's main mission would be accomplished before sundown. Command gave the okay and pagers began to go off all around the airfield.

The operators decided to leave their night-vision goggles at the hangar, as well as extra water and food. Night-vision goggles gave us and the Rangers a huge tactical advantage when fighting at night. Such decisions were left up to them, and since it wasn't even 3 p.m. yet, the sun wouldn't set until a little after 6 p.m. and twilight not for another half hour after that. If this really was only going to take an hour, there was no need to bring the cumbersome goggles or carry the extra water weight. "We'll be back in time for dinner," the guys joked.

The first move was for the AH-6 Little Birds, equipped with rockets and miniguns, to strafe the target area. Anybody carrying a weapon was fair game and would not be given a chance to surrender.

One assault team would follow immediately in Little Birds and be placed on the roof to take down the target building and apprehend its occupants. A second assault team of operators, including mine, in two Black Hawks would land at the designated location and target the building from the ground.

At nearly the same time, four Black Hawks carrying teams of Rangers would arrive and establish a perimeter around the target to prevent interference or a counterattack. While all of this was going on, Black Hawks carrying snipers, one of them with Dan Busch, would hover overhead, ready to provide accurate fire support.

Meanwhile, a convoy of nine Humvees and three five-ton trucks would drive to the target to exfil the assault team and their prisoners back to the base. Tim "Griz" Martin would be driving the Humvee to pick up my team.

In case of unexpected trouble, the Quick Reaction Force of the 10th Mountain Division had been alerted to be on standby. And if things got really hot, the UN peacekeeping elements of the Pakistani and Malaysian armies with their tanks and armored personnel carriers could be called upon.

When the birds lifted off at 3:30, they first headed east, out over the ocean, before swinging west and then south so as to come at the target from the north. At 3:40 p.m., two AH-6 Little Bird gunships were the first to arrive at the target building, blasting away to clear the armed militia and throw the others into a panic.

They were followed immediately by four MH-6 Little Birds, the type modified to carry commandos two on each side, which set down on top of the building. One of the Black Hawks landed next to it. The assaulters rushed into the building and within minutes they captured two of Aidid's top lieutenants without firing a shot—his foreign minister, Omar Salad Elmi, and his top political advisor, Mohamed Hassan Awale—as well as a couple dozen other Aidid supporters and militia members.

Meanwhile, even as the Unit assault team was taking down the target building, the four Black Hawk helicopters carrying about sixty Rangers arrived at the target and the troops began fast-roping to the ground.

Though all seemed to be going well, cracks were already beginning to appear in the plan. The dust raised by the helicopters created such a thick yellow-orange cloud that the pilots had difficulty identifying landing zones, and one of the Black Hawks carrying Rangers took them a block north of where they were supposed to be.

At the same time, Aidid's militia responded much faster than anticipated and the troops began taking fire almost immediately.

The Rangers who'd missed their target had to fight their way back toward their assignment under heavy fire.

Also, the convoy that was supposed to arrive a few minutes after the assault began ran into delays.

In addition, Somali citizens and the militia began throwing up barricades using rocks, the burned out car frames, and the tires I had wondered about when flying over the city, which they set on fire.

The convoy arrived ten minutes late and parked near the Olympic Hotel. They, too, came under heavy fire almost immediately.

A bigger issue presented itself when a Ranger, Pfc. Todd B., fell from a helicopter to the ground and was severely injured. Three Humvees, originally assigned to transport the assault teams back to base, were reassigned to evacuate the injured private. On the way back to the base, Sgt. Dominick Pilla was struck in the head by a bullet and killed. By the time the vehicles arrived at the base, they were smoking and riddled with bullets. It was an ominous sign of what was to come.

The Black Hawk carrying my team was also affected by the cloud of dust. Unable to see the landing zone, the pilot took us several blocks north of the target building. The crew chief had to point in the direction we needed to go after we reached the ground. We then had to fast-rope into a twilight zone in which visibility was limited to twenty feet.

We, too, began taking fire immediately. In that case, the dust probably helped by interfering with the accuracy of the Somali shooters. But that didn't mean we were safe from the fusillade of bullets fired down the street toward us, skipping off walls and snapping as the rounds passed overhead. Surrounded by buildings and walled compounds, which created a huge echo effect that could hide attackers, it was even difficult to tell where shots were coming from.

With the fire intensifying, our leader decided the team needed to get off the street to regroup. We took down a house, finding a frightened family inside trying to survive the battle that had erupted outside of their home.

As I entered the house, I saw one of our men struggling to take down an immense Somali who had his back turned toward him. The man refused to go down. I moved to help, but then saw why the man was putting up such a struggle; he was holding a tiny baby in his dinner plate-sized hands.

Worried about the child and that one of my teammates might misinterpret the man's struggles and shoot him, I tried to wrest the baby from the man. But the Somali wasn't having any part of it and fought harder. Finally, I got the baby away from the man and handed it to one of the wailing women in the room. Only then did the Somali male understand and allow himself to be brought to the ground and cuffed with plastic ties.

WITH A MOMENT TO regroup, Pete determined we were north of the target. The sound of fighting was growing, and we needed to leave before we were cut off. It was clear that we were outside of the Ranger perimeter. With all the dust in the air limiting visibility and the intensifying firefight, the Rangers manning the roadblocks were bound to be jumpy. There was a very real question of whether we would be shot by the bad guys or our own.

The team left the house and began moving south toward the target area. We broke into a wedge and pushed down the street, using the buildings on both sides to maintain distance between each other. Trying to see through the dust, we engaged Somali gunmen while staying watchful for our own troops.

As we continued moving toward the target building, I noticed that the number of Somalis on the streets to the left and right, as well as behind us, was growing. Most didn't have guns, at least not yet. But armed men were mixed in with the crowd, which included women and children, and they were shooting at us.

The Unit's operators shot the men who were wielding guns, taking care not to hit bystanders. I realized that I'd killed more people in the first few minutes of infil than during my entire career in the Unit. But we couldn't stop; the others up ahead were counting on us to show up, so my training took over, targets were shot, and I moved on.

After what seemed like forever, we reached the intersection where Rangers had set up. Fortunately, the dust had started to settle and none of the good guys shot at us as we ran past shouting "Eagle! Eagle! Eagle!" to let them know we were friendlies.

Arriving at the target house, the team ran inside. We found a couple dozen prisoners sitting on the floor with their hands cuffed behind them. But there was plenty more to do.

The building had apparently belonged to the Coca-Cola Bottling Company at some point in the past, as evidenced by bags of sugar piled from floor to ceiling. Tossing the bags off the pile, I discovered a cache of AK-47s and a safe. I coaxed one of the Somalis into opening the safe, which was filled with Somali currency. I stuffed the money in a bag to take back to the base.

Finally, it was time to call in the convoy. It was 4 p.m.; incredibly, only twenty minutes—twenty incredibly long, dangerous minutes—had passed since the assault began. The commander, who'd been monitoring the action from a helicopter said, "Hey, boss, I think we've got the guys you sent us in for; we're ready to get out of Dodge."

The rest of the team and I went outside the house, where we waited with some of the Rangers for our opportunity to load onto the convoy vehicles. The detainees were first, then the rest of the assault force took our turns while maintaining security.

As helicopters circled overhead looking to suppress any attempt to reach the target area, enemy gunfire seemed to have slowed—or at least it wasn't directed at them anymore, though the sound of shooting continued to reach them from nearby streets.

I had just joked that we'd still make it home in time for dinner when a Ranger who'd been leaning against the sheet metal gate of the compound clutched his throat and fell sideways to the ground. A neat hole had appeared in the gate where the bullet had passed through. He was immediately covered by others and dragged from the site so that he could be attended to; then he was sent to a vehicle.

At the same time, I heard a "whoosh" followed by the sound of an explosion above our heads. Looking up, I saw a Black Hawk begin to auto rotate, with gray and black smoke pouring from the rear rotor where it had been struck by an RPG. The helicopter spun so slowly that it seemed surreal as it disappeared to the northeast behind a line of houses.

In that instant, the mission to capture Aidid's lieutenants changed to one of rescuing any survivors and securing the Black Hawk. From his perch above the action, the commander alerted the Quick Reaction Force of the 10th Mountain Division to get ready to roll. The convoy, which had taken a lot of fire already and was mostly loaded with detainees and the wounded, as well as the gunners and drivers who'd rode in on them, was told to drive to the crash site.

At the same time, the Rangers and our Unit operators with the C-1 and C-2 teams were ordered to move to the downed helicopter, rescue any survivors, and secure the scene.

With the crash of the Black Hawk, the shooting intensified again. As we worked our way down the street, I saw armed Somalis running on the streets that paralleled it to the north and south. Each intersection meant a gunfight, as both sides blazed away at each other, but neither stopped moving.

The horde of amped-up Somalis was trying to beat us to the crash site about three blocks away, and we weren't going to let that happen. We had all heard stories about the massacre of the Pakistani troops; some of them had been captured and then killed in cruel ways before being mutilated and dragged through the streets.

We began taking a lot of fire from a shack up ahead. I was working up one side of the street and noticed my friend Earl was working the other. We both stepped from cover into the middle of the road to deal with the threat. Rick launched a 40 mm grenade at the shack while Earl and I blasted away with our M4 rifles.

The grenade struck the roof of the shack and detonated, knocking the militiaman to the ground. I stepped to the side to finish the man off. Satisfied that the man was dead, I looked back and was stunned to see that Earl was down. Two of his teammates were dragging him into the doorway of a building.

I forced myself to focus on my job. I hoped Earl wasn't too badly hurt, but there wasn't time to think about it; we had to get to the crash site before the Somalis.

UP AHEAD, THE BLACK Hawk helicopter known as Super 6-1 lay on its side in an alley. By a twist of fate, it was the same helicopter used to practice a rescue operation just a week earlier. But the coincidences didn't stop there.

As in the practice run, when Super 6-1 crashed, both pilots were killed and two of the crew members were injured. The aircraft also had been carrying three snipers—Steve D., Jim S., and Dan Busch.

With a horde of Somalis bearing down on the helicopter, Jim and Dan climbed out of the wreckage and charged the enemy. At first, their onslaught stopped the Somalis. But then Dan went down, mortally wounded. Jim ran to him and began dragging him back toward where an AH-6 Little Bird had landed, but he too was hit in the shoulder by a bullet.

The Little Bird was piloted by Chief Warrant Officer Karl M. and his co-pilot Chief Warrant Officer Keith J. While the pilot controlled his aircraft with his left hand, he fired a machine gun at the Somalis, trying to get to Dan and Jim. Ignoring the return fire, Keith jumped out of the helicopter and helped the two wounded snipers back to the aircraft. As soon as they were on board, they took off for the airfield base.

While that was going on, a combat search-and-rescue Black Hawk that had appeared over the crash site was struck by another RPG while assaulters were descending. As the pilot fought to keep his wounded aircraft steady, a team of fifteen Rangers, medics, and Air Force Pararescue operators fast-roped to the ground. Some went to aid the wounded crew members and assaulters; others labored to extract the dead pilots.

They were still working at it when two more teams of Unit operators and Rangers reached the location. The teams began to take up defensive positions by occupying houses on each of the four corners of the intersection just south of the downed Black Hawk. The volume of gunfire at this time was still high, but seemed unorganized, frenzied, and not very accurate.

The C-2-G team of Jake, Pete, Rick, Keith, two Rangers, and I took down the house on the southwest corner with a view to the east of the Black Hawk. There was only one male in the house, who we quickly cuffed. We didn't bother cuffing the six females, who ranged in age from a young girl to a woman in her sixties. We moved the frightened and wailing occupants to a room farthest from the fighting and assigned someone to watch them.

Built of the typical mixture of cement, ground seashells, and sand, the house was L-shaped around a walled courtyard with a living room and kitchen just inside the front door, a bathroom with a hole in the floor for waste, and several bedrooms, all with windows facing different directions. Two sides of the house faced the streets and intersection, while a narrow alley ran along the back between it and the neighboring house.

It wasn't long before the Somalis regrouped and came at us again. The near-constant roar of automatic rifles and machine guns was punctuated by grenades and the now all-too-familiar "bang, whoosh, boom" of RPGs. Overhead, the Little Birds swooped down to strafe wherever Somalis gathered in numbers.

At times it seemed the entire city was converging on the intersection where I, along with approximately ninety other Americans, fought for our lives. The Somalis tried everything to get close. They used women and children to shield movements, knowing the ROE would prevent us from shooting into crowds.

At one point, a couple of armed men tried to move across the street using a donkey as a shield. I shot the donkey and then the two men. "Sorry donkey," I muttered.

Hyped up on khat, the Somalis rushed the Americans in mass, shooting wildly and dying by the dozen on the streets, or crawling off after being wounded. Others tried sneaking up, hiding in doorways and courtyards, creeping behind cars, rubble, and even the bodies of their fallen comrades. These too died under the superlative shooting skills of the Unit's operators and the barrage of gunfire laid down by the Rangers.

In order to stay sharp and not get too comfortable between firefights, Unit operators rotated positions throughout the house. As twilight fell, I was pulling guard in a room with a window facing east toward the downed aircraft, when Jake came to replace me. I left the room but then turned around and went back to grab Jake's canteen to refill. Reaching the doorway, I was about to say something when I was knocked backward off my feet and into the hallway by a deafening explosion.

It took a moment for my senses to clear and look back in the smoke-filled room. A small rocket was buzzing around, leaving a red trail behind it until it finally wedged itself into a couch, which caught fire. I realized it was the motor from an RPG.

Entering the room, I saw that the entire corner of the house had been destroyed. All that was left was a gaping hole in the wall through which I could now look directly out at the downed Black Hawk.

At first, I couldn't see Jake or much of anything else because of the smoke. But kicking at the rubble I saw what I thought was my buddy's dismembered leg. I reached for it and discovered that it was still attached to its owner, who was moaning under a large slab of concrete.

Frantically, I pulled the debris off of my friend. Miraculously, Jake only had the wind knocked out of him and a probable concussion. But at least he was alive and otherwise uninjured, though he needed some time to regain his senses.

Unfortunately, not everyone had fared as well. The Rangers manning the machine gun had been closest to where the RPG struck. By the time I got there, other members of the team had pulled them out of the rubble and were dragging them into the courtyard for first aid.

Reaching the first Ranger, I saw that shrapnel had ripped the heel off of one of his feet. I left the man's boot on for support and wrapped it in bandages, then placed his injured foot in a pneumatic boot that would put pressure on the wound when inflated.

I then moved on to the next Ranger. He was worse off; a piece of metal had entered from his backside and exited his groin, taking a testicle with it. He was bleeding profusely and moaning that he wouldn't be able to have children as I packed his groin with Kerlix gauze bandages. My hands covered in blood, I pulled pneumatic shorts onto the Ranger and inflated them to stop the bleeding.

By the time the Rangers were treated and made as comfortable as possible in the house, it was dark outside. A "one-hour" grab-and-go hit had entered its fourth hour with no sign of relief.

We'd been told that a relief column had been formed and was on its way, but we had no idea when it would arrive. In the meantime, we were running low on ammunition and water and, other than a couple of energy bars, there was no food.

I was just wishing that I'd brought my night-vision goggles, when Pete, our team leader, came up to me. "I need you to go retrieve the M60," he said. "We can't chance that they'll find it and use it on us."

Apparently in the rush to get the Rangers to safety and treat their wounds, no one had thought to gather their weapons. Reluctantly, I got up and prepared to do as I'd been told. Although the shooting had abated for the moment, Somalis were still trying to reach the defenders, sneaking up through the dark, and shooting randomly in our direction. There was no telling who I might run into out in the dark street.

I left the relative safety of the house and crept over to the rubble where the Rangers had set up their position. I couldn't use a flashlight without drawing the enemy's attention, so I had to root around on my hands and knees in the dark to feel for the weapon.

After what seemed like an eternity, my hand fastened on a piece of metal that I recognized as part of the M60. I grabbed it and ran back to the courtyard. But it wasn't a large enough piece to be sure that the rest of the weapon wasn't still operable, so Pete sent me back out again. This time I located a bigger, more important piece and returned.

A little later, I had settled in at a window when Pete stopped by to check in with me. Apparently, the convoy was having a rough time reaching us. We could hear a massive volume of firing in the far distance, including the pounding of heavy machine guns, the chattering of Little Bird miniguns, and explosions. Lights flashed against the night sky and the air smelled of burning rubber, trash, and death.

"Do you think they're going to make it?" I asked my team leader.

Pete looked in the direction of the battle being waged in another part of the city. "I hope so," was all Pete, never the talkative sort, said before walking off into the dark.

I was left alone with my thoughts. I'd wanted a little more assurance than "I hope so," but hope was all I had now. It was going to be a long night, and we'd be lucky to survive it. I'd had my fill of combat—of blood, and fear, and death—and I wanted no more of it.

be trapped and attacked. As the Americans' own MOUT training indicated, superior firepower of tanks and armored vehicles could be negated in an urban setting by using buildings to ambush the convoys at close range, as well as provide cover for the defenders.

The helicopters were the second, more important and more difficult, issue to deal with. They were fast, couldn't be slowed by roadblocks, brought a massive amount of firepower to the fight, and could be used to infil and exfil troops quickly.

However, the SNA had help from an outside source. It wouldn't come to light until years later, but they were assisted by a little-known branch of Islamic extremists called al-Qaeda, the Arabic words for "foundation," or more loosely translated to "the base of jihad." Founded in 1988, by Osama bin Laden, the son of a wealthy Saudi Arabian family, al-Qaeda offered advisors to the SNA to teach them how to fight the "infidels."

With Aidid's blessing, al-Qaeda sent battle-hardened veterans from Afghanistan who'd been fighting the Russian army. Historians would later argue how much the al-Qaeda jihadis participated in the Battle of Mogadishu, but their tactics were probably more important anyway.

Their main contribution was teaching the Somali militia how to use RPGs against helicopters. They were first advised, rather than expose themselves to the armored helos by attacking them from the front, to stay hidden until they'd passed overhead. Then pop out and shoot at the most vulnerable part of the aircraft, the tail rotor.

The US command and the CIA informants were unaware that Aidid used a lot of the money raised by Atto to purchase and stockpile hundreds of RPGs. This arsenal changed the course of the battle.

Giumale hoped for one more factor to counter the Americans' technological advantages. His enemies liked to strike at night when it was more difficult to see, and harder to rally the troops when they were home asleep. But the Americans preferred the dark as their night-vision goggles gave them an enormous tactical advantage.

When word got to Giumale at about 3:40 p.m. that the Americans were storming a building near the Olympic Hotel and had captured two of Aidid's lieutenants, he immediately put out the call to arms over a loose network of radios. Within minutes, truckloads of militia men piled into the vehicles, and ran on foot, and headed for the area.

THE TACTICS EMPLOYED BY the SNA worked like a charm. The US convoy sent to pick up the prisoners and exfil the assault teams took a beating just trying to weave its way to the site and arrived late. Bad luck had added to the chaos when Pfc. Blackburn fell from a helicopter and three Humvees were split from the convoy to get him back to the base.

Then Black Hawk Super 6-1 was struck in the back rotor by an RPG and crashed outside of the perimeter, killing the two pilots whose bodies were trapped inside of the wreckage and injuring the crew. That necessitated sending our Unit's operators and Rangers, neither of them designed or equipped—such as with heavy machine guns—to fight through urban terrain or hold a defensive position long. There were also numerous casualties taken along the way that required immediate medical attention.

The crash of the first Black Hawk was then compounded when the combat-rescue Black Hawk flying over the crash site was hit. It limped back to base, but that took another helicopter out of the fight and stranded even more men.

At the same time, the ground convoy that was supposed to exfil the prisoners and the assault teams, but was diverted to the crash site, got lost in the labyrinth of streets on the way and ended up back at the Olympic Hotel. The vehicles and their occupants had been pummeled by Somali gunfire.

Afraid he'd lose the prisoners and the convoy, Major General G. ordered them to give up the rescue attempt and return to base. On the way back, the convoy had to skirt roadblocks and fend off attacks; by the time it arrived, four Americans and three Somali prisoners were dead.

A bad situation turned into a full-fledged disaster when a third Black Hawk, Super 6-4, was struck by an RPG as it, too, was orbiting above the first crash site. The pilot, Chief Warrant Officer Michael Durant, tried to make it back to the base, but the tail rotor blades disintegrated. It slammed into a neighborhood a half mile from the first site.

With each new catastrophe, Task Force Ranger and other US forces leadership were obliged to change plans, which seemed to be falling like dominos. Garrison had planned and practiced for the possibility of one helicopter going down and its crew needing rescue, but not two. There were barely enough troops in Task Force Ranger to defend the first site and certainly not enough for two.

Nothing seemed to be going the Americans' way. The Quick Reaction Force (QRF) from the 10th Mountain Division had alerted when the first Black Hawk went down and moved from its compound at the Somali National University to the airbase. An hour after the crash, a company from the QRF numbering about a hundred men left the airbase and headed for the first crash site. But their vehicles weren't armored, and the troops took a beating after they ran into roadblocks and ambushes and were forced to return to the airbase.

Meanwhile, leadership scrambled to figure out a way to get to the second helicopter. But no one seemed to know how best to do that.

It wasn't from a lack of courage or volunteers. Aviation commander Lt. Col. Thomas Matthews rejected two requests from the crews of four Little Birds to allow the co-pilots to be dropped off to defend the site. Unit commander also twice denied the appeals of our Unit's snipers, Randall D. Shughart and Gary I. Gordon, to land. Only after learning that the company from the 10th Mountain had been turned back, did he consent.

Black Hawk Super 6-2, piloted by Chief Warrant Officer Michael Goffena, with Shughart and Gordon, as well as a third sniper, Brad

H. who'd been with me in Bogotá, rushed to the scene. Knowing full well what they were up against, Shughart and Gordon were dropped in a clearing one hundred yards from the downed aircraft. Brad remained in the Black Hawk to provide fire from above in addition to the crew chiefs who manned the door guns.

Goffena then hovered above the crash site to help our snipers find their way. However, ten minutes into the fight to save the crew of Super 6-4, Goffena's Black Hawk Super 6-2 was struck by another RPG; the blast knocked out his co-pilot and sheared off Brad's leg. Goffena was able to keep the mortally wounded bird in the air long enough to crash land over at the port.

On the ground, there was no sign of the Super 6-4's missing pilot. But the Unit snipers pulled the co-pilot, Chief Warrant Officer Durant, from the wreckage and laid him down next to the craft, giving him a rifle with a full clip. Without more help from above, Gordon and Shughart fought heroically to protect Durant from the swarming Somalis, sometimes shooting it out with the mob from a distance of ten yards. But eventually they were both killed, and Durant was captured after emptying his clip into the angry mob.*

As far as Giumale was concerned, the battle had gone even better than he'd hoped. Four Black Hawk helicopters had been knocked out of commission by RPGs. Two of them had crashed in SNA territory where one was overrun, and the defenders killed or captured; the other was holding out but surrounded by hundreds of militia and irregulars.

Giumale was unaware that the Americans had remained at the wreckage of Super 6-1 because they were unwilling to leave the bodies of the pilots. Such a sacrifice on behalf of dead men was unfathomable to him. Instead, he believed that they were simply trapped by his forces.

---

* The basics of the SNA strategy is taken from "Night of a Thousand Casualties" by Rick Atkinson, *Washington Post*, January 31, 1994.

Also, his "victories" had come at a cost of hundreds of his own dead or wounded, to the point the local hospital was overwhelmed with casualties. But it was a price he and Aidid, who was kept apprised of the battle, were willing to pay. Their al-Qaeda allies also advised them that by killing enough Americans, no matter what the cost to the SNA, we'd give up and go home. Americans, they said, had no stomach for death and would lose the political will at home.*

Huddled in the house near the first crash site, our team wasn't privy to the strategies and tactics of the leaders of either side. We were just trying to survive the night.

At some point in the evening, I learned that another Black Hawk had gone down, but whether it was to keep up our morale, or that the commanders at the scene hadn't been told either, there were few details about what was happening elsewhere.

Nor did we know much about the rescue convoys trying to reach us. We could hear the fierce fighting in the distance, see the flashes of explosions and red tracers arcing into the night sky, and knew that they were fighting for their lives, too.

Except for the two wounded Rangers, we were in pretty good shape, physically. Jake had recovered enough from the blast to get back in the fight. However, we knew others, especially the Rangers, had taken a beating getting to the crash site.

I was worried about several of my friends. I'd heard after they arrived that Dan Busch and Jim S. had been wounded protecting the crash site, but I didn't know their status. My friend Matt Rierson had been in the convoy with the prisoners, but they'd been hit so bad they had to retreat to the airbase. Nor did I know if Earl had made it, and I wondered if Jon, his constant companion, was with him.

---

* Sometimes called "the Beirut effect" after the 1983 bombing of the Marine barracks in Beirut, Lebanon, that led to the withdrawal of US troops there. The success of the suicide car bomb that took out the barracks was considered the beginning of a type of asymmetrical warfare intended to break the political will in the United States by causing casualties, no matter the cost to the attackers.

Otherwise, those of us in our battle-scarred house didn't have a clear idea of the disposition of the other operators and Rangers. Our C-2-G team and the C-2-F team across the street on the southeast corner of the intersection and closest to the Black Hawk were the farthest north and on the front line. Nothing farther to the north or to the east or west of our position was friendly. Behind us to the south, the Rangers and the C-1 operators were strung out in buildings along several blocks.

Although some of the fiercest shooting had slowed down for a bit during the early evening, it proved to be only a respite. The Somalis kept coming at us, following a pattern of advancing on our positions and wildly firing their AK-47s, then all would go quiet again for a bit.

In between beating back assaults, our team had done its best to improve our defensive position by placing mattresses against the walls of the house. As the demolition of the one corner of the house had demonstrated, the home's construction couldn't withstand an RPG hit. But we hoped that the mattresses would at least absorb some of the pieces of wall and shrapnel that would otherwise shred anything in the room.

I grew to hate the sound of RPGs. A pop, a whoosh, and then a detonation when it struck something. Sometimes the Somalis got so close when they fired, the grenades didn't have time to arm themselves and wouldn't explode on contact. At times during the night, when an RPG was launched, I simply put my head against the window sill, closed my eyes and waited for the impact. What else was I to do? I couldn't stop it and worrying about it wouldn't help. I just gave in to it all.

Time and again, I cursed myself for not bringing my night-vision goggles. Without them, we had to wait, squinting into the dark, to identify targets before shooting. The ROE didn't allow for firing indiscriminately into groups of people, some of whom might not be armed combatants. We also had to try to make every shot count because we were running low on ammunition and had no idea if we would be resupplied. This meant having to allow the enemy to get closer than they would have if we'd had our goggles.

On the other hand, the Somalis were allowed to shoot blindly in the dark toward our positions and hope to get lucky. They didn't care who they hit—friend or foe—and they had access to more ammunition.

Still, ROE or not, there were times when the enemy fire grew to such ferocious levels that we had to shoot wildly into the dark to suppress the attackers or else we would be overrun. Then all would go quiet again.

During one lull in the fighting, Jake and I were lying down in the courtyard guarding the approach from the west when we heard the sound of two men talking up the street between us and the C-2-F team across the street. We quickly realized the men were speaking Somali, but we had no clue how the men had gotten in behind us and had apparently walked past the Rangers and other operators who were supposed to have been watching our backs.

We couldn't shoot at them for fear of hitting our own operators in the house across the street and had to wait until they were in the clear. Then Jake lit them up with a light. The men, surprised, stopped in their tracks. They were obviously combatants carrying AK-47s strapped to their shoulders. For that one moment, standing in the brilliant white light, they looked like deer in the headlights of a car.

You fucked up, I thought before we shot them. One of the men dropped to the street, the other ran around a corner and out of sight but I was sure he'd been hit.

The shooting seemed to wake up the rest of the militia who resumed wildly firing their rifles and firing RPGs. Fortunately, their aim with the grenades was generally hurried and not very good so the weapons would zoom off into the sky or past us into the city to detonate.

With each passing hour, the situation was growing more desperate. We were running low on ammunition and were now out of water and food. The lack of bullets was bad enough but dehydration in battle leads to dizziness, cramps, and lethargy—none of them good when fighting for our lives. We needed a resupply. With nothing to shoot, we risked being overrun and slaughtered.

Back at the hangar, Unit command worked on getting us supplies. Finally, a Black Hawk helicopter was dispatched with ammunition, water, and medical supplies.

Hovering in the dark as low as possible above the street between G and F team locations, the helicopter crew pushed the supplies out of the doors to the street below. The ammunition boxes held up, but some of the five-gallon water jugs exploded on impact.

Suddenly, someone on the second floor of the house next to the one I was in, and just below the helicopter, started shooting. A Unit sniper in the helicopter, James, was hit in the face by a bullet.

At first we were stunned. The enemy was right next door, and no one knew about it? But we quickly responded and silenced the enemy gunman in a hail of fire, as the pilot held his position until all the supplies were out.

Now someone had to go out in the dark, find the supplies, and bring them back. Once again, Pete decided that person would be me. It made sense; I was young, uninjured, and one of the fastest runners on the team. But I still wasn't happy about it.

So, I found myself back out in the dusty, pitch-black street, searching on my hands and knees for the ammunition boxes and water. The hovering helicopter had, of course, drawn enemy fire. Although they couldn't see to aim that didn't stop them from shooting blindly up the street hoping to get lucky if some American was out there.

Scrambling around in the dark, I located the supplies. It was too much to take it all back at once and took me three trips to get it all in. I was just starting to relax when Pete said I wasn't done.

"The team across the street needs water," Pete said.

I knew what that meant and got back up again. *Fuck me*, I thought angrily. There was no way in hell I wanted to go back out on the dark street with bullets whistling past and who-knew-how-many Somalis crawling around, waiting for just such an opportunity to slit my throat. But grabbing two five-gallon jugs, off I went.

Reaching the house across the street, I had another problem. I couldn't just run into the dark building without risking getting shot by my own guys. "Eagle, eagle," I yelled as I went through the door, praying that some itchy-fingered Ranger didn't blow me away before recognizing the call sign.

I didn't have to worry. No one was in the front room of the house. I found two Unit operators pulling security in the back off the house, looking east through the window and occasionally firing at whatever they saw out there.

I dropped the water and asked how they were doing. They didn't answer. I shrugged—we were all trying to deal with the situation, and everybody was different—so I left without saying anything more.

Pausing at the doorway to gather my courage, I then ran across the street and was thankful to get back inside with no further incident. But I was damned if I was going to go out again.

The chaos and stressful conditions continued into the night with attacks followed by periods of quiet. The defenders beat back each assault with the help of the Little Birds whose pilots had night-vision goggles and attacked any large groups or when anyone with an RPG was spotted. The pilots were also in contact with a command element flying in a Black Hawk overhead, which had forward looking infrared (FLIR) capabilities and could detect enemy combatants by their body heat.

During one of the quiet moments, I was positioned at a window facing out onto the little alley between the house I was in and the neighbor when I heard an odd sound coming from outside. It sounded like something metal being placed on the ground followed by a shuffling.

There were bars on the windows obstructing my view so I couldn't lean out to see. After a minute, I was able to make out a man, slowly making his way down the alley. He was lifting an AK-47 and as quietly as possible, placing it in front of himself before crawling after it and repeating the effort.

I couldn't get my rifle positioned to shoot the man. So, I waited until the enemy was right below the window and stuck my .45 outside with the barrel almost touching the back of the man's head and pulled the trigger. Nothing happened. I wouldn't know it until later, but sand—probably stirred up by the rotor wash on infil—had jammed my hammer, preventing it from firing.

Fortunately for me, the Somali didn't stand up and start shooting. Instead he froze.

I knew that if I waited, the man might eventually stand and shoot or crawl further forward and shoot someone else. I pulled a small Austrian grenade from a pouch on my vest.

Looking across the room, I showed the grenade to another Unit operator who was standing in the doorway. The other man shook his head vigorously. He didn't want a grenade going off so close to them.

I ignored his silent objection and stuck my hand out the window and dropped the grenade. I saw it strike the man on his head and roll down his back where it lodged in the cowl of his clothing.

I ducked. The blast shook the wall and lit up the room for a moment. Blood, sand, hair, and gore splattered the ceiling. I looked out the window. A headless corpse smoldered in the alley, and the smell of burning hair and blood filled my nostrils.

Several other operators ran into the room to see what was going on.

"It was just a flash-bang grenade," I said.

"He's lying," the operator who'd objected to the grenade yelled.

I felt guilty, like I'd done something wrong, so I admitted to it and demonstrated how the Somali had been trying to sneak up on us. Shaking their heads, the other operators left the room.

As the night wore on and had reached that darkest moment before the dawn, I reached a point where I didn't think we were going to make it. Shooting in the dark, the enemy fire was inaccurate at best, but that would change in the morning light.

Meanwhile, even with the resupply, our ammunition wasn't going to hold out against many more all-out assaults. In fact, I didn't know why the Somalis had not attacked in force and overrun our positions. There were too many of them for us to shoot them all. I knew that, too, would change in the morning.

In the distance, I could hear the rescue convoy still battling to reach us but couldn't tell if they were any closer. If they made it in time, good. If they didn't, I was determined to take as many Somalis down with me as I could. Either way, I was leaving that house as a warrior and glad it was in the presence of other warriors.

I pulled out my knife and set it next to me. I was thankful that I'd written to my parents just a few hours earlier and encouraged them to live their lives fully and let them know that I had chosen this life and, if it became necessary, this death. Again, I gave into the moment and had no other choice. This was my future playing out right now in front of me and I had no idea how long it would be.

With the dawn starting to turn the eastern sky a lighter shade of black, I made my peace and waited for whatever was about to happen.

CHAPTER TEN

October 4, 1993
Mogadishu, Somalia

THE MORNING ARRIVED and so did the cavalry. And just in the prover-
bial nick of time.

At first, I didn't know what to make of the sound of large machinery on the move. No one had slept that night. We were out of water
again and it was tough to think clearly.

A gray pall hung over that part of the city from the smoldering
tires and trash, which burned our eyes and throats. Two Malaysian armored personnel carriers, the source of the sound, followed
by troops from the 10th Mountain Division, lined up and walking
down both sides of the street, appeared out of the haze. I'd never
been so glad to see anybody in my life.

My first encounter was with a sergeant who immediately started
bumming Copenhagen chewing tobacco from us. I wasn't offended.
I knew that the 10th Mountain had been through hell that night just
to get there. But I still answered, "Do we look like we have Copenhagen or cigarettes?"

The sergeant grinned. "Nah, I guess not. But I was hoping."

During the desperate efforts to reach the defenders at the crash sites, it had become apparent that Task Force Ranger's and the 10th Mountain's unarmored Humvees and five-ton trucks were not going to be able to punch through to the beleaguered defenders without help. Major General G. reached out to the Pakistani and Malaysian commanders and asked for their help. He even offered to use only his men if they'd loan their armored vehicles.

In the end, the Pakistanis sent four tanks and the Malaysians sent seventy armored personnel carriers and their drivers and crews to the port. There they hooked up with the 10th Mountain's QRF, and the convoy left a little after 11 p.m.

Diverted into traps with roadblocks of burning tires and shells of cars and ambushed repeatedly, even the tanks and armored personnel carriers had found it difficult to get to the trapped task force. The battle our team heard and saw during the night had been the convoy fighting its way, block by treacherous block.

At one point, the convoy split from a company with the QRF heading for the second crash site. They found the wreckage but no sign of the defenders, only blood trails leading away. The second part of the convoy continued on to the area of the first crash site.

Tanks weren't meant to fight on narrow streets; their weapons systems were designed for distance, not close-up combat. Even the personnel carrier drivers didn't like the close confines. So, most of the second half of the convoy had remained at an intersection near the Olympic Hotel where they could maneuver and fire.

However, two of the personnel carriers, as well as the 10th Mountain had continued on; the latter setting up on each corner, which for the moment seemed to have backed the Somalis off. Only the occasional ineffective shot rang out. It wouldn't last but the respite was nice at the time.

Using a rope attached to one of the armored personnel carriers, they were at last able to move the helicopter enough to retrieve the bodies of the pilot and co-pilot. Now, the only thing left to do was conduct a "sensitive items" inventory—weapons, radios, GPS...check, check, check...

then take a head count to ensure they had everyone, jump in the back of one of the armored personnel carriers, and get the hell out of there.

There was just one problem. I opened the rear of one of the armored personnel carriers only to find out it was packed full of wounded and nonwounded Rangers. The other carrier was the same. In fact, there was no room for the bodies of the pilots, which would have had to be strapped to the roof.

A new plan was hatched. The able-bodied troops—the Unit, Rangers, and members of the 10th Mountain who gave up their seats—would walk behind the armored personnel carriers that would go slow and provide cover.

The plan worked fine at first. The group headed out, with my team and I bringing up the rear as we began heading back toward the Olympic Hotel, the same way we'd come. The shooting had all but stopped so I wasn't sure why what happened next went down. But with a roar, the personnel carriers suddenly took off, leaving those who were walking behind on foot exposed.

So began what would go down in Hollywood lore as "The Mogadishu Mile." However, the distance from the crash site to the tanks was longer than that, all of it through enemy territory. Nor was it a "run" as later fictionalized. The troops moved from cover to cover, usually walking, and stopping often to make sure the element stayed together.

Now the battle resumed. As the US troops moved, hundreds of Somalis—combatants and noncombatants—ran parallel to us on another street a block away. Every intersection where the two sides could see each other meant another gun battle. Mixed in with noncombatants—including women and children—the Somali gunmen let loose with their AK-47s and RPGs. The air came alive with the cracking of bullets passing by or singing off concrete walls and rubble. The RPGs rushed toward us, leaving a smoking trail before exploding when they struck something.

Overhead, the Little Birds poured bullets into wherever the

Somali gunmen gathered. Hot shell casings from the miniguns fell like rain from the sky, burning skin when it touched the men below.

The retreat was a nightmare. My throat felt like gravel. My hands were swollen, and my legs barely responded; only my training kept me fighting and moving tactically forward.

Just south of the location where we'd spent the night and before turning west toward the Olympic Hotel, I became aware of an Apache attack helicopter moving overhead. I knew it was there to send rockets into the remains of the Black Hawk to ensure the Somalis didn't get anything useful from it.

I stopped and turned around. I wanted to watch the Apache at work with rockets and a huge fireball expanding from where we had spent the night fighting for our lives. We'd told the Somali family to stay inside and away from the crash site for just that reason, but it turned out to be an unnecessary warning. For some reason, the Apache never fired.

Disappointed, I turned around to see if anybody else was watching. But I discovered I was all alone; everybody else had gone on.

Panic set in immediately. I was alone and surrounded by hundreds of people who wanted to kill me. My mind hazy with a lack of sleep, dehydration, and now fear, I was wondering what to do when suddenly I was yanked from behind and pulled into a narrow alley. At almost the same time, an RPG whizzed through the space where I'd been standing and exploded against a wall.

Having no idea what had just happened, or who had grabbed me, it took a moment for me to gather my composure. Then I found myself looking into the face of a medic, Kurt S., who'd pulled me to safety at the last moment. Whether the man had seen the RPG coming or was just getting a dazed soldier off the street, I never knew. But the man had saved my life and took some shrapnel to his ear for his efforts.

Back with the other troops, we reached the Olympic Hotel and turned south again, still fighting our way. As I moved down the street, I came upon the burned-out shell of a Humvee. It had been struck by an RPG and the flames had been hot enough to gut the interior. I recognized it as the Humvee assigned to our team that Tim "Griz" Martin drove. I wondered if my friend was okay but there was no time to stop.

After what seemed an eternity, we arrived where the other personnel carriers, the 10th Mountain Humvees, and the tanks were waiting. The tanks were blasting in all directions, as were the gunners on top of the personnel carriers and Humvees. It was violent chaos and yet much appreciated as it kept the Somalis at bay.

Jake, Jason, another Unit operator, the medic who'd saved me, and I were directed into one Humvee. It had no armor, not even sandbags and plywood for added protection, but it was better than walking.

Taking fire from nearby buildings and courtyards, the Humvee top gunner on our vehicle was too frightened to put his head up so that he could see what he was shooting at. That didn't stop him from reaching up and letting off a half-dozen rounds from his 7.62-caliber machine gun. The heavy bullets slammed into a nearby dumpster and nearly hit the F team leader.

Angry at the gunner's cowardice that had nearly caused disastrous consequences, I slapped him across the back of his helmet. "Either get up there and shoot the damn thing right, or don't shoot at all." This seemed to motivate the gunner to do his job properly because then he stood up and started aiming.

As they began rolling out of the hornets' nest, the Humvees continued taking fire at every intersection and seemingly from every window, doorway, and rooftop. I watched in horror as spiderweb cracks appeared at face level in the "bullet resistant" windows from impacts. I wondered how many more hits we could take before the glass gave way.

AT THE SAME TIME, anyone else still capable of it shot from the windows and out the open back. We shot whether or not we saw a target. Fighting in urban terrain was hazardous in the best of circumstances. It's nearly impossible to cover every potential threat or even determine where shots are coming from due to echoes and ricochets and, in this case, the shots were coming from all directions anyway.

Adding to the melee, noncombatants were mixed in with the combatants. It was complete chaos. All we could do as we fought our way down the streets of Mogadishu was lay down enough suppressive fire in all directions to prevent the enemy from feeling safe enough to expose themselves in order to be able to shoot more accurately.

A few blocks into the evacuation, the Humvees came to an intersection where the road ahead was blocked with burning tires. Unarmed Somalis worked on the barriers; aware of the Americans' rules of engagement, confident they wouldn't be shot. Meanwhile, their comrades armed with AK-47s and RPGs fired from a distance.

The Humvee driver began to slow. "Don't you fucking stop or turn!" I yelled over the whoosh of RPGs flying overhead, exploding against buildings, and the hammering of bullets striking the vehicle. I knew now what the tires I'd previously seen from the air meant and that the people on the barriers were trying to steer them into traps.

The driver punched the accelerator and the two-and-half-ton Humvee plowed into the barricade, sending flaming tires and surprised Somalis flying. The same scenario was repeated several more times as we continued down the road as the enemy continued trying to steer us into deathtraps. Every wall of every sand-colored building was pockmarked from bullets and RPGs, the normally rancid air of Mogadishu mixed with the acrid smell of burning rubber.

Somewhere on the way back, the Humvee I was riding in got separated from the others, but all we could do was press on.

Meanwhile, the occupants continued to shoot at any Somali

who appeared. Some of the gunmen would put their weapons down on the ground as they approached and pretend to be noncombatants. But then they'd pick them up again and start shooting when the Americans got close. So, we quickly recognized the ruse and treated anyone we saw as a potential threat.

After what seemed an eternity, the sound of rifle fire and rockets appeared farther away as we crossed a major boulevard. At that point, my friend Jake yelled at me to stop shooting. We'd just passed 21 October Road, which was the demarcation line between the Aidid clan we'd been fighting and a friendly clan.

Exhausted and running on pure adrenalin, it took me a moment to realize that the Somalis I saw now weren't carrying weapons or shooting at us. In fact, they looked like they'd just crawled out of bed, bewildered and exhausted after what had been a night of listening to a battle rage just a few blocks away.

Without the sound of war, the occupants felt a sense of relief. It wasn't the same as the All Secure command given when a mission was complete. Although we weren't safe to let our guard down, we were still close enough to know that the imminent danger had passed.

I stopped sighting down the barrel of my M4 rifle. I remained vigilant and on edge, but with an increasing sense of security and the growing realization that I was going to make it out alive.

However, the survivors and rescuers were soon confronted by another setback. According to the original plan, after we'd secured the targets near the Olympic Hotel and Crash Site 1, Unit operators and the Rangers were to be taken back to the airfield. But when everything went horribly wrong, the new plan hashed out in the Joint Operations Center (JOC) had been to evacuate everyone from Crash Sites 1 and 2 and take us to the Pakistani stadium, named by its occupants who had taken it over from Pakistan while assisting in Operation Restore Hope. The stadium was closer to the target area, secure, and easy to reach under normal conditions. From there, we'd be flown back along the coast to the airfield.

However, whether the route to the stadium was impossible to navigate or the drivers simply lost their nerve, the Humvees carrying us arrived at the back gate of the airfield instead of at the stadium.*

There was no movement inside the perimeter of the airfield, nor were we joined by the rest of the evacuation convoy. The silence and lack of human activity were unnerving, and disconcerting. I didn't even smoke, but I bummed a cigarette and lit up as I shifted my weapon and looked around.

We waited at the back gate for twenty minutes, listening to radio traffic. When it became obvious from the chatter of the transmissions that no one else was coming, we drove around the airfield to reach the hangar to look for others and to decide what to do next. But the airfield appeared to have been abandoned.

The scene became even more surreal when we stopped on the tarmac between the field hospital on one side and the enclosed parking lot and hangar. Lying on the asphalt, side by side in front of the hospital, were the bodies of a dozen American soldiers, one of them surrounded by sandbags due to the unexploded RPG sticking out of his ribs. The sandbags were to protect the living in case the weapon detonated.

I could tell by the dead men's uniforms and gear that most were Rangers. But I did not allow myself to focus too closely on the faces, knowing that some of the dead would also include close friends. I hoped I wouldn't catch a glimpse of something that would identify someone I knew; I didn't want to see any of my friends lying there. I wasn't ready to deal with the reality of death so soon after experiencing the joy of having survived.

The thought crossed my mind that mine could have easily been one of those bodies waiting to be inventoried, my personal effects

---

* Tom would find out twenty-five years later, when he ran into one of the 10th Mountain Division soldiers at a reunion, that they had gotten lost in the battle and decided to drive back to a location they knew.

bagged, being prepared for the long ride home in a flag-draped coffin. I felt sorrow—not just for the fallen soldiers—but for their families and friends. I was concerned about Debbie, wondering if she knew what was going on and if she was worried. I felt sadness that it was them, and not me.

Dismounting from the Humvee, I walked toward the hangar. Three battle-scarred Humvees were neatly lined up outside. Their windows were riddled with bullet impacts, and some of the glass had even been shot out. I shuddered knowing that probably meant someone had died or been wounded when the glass gave way.

The vehicles were also pockmarked and punctured by bullets. Several bore the signs of having been hit by RPGs—perfect circles with flowerlike petals extending from the center—that fortunately had not had the time to arm themselves in the close confines of urban warfare and so had not exploded.

The backs of the vehicles were open and when I looked inside I saw that they'd been filled with sand to soak up blood, some of which had already escaped to pool on the ground beneath them. I later learned that the Humvees and their crews had been sent out repeatedly during the battle to pick up the dead and the wounded who were ferried back to the hospital.

Bleach had been poured on the sand to sanitize the blood, and the cloying metallic smell of blood added to the bleach was overpowering. It would be the stench of war that I would remember long after I'd left Africa.

CHAPTER ELEVEN

October 13, 2003
Somewhere over the Atlantic Ocean

EVERYTHING HAD CHANGED. Not just the empty seats of men who had made the ride over but were absent for the ride back. Something else. Something not visible. Something in a man's heart and a man's mind. Hard to put a finger on but we all knew we'd been changed by what happened in Mogadishu.

Certainly no one talked about being afraid, the loss of invincibility, or the overwhelming sadness we felt when we thought about our absent friends. *We're all men. We knew what could happen. No need to talk about it.*

A few played cards or Risk, but no longer with the laughter or competitive spirit that marked the games before October 3. Others swallowed the Ambien the medics offered and slept. Still more, like me, sat lost in thought.

I understood that I was different now. That my expectation of what combat would be like had been false. The movies, the TV shows, the parades—they got it all wrong. I now knew war at its most basic level and was no longer under the illusion that it was glorious or honorable, even if the individual sacrifices of soldiers fighting for

129

their brothers was both. War was hell. It was horrible, destroying lives and property, all for some assholes' desires for power and control…the worst thing I could have imagined anyone going through.

Surviving war, and its aftermath, was all about hatred, anger, and unbelievable violence. I knew that from now on, in order to do my job right and survive, I would have to focus on those aspects. Remove empathy and compassion for others, and I wouldn't feel the pain.

Sitting in my seat as the transport jet headed west to the safety of the United States, the sights, sounds, and smell of what I'd experienced in Somalia stayed with me. The memories flooded my mind. The hole in the wall of the home where I thought I would die, looking across the street at the wreckage of the Black Hawk. The bodies of the Black Hawk pilots strapped like luggage on top of the Malaysian armored personnel carrier. The back of the Humvee, full of blood-soaked sand, with the mental image of a single army-green sock lying on the ground next to it. Bodies lined up on the tarmac beneath ponchos, booted feet sticking out from beneath the bottom edges, toes pointing to the sky. Earl's limp body being dragged from the sidewalk.

The screams of wounded men echoed down the corridors of my mind. The deep bass "WHOMP" of a mortar landing. The chatter of a Little Bird's miniguns and hiss of rockets, and the "whop whop" of the blades. An RPG's three-part act. Bullets cracking overhead as they passed at supersonic speeds—if they didn't hit you in the face as one did Earl. Those you don't hear.

Of all the senses, scientists say that smell may be the most closely linked to memory. Somalia was all about odors I couldn't forget. The rotting garbage on the beach that included human body parts. The burning trash and tires turning the sky ashen. The mixed odors of iron and chlorine in the reek of blood and bleach. I could still smell them, remembering while sitting in a jet on my way home.

As I'd stood there in the African sun, and the safety of our base, on October 4, looking in the back of the blood-splattered Humvee, the scent of war filling my nostrils and taking up residence in my mind, I'd wondered what had become of the rest of the rescue convoy. Had they been trapped and overrun? Were they waiting for help? I began cleaning my weapons and getting more ammunition so I could return to the fight, a white-hot desire for revenge burning in my mind.

Still, even as I prepared to go find my comrades and kill Somalis, I was torn by the thought of leaving the relative safety of the airfield and returning to the vicious streets of Mogadishu. Although I didn't know it yet, I had just survived the longest sustained firefight in the US military since the Vietnam War. While I was still willing to go for my brothers, I realized I'd had my fill of fighting.

Fortunately, my preparations were interrupted by the sound of approaching helicopters. As it turned out, most of the Ranger company and our Unit's squadron had been taken to the Pakistani stadium and were now being transported to the airbase.

Soon after our arrival, information started trickling down to the survivors. There were thirteen known dead, six missing, including one believed to have been captured, the helicopter pilot of the second Black Hawk, Chief Warrant Officer Durant. Seventy-three others had been wounded; the call went out for blood donations and all those who could lined up.

Griz Martin had been killed the previous night trying to reach the trapped defenders. As I had feared, he'd been driving the burned-out Humvee that I passed during the exfil. It had been struck by an RPG that entered the unprotected wheel well and detonated. The resulting fire had been so intense that Griz's .45 melted and discharged into him. He wouldn't be retiring and starting a small business or going home to his wife and three daughters except in a flag-draped coffin.

Earl was dead. He'd been shot in the face and was already gone when I looked back and saw him being dragged off the sidewalk. It was hard to accept that I'd never talk to that fun-loving guy again, a guy who'd mounted a pair of warthog tusks on his helmet and paraded around the hangar half naked. He looked like a kid, but had been fearless, a medic and assaulter who both healed and killed. Now his goofy smile and sense of humor were lost to the world, which might not notice his absence, but his family and friends would.

I couldn't imagine what Jon Hale was going through. He'd been with Earl when he got shot and spent the night fighting to survive with the lifeless body of his best friend in the room.

Dan Busch had been shot four times defending others before he succumbed to his wounds. At the time of his death, he had a pregnant wife waiting for him back home. He'd never hunt or trap game in his beloved woods again, or worship his God, or know his child.

Meanwhile, everybody waited to learn the fate of the pilot and crew of the second downed Black Hawk, as well as our Unit's snipers, Gary Gordon and Randy Shugart, who'd requested three times to be allowed to land and defend them. When the 10th Mountain troops reached the site, they'd found only the wreckage of the helicopters and trails of blood leading away from the scene.

Knowing there were still Americans that were not accounted for, all able-bodied troops quickly went about cleaning their gear, readying the vehicles, and devising ways to carry more water and ammunition in preparation for going back out. This time we packed our night-vision goggles. We'd fought for eighteen hours, lost so many men, to recover the remains of the crew from the first downed Black Hawk, and then a second; we weren't about to leave any American soldier, living or dead, behind.

As we gathered in front of a small television nestled in the back corner of the hangar, the images of dead Americans being dragged through the streets—half or fully naked—by jeering mobs appeared on the screen. One journalist said he'd seen a group of children pulling a corpse that had been burned beyond recognition with ropes. We now knew the whereabouts of at least some of the crew from the second downed Black Hawk and the Unit snipers who'd gone to their rescue.

A visceral reaction rippled through the room and spread through the hangar as the word was passed. Somebody needed to pay for that atrocity. It only got worse when body parts of the dead men started showing up at the front gate of the airbase in garbage bags.

A bloodlust arose among the Unit's operators. A seething anger and hatred toward the Somalis. Every man was ready to go back into the city and slaughter the bastards. Kill them all. The brass knew we would do it, too, and put an end to it. Our battle was over.

However, we were not through dying. On October 6, two days after the battle ended, Task Force Ranger assembled for a memorial service for those killed in action. The Unit's replacement forces, A Squadron, had just arrived and lined up with C Squadron on the tarmac directly outside our hangar, the traditional empty boots and bayoneted rifles lined up in a row in front of Little Bird helicopters. That was all that remained of our friends to mourn.

As I was standing there, listening to the bugler playing taps, I considered the implications if the Somalis got lucky and landed a mortar round in our midst. Nowhere felt safe anymore.

Jake and I were returning to the hangar that evening when we walked up on our Squadron Commander who was talking to the lead surgeon, Maj. Curt A., as well as with C squadron team leaders and newly arrived team leaders from A, outside the entrance. After stopping for a few minutes to greet friends in A Squadron, I continued to my bunk just inside the entrance, leaving Jake to shoot the breeze.

Without warning, there was a deafening crack and then the roar of an explosion, followed by debris flying through the air and a cloud of smoke. Something hard struck me on the leg and I was deafened. It took me a moment to realize what had happened: the Somalis got lucky; a mortar round had landed a few feet from the men outside.

As my hearing returned, I was shaken by the sound of a man

screaming in pain. I started to head for the entrance just as Jake hopped into the building on one leg and fell into my arms, a piece of shrapnel having severed an Achilles tendon.

As I laid Jake down on a cot, he looked up and yelled, "Avenge me, Tom! Avenge me!"

Under other circumstances, his plea for vengeance might have been humorous for its dramatic flair. But while serious, the wound was not life-threatening or permanently debilitating. I left him and ran outside to check the others.

The Commander was on the ground, his legs punctured in dozens of places by shrapnel. He was shrieking so loudly that I could almost feel the man's pain in my own body. It was unnerving, and a chill ran down my spine.

The lead surgeon, Curt, had been struck in his torso and legs by the flying pieces of metal. But he'd been knocked unconscious by the blast and no sound came from him.

Matt Rierson, who had been standing between the others and where the mortar round landed, had absorbed the worst of it. He was still alive, but it was obvious that he wasn't going to make it.

Of all those injured, his fate seemed the most unfair. There were many stories of heroics that took place during the Battle of Mogadishu. Tales of clerks, cooks, and support staff who'd volunteered to join the effort to fight their way into the city to evacuate the wounded and try to break through the defenders. The 10th Mountain Division had lived up to its reputation for courage, as had the Rangers. And the Little Bird pilots had refused to let the enemy overrun the defenders, exposing themselves to RPGs while living up to their motto "Night Stalkers Don't Quit!" Many men had sacrificed themselves for their brothers-in-arms.

However, Matt Rierson had achieved near-legendary status for his actions, even among the elite warriors of the Unit. He'd been in on the initial assault of the target building, and was then with the convoy that brought back the prisoners. Getting out of the vehicle when they came to roadblocks, Matt took the fight to the enemy and overcame overwhelming odds to get the convoy moving again.

By the time he got back to the airbase, Matt had been through hell. But he immediately grabbed more ammunition and then jumped in a Humvee and headed back into the city to bring wounded troops back to safety. Each time he returned with a vehicle full of wounded, he'd turned the bullet-riddled vehicle back around and gone out again, knowing that with each trip he'd be subjected to constant attacks and the likelihood of death.

Somehow, miraculously, Matt had survived. But now, fate had caught up to him, delivered by an unseen enemy. He died shortly after arriving at the field hospital; he'd lost too much blood, suffered too many wounds.

More calls for blood donations went out as the remaining troops huddled in a bunker at the back of the hangar, listening to the wounded scream in pain, and no longer making jokes about the Somalis' lack of accuracy. That night I fell into an uneasy sleep, the sound of Harrell's screams reverberating throughout the building, and up and down the hallways of my mind.

A dark cloud settled over the men of our Unit. We'd learned a tough lesson; we were not invincible; we were not untouchable. Nineteen Americans had been killed, including Unit operators Rierson, Busch, Fillmore, Shughart, and Gordon. Seventy-three were wounded.

Somali combatant casualties were horrendous, though the actual numbers varied according to the source. Whether they were all noncombatants, shot while intermixed with combatants, or hit by bullets or RPGs far from the battle was unknown.

Following the newscasts, the men of Task Force Ranger wondered what our families had been told. People in the United States were seeing the same broadcasts we were, including the bodies being dragged through the streets.

The families of the deceased would, of course, be notified as soon as command was sure it had the correct information. However, other families would be worrying. Usually Unit families assumed that no news was good news, but if they'd heard about the battle, they'd be sure to be lighting up the call center at Fort Bragg.

The day before the mortar attack, Jake and I had located a satellite phone and secretly made calls back to Debbie and Jake's girlfriend, Shari. We didn't say much, just enough to let them know we were okay. Of course, the next day that changed for Jake with his severed Achilles.

AFTER THE MORTAR ATTACK that killed Rierson, command decided that the best thing for the operators was to get back to training and preparing for whatever lay ahead. The survivors of the Battle of Mogadishu filled in the new arrivals of A Squadron on what to expect if they went into bad-guy territory, including the reality of war and combat for those who had not experienced it before but were willing to listen. Those of us who'd been in the fight could see in the untested men the same look we knew we'd had before everything had gone to hell: eager to fight, unafraid, believing in our invincibility.

In an After-Action Review, we passed on the lessons we'd learned, such as not leaving night-vision goggles behind, taking plenty of water, and having resupply ammunition prepackaged and ready to deliver before going on missions. Within days we'd received Kevlar helmets to replace the bicycle helmets.

We also talked to the new guys about the battle tactics of the enemy, including their propensity for hiding behind unarmed civilians while they shot. Normally, the rules of engagement were that in such circumstances the American soldier was to shoot back only when shot at first, and only at the person imposing a direct threat. However, the Somali combatants blatantly used noncombatants as shields, believing that the US forces would not shoot back, which made the decision to shoot into a crowd more difficult. It weighed heavily on those forced to shoot in such circumstances in order to survive and to protect their brothers-in-arms. The commanders left it to each individual team member to decide how to react in those instances. No matter what you tell yourself if you have not been in combat, it is not an easy task to shoot toward civilians even when getting shot at. It's very easy to say you would do so having not been put in that position before.

In the meantime, both groups trained at an abandoned village near the sea, each clearing buildings on opposite sides of the street. Right away, I noticed a marked difference between how the newcomers and those who had already been in battle went about their business.

The newcomers charged up stairways, stood in doorways or windows, and stopped to talk in the open, leaving themselves exposed. I could see them and that meant so would the enemy in battle. On the other side of the street, the survivors of the battle were invisible even during daylight hours. They crawled up stairways and avoided standing where they'd make good targets.

There were individual lessons as well. My .45 had jammed when I tried to kill the man creeping down the alley. That was because we kept our weapons so finely tuned—practice range ready—that a little bit of sand had prevented it from firing. A "sloppy" weapon might not be as accurate shooting targets on the range, but in the field, it was more reliable.

The most important lesson of all, one that would change the way special operations were performed in the future: don't have helicopters hover over the target area, essentially broadcasting to the locals where to find Americans and providing easy targets for RPGs. If the Black Hawk had not gone done, the mission would have been accomplished quickly and with many fewer casualties.

As the days passed, one unsolved question weighed on the men of Task Force Ranger. Everyone had been accounted for except Chief Warrant Officer Durant, who we'd learned from the television was being held hostage. He'd even been interviewed on television.

Following the interview, Robert Oakley, the US special envoy to Somalia, warned Aidid and Durant's captors that if the pilot was not released there would be dire consequences. Americans were enraged by images of the bodies of servicemen being dragged through Mogadishu and were in no mood for more atrocities.

"There's going to be a fight with your people," Oakley told the media for Aidid's consumption. "The minute the guns start again, all restraint on the US side goes. Just look at the stuff coming in here now. An aircraft carrier, tanks, gunships…the works. Once the fighting starts, all this pent-up anger is going to be released. This whole part of the city will be destroyed."

President Clinton had backed up the threat with the deployment of a mechanized infantry unit—including Abrams tanks and Bradley fighting vehicles—an additional 10th Mountain battalion, AC-130 Spectre gunships that could level a block in minutes with their armament, the USS *Abraham Lincoln*, and a fresh squadron to replace the battered C Squadron.

Aidid got the picture. Durant was released after eleven days of captivity. It was through his account that the men, and then the world, learned the story of the heroism of Shughart and Gordon. He described how they fought ferociously, even after being wounded, outgunned, and outnumbered. They'd had to have known that it was hopeless, especially after losing their air cover, but they'd taken many of the enemy with them.* I was among those who put Durant on a plane back to the States.

Those who'd been killed had already been sent home in flag-draped coffins to their grieving families who were tasked with making funeral arrangements, their lives changed forever. The wounded were spread out among military hospitals in Germany and Walter Reed Army Medical Center in Bethesda, Maryland.

Then, finally, on October 13, it was time for what was left of C Squadron to go home. Our team members were waiting to board the

---

* The Somalis reported twenty-five dead and many more than that wounded.

massive C-5 transport aircraft when we were approached by a psychiatrist sent by the Unit. There was always a psychiatrist attached to the squadrons to ensure that the soldiers were psychologically fit to do their jobs. But we weren't expecting what he wanted to talk to us about this time around.

"Hey," Larry L. started, "when you guys get home and have time to think about what happened, don't be surprised if you break down, maybe cry for no apparent reason. After what you went through here, it's bound to happen at some point. Just remember, it's perfectly normal."

No one quite knew what to say. What the doc told us baffled most men. Yes, it had been bad, but weren't they the best in the world? The toughest? The most highly trained? Besides, breaking down was a sign of weakness, and the Unit wasn't a place for the weak. It could get you kicked out. An operator had to be able to count on the guy next to him in situations where a moment's hesitation could be the difference between life and death.

Out of respect for the doctor, we just nodded and didn't question his comments. But I was still perplexed as to why the shrink would even bring it up or, even more so, why a breakdown would occur after we all reached the safety of the States. I chalked it up to just something psychiatrists needed to say.

Arriving in the States, C Squadron wasn't flown directly to Fort Bragg but to a different airfield and then bussed to Bragg for secrecy. The press was all over the events in Mogadishu and the Unit's participation was still classified.

After storing my gear, I walked to the front gate where I was met by Debbie. Our conversation on the ride home was mostly small talk about the things that needed to be fixed around the house, the weather, and her work.

She'd heard about Mogadishu, but only the sanitized version—as bad as that was—that had appeared on the news. And she didn't ask for more details...not until after we got home.

"So how was it really?" she asked as we walked in the door.

I stopped and turned to face her. I thought for a moment about how to answer, but before I could speak, I felt the memories welling up inside of me like flotsam on a rising tide. The sights, the sounds— the screams of men and the scent of blood and bleach.

In my mind, I saw dead American soldiers lying side by side on the tarmac, and the faces of Earl, Griz, Dan, Gary, Randy, and Matt—friends I'd laughed with, eaten with, gotten drunk with, and now gone forever. I was racked with guilt for having survived what my friends, my brothers, had not.

My shoulders began to shake. My gut knotted. I covered my face with my hands and wept.

CHAPTER TWELVE

October 1993
Nevada, Iowa

IT WAS TWENTY DEGREES OUTSIDE and cloudy, fitting for the mood of the day. Winter was definitely on its way. Ignoring the cold, I stood outside with the honor guard looking in through the open double doors that led to the high school gymnasium. In a few minutes, the seven of us on the rifle squad would send three volleys into the gray skies, a final goodbye to our friend Matt Rierson.

The gym was packed with Matt's family, friends, and townspeople who'd come to pay their respects to the hometown boy who'd given his last full measure. Most were seated in the rows of folding chairs in front of a podium. Matt's young widow, Trish, dressed in black, sat in the middle of the front row, her two young sons on either side of her, with other family members surrounding them.

Photographs of Matt and his family had been placed front and center for all to see. It was the sort of turnout and service one might expect in small-town America: the US flags, the high school band, the funny stories recalled by former classmates, and the tearful farewells of friends and family.

All of the remaining members of C Squadron had flown into Ames

Municipal Airport and then had driven ten miles to Nevada for the memorial service, which had been delayed so we could attend. It was the only chance we'd had to attend a funeral or a memorial for one of our fallen comrades.

By the time the squadron flew back to the United States from Somalia, all of the dead from the Battle of Mogadishu, as the media was calling it, had been buried. Matt had been laid to rest at the Fort Bragg Main Post Cemetery.

As with the others, he'd been buried with full military honors, including the folding of the flag which had been presented to Trish *on behalf of the president of the United States, the United States Army and a grateful nation...for your loved one's honorable and faithful service.*

The Unit had had its own private ceremony—just operators and families—in the courtyard where the names of the newly dead had been inscribed on the memorial wall with the others. The names of the Rangers and airmen from the 160th SOAR who'd died had been added to a separate monument nearby. The ceremony was simple. It started with a prayer and reading of scripture, followed by comments from command, family members, and then the men they'd served with. It concluded with more scripture.

ONCE THE OFFICIAL CEREMONY was complete, the operators moved to their squadron bar—each had one in their building—for a proper sendoff with the telling of stories, both funny and poignant, all of it fueled by copious amounts of alcohol. The wake had lasted well into the next morning.

Back in Iowa, an article about Matt had appeared in the *Des Moines Register*, in which reporter Ken Fuson wrote that after arriving back at the airbase with the convoy and prisoners, Matt had returned to the city "in a frantic attempt to rescue fallen friends or recover their bodies. He followed the Ranger Creed: 'Never shall I fail my comrades.'"

The story quoted Trish as saying, "These men weren't super-heroes. They were husbands and fathers and average Joes who went to church on Sunday and signed up for Neighborhood Watch. They taught their children how to throw a spiral and catch a fish. Then all of a sudden, they go to work, and it's like this new personality comes out. They were just so determined that you can't leave anybody, no matter what."

The story noted that Matt had turned thirty-three years old while in Somalia. And that his two young sons, Jacob and Kaleb, had been "postponing his birthday cake until he returned home."

Arriving in Nevada, Iowa, I was struck by how much it reminded me of the small Indiana towns where I'd grown up. Smack dab in the middle of Iowa, and surrounded by cornfields, it was a town of six thousand people who remembered Matt not as an elite soldier but as a high school sports legend who'd married his high school sweetheart. The people I met before the ceremony had that small-town friendliness that gave the impression that they actually cared about each other and appreciated that Matt's brothers-in-arms had come "all this way" to say goodbye to one of their own.

As I stood on the grass outside the gymnasium waiting for the eulogies to end, I considered how, but for the grace of God, there might have been such a small-town service for me. Only Debbie would have been the grieving widow—no children at her side— surrounded by my parents and my siblings, Shelly and Steve. It could have been my high school buddies and family recalling funny anecdotes and tearfully saying they'd miss me, followed by the color guard firing three volleys, and then followed by the playing of taps. Instead, I stood at attention in uniform—a rarity since joining the Unit—waiting to do the honors for my friend Matt.

To be honest, I was relieved that I wasn't sitting with other squadron members near the family. Burdened with the guilt of having survived when some of my friends and comrades didn't, I wouldn't have known what to say to anybody. Just like I hadn't known what to say to Debbie when I got home and broke down in front of her a few days earlier.

As I sobbed, Debbie had gotten a bewildered look on her face. She'd never seen me cry or lose control before. It didn't last long. I quickly pulled myself together, wiped my nose, cleared my throat, apologized for "being a pussy," and the subject never came up again. I recognized at that moment, that I would never be able to talk to anyone outside the Unit about Somalia.

Jake was the only person I ever mentioned the breakdown to—a few days later when we were working out at the base. Even then I minimized it by saying I'd had one of those moments the psychiatrist had mentioned in Iraq, without going into the whole sobbing like a child description. "Weird, huh?"

Jake, who was rehabbing his injured ankle, conceded he'd had a few moments that had troubled him, too. Then, as if we'd wandered into forbidden territory, we dropped the subject as quickly as it had come up and went back to work.

Some of the reluctance to talk about the after-effects of Mogadishu was not wanting to appear fainthearted or "less of a man" in the hyper-alpha-male culture of the Unit. So much had gone into proving how tough and resilient I was during selection and OTC, I was surprised by what I perceived as weakness, a "chink in the armor." After all, wasn't the whole point of my training about preparing for war?

However, personal embarrassment or being perceived by my teammates as a weak link wasn't the only thing contributing to an unwillingness to discuss the emotions I was experiencing. It was an unspoken truth that admitting to having mental health issues, especially as they related to the job, could get an operator kicked out of the Unit.

I understood the reasoning. Command's first duty was to the Unit as an entity, not the individual soldier. Part of that went back to the necessity of a team having to count on each member to do his part without hesitating or making a mistake, and therefore putting other team members and the mission at risk. But there was more to it than that.

Operators for the Unit often worked in far off parts of the world without much direct supervision. We were expected to make snap decisions—whether taking out a terrorist or drug lord—within the limitations of international law and our mission. Command couldn't have a highly trained, but mentally unstable, killer going off the rails and doing something illegal or crazy.

There was nothing malicious or purposefully humiliating about getting "fired" from the Unit. No aspersions were cast as far as a man's competence as a soldier. Quite the contrary, the operator would be returned to another Army unit with the Unit commander's commendation. Of course, it was heartbreaking to the individual who, after having worked so hard to get in, would then have his dream crushed by being told that he was no longer good enough to be in the Unit.

However, while the rationale was protecting the Unit as a whole, it also meant that soldiers who were struggling with the complexities of what they'd seen or done while in combat or carrying out missions wouldn't talk about them with a Unit psychiatrist for fear of being flagged. It was okay to tell a shrink about marital problems or other everyday issues. But mention that you had suicidal thoughts, drank a lot in part to forget or deal with the problem, and were confused about having taken a life or having difficulty in dealing with the death of a friend, and you might find yourself in front of the squadron commander and possibly reassigned to another unit. If I had felt like I was able to talk about these issues with a psychiatrist, I might have been able to deal with them better.

I was certainly experiencing all of those symptoms and more. Nightmares of being trapped—both in a combat sense, but also in everyday life—jolted me from my sleep. The dream images played in my mind like a horrifying slideshow with blood, explosions, and the faces of the dead.

The effects of Mogadishu weren't just at night or when I was sleeping. Even though I trained daily on the firing range, and constantly rehearsed CQB, unexpected loud noises made me jump both physically and internally. The sound of a helicopter's blades slapping the air could trigger memories of Somalia and brought on a sense of impending doom. If I woke up to Debbie doing the laundry and using bleach, I was instantaneously reminded of the smell of death on a hot October morning in Mogadishu while looking in the back of a blood-soaked Humvee.

Sometimes I'd look at the photographs of the fallen on the memorial wall and feel such a profound sadness as I tried to recall their voices and the times we'd spent together as young men, full of life and confident about our place in the world. No one ever talked about "survivor's guilt" or what to do when the sound of their voices and the memories we have of them started to fade.

As I stood at Matt's service waiting for the ceremony to end, I wondered if I was the only one going through hell. I'd noted that the mood around headquarters was much more somber than before we'd left, but I ascribed that to the process of recovering from the longest and bloodiest fight since Vietnam.

So, I kept my mouth shut and devoted myself to training even harder to be a better operator for the Unit. No matter what I was going through on the inside, I wasn't going to let my team or the Unit down.

Most of 1994 was spent rebuilding C Squadron. The new guys, fresh from OTC, of course, all wanted to talk about "what it was like" in Mogadishu. Within the Unit, the veterans of the battle were regarded by the younger guys with awe, especially when the commendations were awarded.

In keeping with the secretive nature of the Unit, in which our exploits were rarely mentioned and never publicized, most members of the Unit were not the sort who cared much for medals and commendations. The awards only really mattered when it came to competing with soldiers in other units for promotions.

Les Aspin, the secretary of defense in October 1993, had handed out the numerous medals awarded to veterans of the battle at a large ceremony at Unit headquarters attended by members of the Unit and their families. He wasn't a popular choice for the task because prior to the battle he'd turned down a request from General Montgomery for tanks and AC-130 Spectre gunships, which many felt would have saved American lives.*

Matt Rierson was posthumously awarded the Silver Star for "conspicuous gallantry and intrepidity in action against hostile enemy forces while serving with the 1st Special Forces Operational Detachment during combat operations in Mogadishu, Somalia."

Dan Busch was also awarded the Silver Star, according to the commendation, for "gallantly defending the crew of a downed MH-60 Black Hawk helicopter against a numerically superior enemy force.... His actions were in keeping with the highest traditions of the military forces, and reflect great credit upon himself, the Special Operations Command, and the United States Army."

"He told me his unit was going someplace later that summer, but he couldn't say where," his mother, Virginia Johnson, later told a reporter for a website dedicated to the battle. "He just told me not to worry. He said, 'I know this job is dangerous, but remember that it keeps me close to God. A Christian soldier is just a click away from heaven in this type of work.'"

Dan had been planning on getting out of the military in September 1995, his wife, Traci, said for the same article. He wanted their infant son, Mitchell, "to grow up in an atmosphere that had nothing to do with the Army and the constant deployments." Shortly before

---

* Randy Shughart and Gary Gordon were later posthumously awarded the Medal of Honor, the first since Vietnam, by President Clinton. The commendation noted their *"extraordinary heroism and devotion."* However, Shughart's father refused to shake Clinton's hand and openly criticized him: *"The blame for my son's death rests with the White House and with you. You are not fit for command."*

the battle, he'd written a letter to his unborn son urging him to be a man of "morals and values."

Tim "Griz" Martin and Earl Fillmore were both posthumously awarded the Bronze star given for "heroic or meritorious achievement."

I was also awarded the Bronze Star with the additional "with Valor" designation. But I was uncomfortable receiving the medal. I didn't feel like I'd done anything particularly heroic that night other than the job I was trained to do. And trying to survive.

Numerous other Mogadishu veterans received commendations, including Purple Hearts for my friends Jake and Brad, my companion in Colombia who lost his leg when the Black Hawk he was on above the second crash site was shot down. Both had returned to our Unit.

When new guys brought up Mogadishu, I tried to stick to the teaching points that had come out of the engagement. Remember your night-vision goggles, as well as sufficient food and water, and always carry extra ammunition. I didn't like talking about what they wanted to hear, the "war stories," and tried to avoid getting into blow-by-blow accounts of the details.

Nor did I talk about it with my wife or my family. Frightened and lonely, Debbie had confided in Shelly that she didn't know what was going on with me. Even before Mogadishu our relationship had essentially become like one of housemates, each with their own circle of friends and interests—mine being centered around the Unit. But, she confided to my sister, that ever since I got back, I'd been especially cold toward her and spent my social hours drinking with my Unit buddies.

Shelly thought she knew why. She'd been home in the evening when Debbie called and told her to turn her television to the news. The scene of a mob of jeering Somalis dragging the burned body of a US soldier through the streets had horrified her. She was frightened for me and prayed that I was okay. Then Debbie called to say she'd heard from me and I was safe, which was a relief to both of them.

However, the Tom who went away to war was not the man who came back. After making the Unit, I'd been confident and looking forward to testing my mettle, but I was still my sister's tenderhearted baby brother who liked to joke and was loving by nature whether with a friend or a family member. After Somalia, though, it was as if I was wearing a mask over the other boy's face and had buried my heart, my empathy for others, and my emotions. But I wouldn't talk about it, not to her, not to Debbie, not to my parents, and none of them knew how to get through to me.

Shelly counseled Debbie to give me space. "Just be there for him. It's crazy what he went through, and he's probably dealing with some survivor's guilt." They all hoped that with time, I'd come back out of my shell.

GENERAL G.'S PREDICTION THAT Task Force Ranger would "win the gunfight but lose the war" had proved to be true. On October 6, 1993, the same day Matt Rierson was killed, President Clinton ordered all combat operations against Aidid to stop except in self-defense. After issuing the threats that resulted in the return of Michael Durant, the US military basically remained on base and in their ships.

In February 1994, the UN Security Council voted to end its efforts in Somalia. President Clinton ordered the withdrawal of all US forces, while humanitarian and security objectives remained unmet.

Fearful of other Somalia-like entanglements, the administration also scaled back other humanitarian efforts in the region that might have called for US military support. The Battle of Mogadishu was cited by critics as the key reason the United States didn't intervene in the Rwandan genocide that resulted in anywhere from five hundred thousand to a million deaths.

"The ghosts of Somalia continue to haunt US policy," the former

US deputy special envoy to Somalia Walter Clarke said in a PBS interview. "Our lack of response in Rwanda was a fear of getting involved in something like Somalia again."

Two more years would pass before it became common knowledge, but the public relations success of the Somalis against US troops, and subsequent ignoble withdrawal, encouraged Osama bin Laden and al-Qaeda. He now believed that he had a template for how to defeat the US military by shaking its political will. That template would lead to unimaginable consequences in the future.

Rubbing salt into the wounds of the US veterans of the battle, Aidid's lieutenants, including Atto and the two captured on October 3, were freed as part of the agreement to release Durant. The men of the Unit complained bitterly among themselves; while they were grateful for Durant's release, they'd fought bitterly, lost friends, and ultimately, for what? Nothing.

However, they were soldiers and, in the end, had to leave political decisions to the politicians. Unfortunately, it was a fact of military life that politicians would continue to insert themselves into combat operations planning and decision making, often with unforeseen and dangerous consequences.

The first anniversary of the Battle of Mogadishu was an emotional one for the men of C Squadron. We gathered at the squadron bar to draw closer and toast our lost brothers. There was a lot of love in that room to go with a lot of alcohol. But the memories still stung, and I wondered how long I would have to deal with the consequences.

Shortly after the anniversary party, my squadron was sent to Israel for desert mobility training.

When I returned to Fort Bragg in November, I packed up all of my gear and drove home, tired but happy. That is, until I walked into my house.

It was completely empty. No furniture. No art on the walls. None of the personal items I'd spent years collecting from different parts of the world. Even the washer and dryer were gone.

Writing home from Germany, 1986.

Graduation from German Ranger School, 1988.

At Ft. Bragg, NC, back in my engineer days prior to Special Forces.

Don't mess with Kuwait and try to get away with it:
Touring the Highway of Death.

After running the Mogadishu Mile. In 2018, I was approached by the driver of the vehicle, who told me his story of coming in to get us out. I was never so relieved to see the 10th Mountain Division as I was that morning.

Moments after our return to the hangar from the Mogadishu Mile. I had just learned of the devastation when my buddy snapped this. "You'll thank me for this one day," he told me.

Boots of the Fallen memorial dedication in Somalia, October 6, 1993. A mortar round landed just hours after the service, killing Matt Rierson.

Viewing a special exhibit on the Battle of Mogadishu at the Airborne and Special Operations Museum in Fayetteville, NC.

It was an honor to train with the best. I got my ass kicked, but that's how you learn.

Having to dress in uniform to attend ANCOC at Ft. Bragg, NC.

Reenlisting with my team in an undisclosed overseas location.

Just a little workout with some of my teammates and closest friends.

Testing the next generation of hopeful Special Operators.

Training stateside: Nothing like a little Hellfire.

Desert training in our modified vehicle.

Taking advantage of a great photo op in Jordan.

When it's dangerous, they call in the Unit.

On leave from Ft. Bragg, I spent some time with my parents. My dad was always cracking jokes, and he always made everyone feel good about themselves.

No matter where we are in the world, we check in.

Providing security for President Bush's visit with the troops, Thanksgiving Day, 2003.

Kings Challenge in Amman, Jordan, post-service.

The night before I attempted to kill myself. I didn't know how visible
my misery was until I saw this picture years later.

Working alongside Jen as we trained Special Operation warriors across the country with a military company we helped found. She never hesitated to get in and get the shot no matter what it called for, which only made me love and respect her more.

Special Operations mission training. Never afraid to get right in the thick of it, Jen was blown over by the rotor wash.

Happiest day of my life. The ceremony was rushed but turned out perfect, the rain earlier kept everyone away, and we had Tybee Island to ourselves.
(*Amanda Knox Photography*)

I can see it in my face now, the feeling that I was undeserving of happiness and love, still spiraling down to rock bottom, which I hit that night.
(*Amanda Knox Photography*)

Working alongside my love, Jen, to help others heal from the invisible wounds of war.

Continuing in life with my new mission, to save Special Operation warrior families battling on the homefront, alongside my partner in life and work, Jen.

Graduation from Basic Training, Oklahoma, 2017.

I never take for granted getting a second chance to have a family again, and I'm grateful for my relationship with my stepkids, Claudia and Luke.

Speaking on behalf of the All Secure Foundation at a congressional briefing on suicide among veterans, alongside Jen Satterly and NAMI.

Walking into the master bedroom, I could see that Debbie had left the waterbed mattress, but not the frame, and piled my clothes on top. I discovered that she'd even taken my wedding ring, which I left when deployed, and my favorite pair of Boa Constrictor cowboy boots I'd purchased in Bogotá. She didn't even leave me a spoon to eat with.

I was completely caught off guard. I knew I'd been absent both physically and emotionally with Debbie, but I didn't expect this. Nor did she leave a note explaining.

Then I realized that I wasn't sure I even cared. I didn't really have strong feelings for her anymore. I pretty much lived for the Unit and she had become someone who stayed in our house, cooked, did the laundry, and otherwise had a separate life from me. Admittedly though, through no choice of her own.

I walked out to the backyard and got a lawn chair out of the shed. I set it up in the living room and went to sleep. When I woke up in the morning and went outside again, I noticed that Debbie had removed one more item. This made me mad enough that I called Jake.

"Debbie left me," I said. "But you know the one thing that pisses me off more than anything? Even more than the fact that she took my wedding ring and my boots. She even took the shingles you and I ripped off the roof!" Jake laughed and told me that he had removed the shingles we had left on the side of the house after re-roofing my house just prior to leaving.

CHAPTER THIRTEEN

Fall 1996
Sarajevo, Bosnia

"WHAT'S THAT?" I said, pointing to a red floral design seemingly imbedded in *Ulica Zmaja od Bosne*, the main boulevard from the airport to the city. It looked like a flower with petals radiating from the center.

"Those are the 'Sarajevo Roses,'" replied the operator I was replacing. "They're where mortars landed, and somebody was killed. They fill the crater with red resin as a reminder."

I was stunned. We'd passed seemingly hundreds of such "roses" once we reached the city and I could see more on the road and sidewalks up ahead. *God, somebody mortared the hell out of these people,* I thought.

It wasn't just the road either. The entire city looked like an old World War II documentary from Germany in which every building was pockmarked by bullets, and entire blocks devastated by artillery and tank shelling. Office and apartment buildings had crumbled, leaving gaping holes, shattered windows, or exposed interiors missing entire sides. Every street and sidewalk were seemingly linked by the Sarajevo Roses.

I had just arrived with my team, as well as other teams, as part of a NATO peacekeeping force following four years of brutal war that had included the siege of Sarajevo. The other teams were assigned to hunt down war criminals indicted by an international tribunal. My team was to provide security for the commander of the NATO forces, US Gen. Montgomery Cunningham Meigs, as well as other military and civilian dignitaries who visited the city on official business.

In the nearly two years since returning from Israel to find my wife gone and the house empty, I had been through a lot of changes. One was that that I'd already remarried and to someone who was the exact opposite of Debbie in just about every way possible.

"Brandy" was a stripper I met in early 1995 shortly after Debbie left me. I was attending the Advanced Non-Commissioned Officers Course at Fort Bragg when several Special Forces soldiers attending the course from out of town asked where they could find a strip club. I offered to show them.

While at the club, one of my new friends started talking about how beautiful one of the strippers was as she performed on stage. But, he said, he was too shy to approach her.

I told the other soldier to watch me to see "how it's done." I walked over to the stage and got the young woman's attention after she finished her dance. After the obvious question of "Why do you work here?" I added, "I bet you get a fifty-dollar tip before your set is over."

"You're crazy," she replied nodding at the young, and poorly paid, soldiers that made up the club's clientele. "Nobody in here tips that kind of money." She smiled. "What do you get if I lose?"

"You'll let me take you out."

Brandy said she'd take the bet. I then pulled a fifty-dollar bill from my wallet and handed it to her. "Looks like you lost, and I'm taking you out to dinner."

That was pretty much the extent of our courtship. It wasn't long before we were married. The sex was great, and she liked to party, which fit my lifestyle. I was looking for validation and I'd found it by marrying a beautiful stripper. Plus, she made more money taking her clothes off than I did as a staff sergeant in the Army.

Just the fact that I married Brandy reflected some of the changes I'd been going through. For all my big talk about showing the Special Forces visitors *"how it's done,"* I'd never been a ladies' man as far as pickup lines. In spite of my status as a warrior, I wasn't really very self-assured around women, which was probably why I'd stayed with Debbie as long as I had, long after any romantic feelings had disappeared.

I was often depressed and angry. I also felt inferior to the other operators, but I didn't let it show. No matter what evidence there was to the contrary—on the shooting range or my level of physical fitness—I had a growing sense of "not measuring up." We'd all been warned that selection never stopped in the Unit; we would be continuously judged, and if somebody didn't measure up, they were out.

The Unit was constantly being pruned. Weak branches had to go. Afraid that someone would think I wasn't capable of the strength required, I worked even harder at being the best, and then handled the stress of that like many of the other operators by drinking. I had noticed that a lot of the other combat vets, especially those who'd been in the fight in Somalia, seemed to handle it the same way.

There were certainly Unit operators who were family men who put their guns away at the end of the day and went straight home to their wives and children. But for most, the culture was about boozing it up and making a lot of poor personal decisions—whether it was choosing to drink and drive, or chase women while married. As a result, a lot of Unit guys got DUIs and were on their second, third, or even fourth wife, watching their paychecks disappear into child and spousal support obligations.

Essentially, I was a high-functioning alcoholic. I got up early, went to work, and even stayed late working sometimes. But most days, after quitting time, I was off to the bar. If I went home, I started drinking there. The next day, hungover, I went back to work but always with the concerned thought in the back of my mind that "today's the day" that command would call me into his office and tell me I was fired.

In the meantime, the world remained a dangerous place. In particular, the threat of Islamic extremism was growing, even if most Americans were still in the dark about the storm clouds gathering in little known corners of the world.

In January 1996, Gary K., a member from another team, and I were sent to Algeria for three months to provide security for Ambassador Ronald E. Neumann, an American expert on Middle Eastern issues.

Algeria had been locked in a brutal civil war between its government and Islamic rebels since 1992 and being the US ambassador there was a dangerous job. Although the State Department had a diplomatic security unit, in countries where the threat was higher than normal, Unit operators would be requested, as we were by Neumann.

THE UNREST IN ALGIERS, and the animosity directed at the United States, seemed endemic to the Muslim world and the threat level was increasing as evidenced by two events prior to our deploying to Sarajevo.

On June 25, 1996, a truck bomb detonated outside the Khobar Towers, an apartment complex in Khobar, Saudi Arabia, that was being used to house coalition forces assigned to Operation Southern Watch, part of the no-fly zones over Iraq. Nine US Air Force personnel and one Saudi resident were killed and nearly six hundred people were injured. The Iran-sponsored terrorist organization Hezbollah claimed responsibility.*

Then in August 1996, a little-known Islamic demagogue named

---

* In 2008, a US federal court found Iran and Hezbollah guilty of orchestrating the attack.

Osama bin Laden published his first *fatwa*. He called it a "Declaration of War Against the Americans Occupying the Land of the Two Holy Places," meaning US troops in Saudi Arabia.

The *fatwa* gained little attention. At the time, bin Laden was still only a wanted man in his own country of Saudi Arabia and hardly known to anyone outside of the intelligence community. However, one of his comments about American involvement in Somalia caught the attention of Mogadishu veterans.

"You left carrying disappointment, humiliation, defeat, and your dead with you," he taunted.

Shortly after the statement, we were sent to Sarajevo. The irony was that we were protecting Bosnian Muslims from Serbian Christians.

Assisted by the government of Serbia and its powerful military, the ethnic Christian Serbians in Bosnia held the upper hand that included the siege of Sarajevo. With a force of about thirteen thousand troops situated in the surrounding pine-forested hills, the city had been assaulted on a daily basis by heavy artillery, tanks, and street-to-street fighting.

At the height of the siege, more than three hundred rounds of artillery, tank, and mortar shells pounded the city. The Serbs didn't just destroy military objectives; they destroyed hospitals and medical clinics, and even used incendiary bombs to destroy libraries that housed ancient, irreplaceable manuscripts.

Nearly fourteen thousand Sarajevans lost their lives during the siege, which lasted three times longer than the Battle of Stalingrad and a year longer than the Siege of Leningrad during World War II, through a combination of military action, starvation, disease, and exposure in a city without electricity or running water. Of the dead, 5,434 were civilians.

At first, the rest of the world was hardly aware of the atrocities being committed in the former Yugoslavia. But in 1993, reports of mass killings of civilians, primarily in mortar attacks, began to make headline news around the world.

Then in July 1995, elements of the Bosnian Serb army under the command of Ratko Mladić massacred more than eight thousand Bosniaks, mostly men and boys, from the town of Srebrenica. They followed that up on August 28 with another mortar attack on the Markale Marketplace in Sarajevo, killing forty-three more civilians.

NATO responded with widespread airstrikes and artillery attacks on Bosnian Serb positions, and finally the Serbs had absorbed enough punishment. In September, the NATO airstrikes were suspended to allow the Serbs to withdraw heavy weapons from around Sarajevo. Twelve days later, the sides agreed on basic principles for a peace accord. A sixty-day cease-fire went into effect on October 12 and peace talks began on the first of November, followed by a signed peace agreement that day.*

Following the cease-fire, an eighty-thousand-strong NATO-led force was deployed to Bosnia-Herzegovina under the command of General Meigs, the commander of the US 1st Infantry Division. I was assigned to his security.

I was shocked the first time we drove into the city after landing at the airport. I recalled watching the 1984 Winter Olympics which were held in Sarajevo, then a beautiful, modern city nestled into pine-forested mountains. We drove up to see the site of the 1984 Olympic Games and found the buildings and event areas overgrown with weeds and covered with graffiti. It was horrifying to see the impact of bullets in structures where innocent men, women, and children had been lined up and shot by Serbian death squads. The bobsled run had been turned into an artillery installation, as well as a site for public hangings.

As I got to know the city and its people, I saw the psychological

---

* More than 101,000 died or remain "missing" from the Bosnia conflict, according to a 2012 report from the Sarajevo Research and Documentation Center. Of those, 61 percent were Bosniak, 25 percent were Bosnian Serb, and 8 percent Croatian (the remainder were unknown ethnicity). The dead included 38,000 civilians; 81 percent Bosniak, 11 percent Bosnian Serb, and 7 percent Croatian.

effects of living in a war zone for years. While many relied on a dark, fatalistic humor to get through the day, fear seemed to be their constant companion.

Many of the people I met lived in collapsed buildings. Few had any power or running water, and I knew neither did most residences. The schools weren't open, so children wandered the streets, endangered by the land mines and thousands of rounds of unexploded ordnance—some of which I saw stuck in trees when out for a morning run with General Meigs.

In a way, the devastation in Sarajevo was even more shocking than the war-ravaged streets of Mogadishu. I guessed part of that was because countries in Africa always seemed locked into brutal and devastating conflicts. But also, while Mogadishu had at one time in its colonial past been a prosperous city for the Horn of Africa, it was still predominantly a city with dirt roads, modest homes, and even shacks without running water. There were only a few modern buildings, and those seemed built for efficiency, not style.

On the other hand, Sarajevo had been a blend of modern and beautiful centuries-old architecture from the Ottoman Empire. Prior to the war, the city boasted big apartment buildings, tree-lined neighborhoods, good roads, modern infrastructure, fine hotels, and the sort of nightlife and amenities one could find in any European city.

What had happened to innocent people in both cities was equally tragic. But the devastation to Sarajevo was a wake-up call for me that the horrors of war could come to any people, including my own country.

Even though a cease-fire was in place, tensions and the threat level remained high. Although the limousine I drove when transporting Meigs or US dignitaries was armored, I didn't count on the vehicle alone to protect my passengers. Traffic in Sarajevo was a mess. The city was without electricity, running water, or a law enforcement presence. There were no traffic lights to direct traffic, even in the absence of police officers. So, I drove like a bat out of hell to keep anyone from anticipating my movements. There was always the possibility of threats, or that someone would detonate an IED by remote control if I stopped at an intersection, which meant I didn't stop, and it didn't matter who I had to run off the road.

Anywhere General Meigs went, our team was there. No one knew we were Unit operators because we carried State Department credentials. But we were identifiable as the general's security team by our "uniform" of photo journalism vests—good for carrying camera equipment and film, or ammunition and a grenade, with M4 rifles at ready, and the ever-present Oakleys hiding our eyes.

Most of the time I spent in Sarajevo was uneventful. But one incident would haunt me, forever resurfacing in the chilling panoply of my nightmares.

One night, Jake and I were sitting at the house we occupied when someone shot out the porch lights. When it happened again on another night, we started worrying that someone "on the other side" was targeting us, maybe setting us up for a sniper attack.

We decided to try to catch whoever was doing it. So, one night Jake went upstairs with a hand-held radio while I waited by the front door with my pistol drawn.

It wasn't long before Jake called in. "There's a guy outside with a rifle aiming at the house."

Without thinking about the danger, I threw open the front door and charged out onto the deck. I saw a man with a rifle running away and gave chase, joined by Jake. At one point, he stopped for a moment in the dark, and I nearly shot him before he darted off again.

Finally, when we caught him, we learned he was just a teenager with a BB gun. Apparently, the boy and his friends were out causing mischief while their parents were away on vacation.

I was reminded of the shenanigans my friends and I used to get up to in Indiana. The difference was these kids lived in a city where carrying a weapon could get them shot. I would have been devastated if we'd killed a boy, and feared there'd be a day when I wouldn't have a choice.

CHAPTER FOURTEEN

Summer 2000
Lahore, Pakistan

WE WERE CRUISING PAST the golf course on the outskirts of Lahore when Jake nudged me. "Check out the caddies."

Taking my eyes off the road for a moment, I glanced over to where a traditionally garbed foursome and their caddies were getting ready to tee-off on the first hole. But what got Jake's attention was that in addition to humping golf bags for their bosses, the caddies all had AK-47s slung over their shoulders.

The caddies had noticed us, too—a couple of white guys in Western-style clothing, Oakley sunglasses, driving a rental car. There was nothing hostile in their look, just bodyguards pulling security, wondering who the "new guys in town" might be. The AKs stayed on their backs, and they went back to digging out the proper clubs for their bosses.

I shrugged and cracked a smile. While the rifles might have been out of place on any green and well-tended course in an American city, this was Pakistan. AK-47s were everywhere. Every nice house had a guard shack in front with an armed guard who spent all day sleeping. Every hotel and professional office with the financial means also had guards with rifles standing out front. Even the cops strolled around with the ubiquitous assault rifle.

It didn't particularly alarm us. Along with our experience and confirmation from a contact at the US Embassy, we knew that the plethora of weapons was due more to the high crime rate than because of terrorists. Jake and I weren't there to get in a fight, anyway; we weren't even armed. Our objectives were to assess security at the embassy and get an impression about feelings toward the United States in some of the major cities and tribal areas.

A lot of water had passed under the bridge, carrying with it many life changes, since my deployment in war-torn Sarajevo.

Returning from a mission in early 1997, I learned that my second wife, Brandy, was cheating on me with a Special Forces soldier who was trying to get into the Unit. Her paramour didn't make it in, and I kicked her out of the house.

However, I made a strategic error in not having the locks changed before I went on another training mission to Israel. So, for the second time in as many wives, and trips to the Holy Land, I came home to find out that I'd been cleaned out. Given the circumstances, I decided I wasn't going to miss Brandy, but I concluded that trips to Israel were bad for my marriages and keeping my home furnishings.

A more mixed blessing was that I was made the leader of the team I'd been assigned to since the beginning. On one hand, it meant that the Unit command felt that I'd earned the right to lead other operators, which due to their independent nature could be a challenge of its own. On the other, it added more stress—not just in what was required of me as a team leader, but also the recognition that in a combat situation, my decisions would impact the lives of my men and could even cost someone his life. This burden of leadership weighed on me.

In the years since my first deployment to Sarajevo, there'd been several more, including in April 1997, when my team was assigned to provide security for Pope John Paul II. Our diligence paid off when we discovered bombs had been placed beneath a bridge the pontiff's motorcade was scheduled to cross. Of course, others received credit for possibly saving the pope's life, and as with everything else, we laughed it off. A job well done is still a job well done no matter who actually does it or takes credit for it

As with the trip to Pakistan, when not otherwise deployed on specific security assignments, the members of my team—sometimes together, sometimes in groups of two or three—regularly traveled the globe, training in our specialties or conducting area familiarization to gain knowledge that could come in handy later in a crisis.

However, the major change in my life was that I'd married again in November 1998 and now had a son. I'd met "Christine" at a local hangout for many unit members after I kicked Brandy out of the house. Originally, we were just friends; she was more like "one of the guys" and easy to talk to. But eventually friendship led to intimacy which, in turn, led to her announcing that she was pregnant.

At first, it had taken a little adjusting to the idea of being a father, but then it started to grow on me. I was the one who suggested we get married and "do the right thing," and we'd tied the knot.

When we found out our baby would be a boy, I was excited. As a thirty-one-year-old special operations soldier, there was an appeal to having a son to carry on the family name, maybe even follow my footsteps into the Army. I also hoped that having a child might bring stability and a sense of normalcy to my life.

By this time, I recognized that I was dealing with some serious mental health issues such as depression, bouts of anger, and high levels of anxiety, coupled with suicidal ideation and the constant nagging belief that I was never quite good enough. The worst memory fallout from Somalia had faded, though all of my wives, including Christine, had said I cried out, yelled, and struggled in my sleep. Those things that triggered flashbacks or anxiety remained even if my reactions weren't as noticeable.

I was getting better at hiding my issues, but not in all situations.

When the World War II film *Saving Private Ryan* debuted in 1998, I had to leave during the violent and graphic opening scenes depicting the D-Day invasion. I walked out of the theater in tears and couldn't return.

Despite the issues that plagued me, I still didn't seek help. I already lived with the anticipation that I would fail at a task and that I wouldn't be able to compete with men who were the best on the planet at what they did. I was getting older and new hungry young operators were coming on board every six months. It hardly mattered that they looked up to me and the other Mogadishu veterans with a sort of awe, hanging on our every word and instruction.

I had traveled to many places in the world, most of them dangerous to one degree or another; I'd survived violent, heartbreaking combat, and killed the enemy as I'd been trained. But I sensed that I was losing control of who I was at the core. I no longer felt like the innocent kindhearted boy from Indiana who loved my friends and family, or even the young man who'd joined the Army seeking adventure, or even the Special Forces soldier who'd persevered through the Unit's selection process as well as operator training. I was someone different from all of my former selves.

I had become a hard-nosed, cynical young man who didn't trust people or emotions—mine or anybody else's. I'd seen what humans were capable of doing to one another in Mogadishu and Sarajevo, and, on a personal level, I was still focused on feeling that I'd been betrayed by my two wives, still without acknowledging my own role in what happened to my marriages.

The world was a dark and dangerous place. Those I didn't know well and trust didn't matter to me. The "enemy" was always less than human and was the cause, and therefore got the blame, of all of mine and my friends' issues. Even my own men thought I was an asshole who was anal about the team room being kept immaculate, but those same guys knew I was an honest, fair, and prepared team leader. The truth was that the only people I really had any time for were the other men in the Unit, and the only thing I really cared about was my job...and drinking to forget.

Marrying a third time and having a son was my hope to live a "normal" life. Maybe the responsibility of caring for a family would settle me down, help me rediscover the person I'd once been. But, of course, none of it had stopped me from drinking with my friends. In fact, now I had a new reason. I could toast to my unborn son.

However, a few weeks after Thomas's birth, my team was deployed again to Bosnia. I felt both relieved and guilty. I knew it was a terrible time to leave Christine alone with a newborn, but I rationalized that it was my job and I had to make a living to support my family. I knew in my heart that I should be home, but in my mind, the work was more important. Regardless, I didn't have a choice. I was ordered to go.

On the flight to Sarajevo, the guilt weighed on me. But with every mile that passed, I forced myself to transition to what I needed to do. Protecting the general in charge of the peacekeeping forces and any other VIPs was a "no fail" mission, and anything that didn't help me accomplish that had to be put out of my mind.

Outwardly, Sarajevo had continued to recover from the horrors of war. Most of the buildings that had been destroyed by shelling were being torn down, the streets repaved, and businesses were opening. There were still reminders of what the people of Sarajevo had suffered—the skeletons of apartment buildings on weed-covered lots, Sarajevo Roses preserved for posterity, and massive graveyards, such as one outside the former Olympic stadium. But otherwise life there was becoming a new normal.

However, I was also hearing disturbing information, both from intelligence sources and the news, that Bosnia and Herzegovina, both Muslim countries, were becoming "safe havens" for Islamic terrorists from other countries. I found it ironic that NATO had stepped in to protect the Muslim population from the Christians in Serbia. But now some of those people were harboring the enemy, including those with ties to Osama bin Laden and al-Qaeda.

Returning from Sarajevo, I looked forward to seeing my wife, and especially my son, again. But after three months I wondered if Thomas would even remember me.

I quickly learned that Christine was still dealing with postpartum depression and was angry that I'd left her alone for three months to raise a newborn. Her family had helped a lot while I was gone, but it wasn't the same as having her husband at home to help. I dealt with it by not dealing with it. After a few days of trying to reconnect with my son, I went back to my life in the Unit.

As a team leader, I tried to set an example by training more than ever, whether it was on the firing range or in CQB, or by just working to increase my physical strength I felt like I needed to in order to keep up with the new operators.

I was also taking my team on an increasing number of special training exercises, such as an off-road driving course, parachuting, and other focused preparation to improve our abilities to deal with an ever-changing international environment. I was determined that we'd be ready for the day we were called back to combat.

Sometimes the squadron would run through training exercises in US cities. We'd locate an empty building and then swoop in at night to take down the "terrorists"—role players—emulating a hostage situation or "direct action," short-duration strikes. These drills generated reports from citizens to the local police department, who would have already been apprised of the maneuvers, about mysterious black helicopters and the sound of explosions and gunfire. But by morning, Unit operators would be long gone.

Operators were given a lot of latitude deciding what missions to undertake. We were expected to read intelligence reports, generate proposals, and, even though we were trusted to make the right decisions when traveling, the proposals had to be approved by command. These were never "vacation" assignments and usually the destinations were unpleasant at best. Upon return, we had to generate extensive reports detailing what we had learned.

Of course, the mission had to be run through the Unit's operations, who kept tabs on which operator was doing what and where. There was always the chance that there might already be something going on in the area of interest. Operators didn't talk about their missions, even with other operators, so any new proposals had to be checked off so that we wouldn't meddle with operations already in progress. Although the public would never hear about them—other than perhaps some reference in the media to a drug lord being captured, or a wanted terrorist being killed, none of which was ever attributed to the Unit—operators were constantly on missions of national security all over the world.

The job never stopped. I was either traveling on missions, or thinking about the next mission, or off training. My home life just seemed to get in the way.

When Jake and I spun up the mission to Pakistan, the idea was to assess the situation in the tribal areas known to be friendly with the Taliban government of neighboring Afghanistan. The second part of our mission was to check on the security of the US Embassy in the capital of Islamabad and get a handle on any anti-American sentiment.

The government of Pakistan had a long-standing relationship with the Taliban. During the 1980s, the United States and Pakistan had worked with Muslim fighters in Afghanistan trying to throw the Russians out of their country. When the Russians finally left, the country was then embroiled in a civil war that lasted until 1994. That's when the Taliban, who believed in a harsh interpretation of Sharia law, rose to prominence, financially supported by Pakistan's Inter-Services Intelligence agency, and logistically with Pakistani troops and fighters recruited from Afghan refugee camps in Pakistan. The Taliban and their Pakistani allies were joined by several thousand al-Qaeda jihadis from training camps located throughout Afghanistan under the leadership of Osama bin Laden and Ayman al-Zawahiri.

Although bin Laden still wasn't on the radar for most Americans, the Unit was well aware of him. In 1997 the CIA learned that the terrorist leader had actually sent military advisers to train the Somalis to shoot down helicopters.* That made it personal.

Then in February 1998, bin Laden and Ayman al-Zawahiri cosigned another *fatwa* that declared killing Americans and their allies was an "individual duty for every Muslim." The goal, they said, was to liberate the al-Aqsa Mosque in Israeli-controlled Jerusalem and the Grand Mosque in Mecca, demanding that US troops be kicked out of Saudi Arabia and all Muslim lands.

In announcing this second *fatwa*, and its "declaration of war," bin Laden described Americans as "very easy targets." He told the press, "You will see the results of this in a very short time." He'd then made good on his threat in August 1998, when the US embassies in the East African cities of Dar es Salaam, Tanzania, and Nairobi, Kenya, were decimated by simultaneous truck bombs. Hundreds of people were killed and many more wounded.

The Unit responded by sending teams into Sudan and Afghanistan to secretly locate and target al-Qaeda training camps, which were then struck by cruise missiles. Under pressure from the United States, Sudan kicked bin Laden out of the country. He then moved to Afghanistan where he developed a relationship with Mullah Mohammad Omar, an Afghan mujahideen commander who had founded the Islamic Emirate of Afghanistan in 1996 and was recognized by the Taliban as "commander of the faithful." In Afghanistan, bin Laden began setting up terrorist training camps and recruiting foreign fighters from Muslim countries, including Pakistan.

---

* On November 4, 1998, Osama bin Laden was indicted by a federal grand jury in the US District Court for the Southern District of New York on charges of "Murder of US Nationals Outside the United States, Conspiracy to Murder US Nationals Outside the United States, and Attacks on a Federal Facility Resulting in Death" for his role in the East African truck bombings. The indictment, which was sealed, also stated that "members of al Qaeda participated with Somali tribesmen in an attack on United States military personnel serving in Somalia."

It seemed to Jake and me that a visit to the area made sense. After digesting all that the intelligence people could give us about the Taliban, Afghanistan, and Pakistan, we flew to London where we spent the night, and then left for Pakistan in the morning. Upon arrival, we checked in at the Marriott Hotel, a modern hotel frequented by Western businessmen and journalists in downtown Islamabad.

We then headed over to the embassy to check in. To most everyone, we were introduced as low-level State Department employees who were just visiting. Only the ambassador and a few select others were briefed on who we really were and the true purpose of our mission.

Jake and I toured the embassy to familiarize ourselves with the layout so that if something happened and the Unit needed to take action, a plan could be formulated based on our reports. We checked out the situation rooms where the ambassador and embassy staff could hole up and await rescue if the need arose. We also inspected the grounds to determine if there was sufficient space for a helicopter landing zone for extractions.

After assessing the situation at the embassy, we spent some time wandering around Islamabad to determine if we detected any anti-Western sentiment. A member of the embassy staff had briefed us on the political situation in Pakistan but had never mentioned Islamic extremism or issues with the Taliban in neighboring Afghanistan.

After a couple of days, we rented a car intending to drive to the cities of Peshawar, in the northwestern portion of the country and close to the border with Afghanistan, and Lahore, a wealthy city on the east border near India. Of the two, Peshawar seemed destined to be a problem because of its proximity to the extremists in the neighboring country.

During the Russian-Afghan conflict of the 1980s, Peshawar was a base for the Central Intelligence Agency and the Inter-Services Intelligence–trained mujahideen fighters who were recruited from Afghan refugee camps. It was now a recruiting area for the Taliban.

We decided to head to Peshawar first, which meant traveling through the mountains on narrow, poorly maintained roads that skirted frightening precipices. The driving was treacherous, especially when confronted with the local buses overloaded with luggage on top and so crowded that many of the passengers rode clinging to the sides or up with the baggage.

After a few days in Peshawar, we crossed the country to Lahore, which was an obviously wealthier city. In neither location did we detect any Islamic extremist sentiments. Nor were we ever confronted. However, our report would indicate that outside of Islamabad, nowhere in Pakistan should be considered safe.

At thirty-three, I was an "old man" to the new operators, all of whom wanted to hear about Mogadishu, though I avoided the topic as much as possible. This was the year that the movie *Black Hawk Down* came out and we'd been given a special viewing of the film at a local theater.

In general, the film did a decent job at presenting the chaos and intensity of the fighting. It also gave those of us who'd been on the ground fighting for our lives, the "bigger picture" of some of what others went through and some of the command decisions we weren't privy to before. Because of our penchant for secrecy, Unit operators had not cooperated with the writing of the book on which the movie was based, or the movie itself. So, it was mostly from the point of view of the Rangers who were there.

No film can accurately depict war's assault on the senses—the smell of blood mixed with gunpowder, the sound of a bullet passing a few inches from your face or the screams of the wounded. They can't let you experience the shock wave of an explosion that feels like you just got slammed in the face by the heavyweight champion of the world. There is no substitute for the fear and sorrow, or the guilt over the fact that you survived while some friends died.

Most of us seemed to think the movie was done about as well as it could have been; it wasn't too typical of a Hollywood war movie, and it didn't make anyone look stupid. I think as a group, no one wanted to bring up the dark memories; so even the Mogadishu vets watched it with our shields up and just tried to appreciate it for what it was. There was a lot of kidding around about which actor was representing which real soldier. *"Hey that was me that did that!"* But in truth, a lot of the movie characters were drawn from several people or fictionalized.

Movies, however, are not real life, even those based on real events. But all too soon, all of us, along with the rest of America, would experience a real event that would change our lives forever. On the morning of September 11, 2001, I wasn't thinking about Afghanistan or Pakistan or Islamic extremists as I gazed out the window of a commercial jet on the way to Boston.

I WAS TAKING BOTH MY team and another to conduct vehicle extrication training, followed by a trip to New Hampshire to drive rally cars. Mogadishu and the threat of Islamic terrorism seemed a long way off as I admired the bluebird-colored skies as we entered New York airspace. Then I noticed the smoke. I couldn't see what was causing it, but when I checked my GPS, I determined that it was coming from New York City.

A moment later, the pilot came on the intercom and asked if there were any military personnel on board. I paused, then raised my hand. A flight attendant approached and asked me to accompany her to the cockpit. There, the pilot told me that terrorists had apparently taken over several commercial airliners. At least one had crashed into the World Trade Center. He asked if I would stand outside the cockpit and make sure no unauthorized person tried to get in.

As I took up the position, I wasn't worried about the plane being taken over. In addition to myself, there were eight other Unit operators aboard, and no terrorist would have survived an attempt. But the other people on board began freaking out with many of them crying out in terror and bursting into tears.

Although my mind was racing with the implications of this terrorist attack, I remained outwardly calm for the sake of the passengers. Without question, things were going to spin up quickly, and a response was inevitable. But first there would be a period of time to determine who had committed the heinous attacks on America and where to find them. And if there was going to be war, it would take time for our government to decide the direction and timing of our military response.

Meanwhile, the best thing the Unit could do was prepare for what was coming. Always in the past, I'd talked to my guys about training to go to war. Now I knew we wouldn't just be training for war, we would be going to war, and Somalia weighed heavily on my mind.

CHAPTER FIFTEEN

Early October 2003
Mansour, Iraq

THE WHITE UNMARKED van rolled slowly down the narrow street of the neighborhood just outside of downtown Baghdad. Inside the van, a squadron electronics technician was monitoring equipment to get a fix on a cell phone signal belonging to a "facilitator," someone known to be supplying money and passing orders to insurgents still loyal to the previous regime's leaders.

Tall apartment buildings loomed on either side of the street, each with its own storefronts on the ground floor. Behind the buildings, the neighborhood morphed into streets lined by small houses with tiny yards, carports, and palm trees, much like a blue-collar community in Arizona.

However, this was Iraq and it was just beginning to get dark as a *muezzin* called to the faithful from a nearby mosque to begin *Maghrib*, the sunset prayer. Following the van a few blocks back in armored vehicles, three teams of operators and I waited on word that the technician had a fixed a location.

An hour earlier, I had been at our living quarters in the Green Zone when I was notified by the Tactical Operations Center that one of the cell phones the squadron was tracking had pinged off a cell tower near downtown Baghdad. As a newly minted troop sergeant major, I decided who would go on a "hit," as these missions were called, to capture or, if necessary, kill high-value targets and their subordinates.

As the troop "kitted up"—donning our Kevlar jackets and helmets, checking our ammunition and performing function checks on our weapons, making sure the other guys were ready, too—I briefed the team leaders. The ping off the cell tower only gave us a general sense of where the cell phone had last contacted the tower. So, the van with the tracking equipment would be sent ahead of the assault teams to try to pinpoint the location.

Following the attacks on the World Trade Center and Pentagon, I'd flown with my team medic and communications specialist to White Sands, New Mexico, to make preparations for my Squadron to follow for desert mobility training. After checking into my hotel room, I opened my suitcase and found a note from my wife Christine. It read: *Don't bother to call, send a card, or flowers. It won't mean anything.* I grimaced and swore—for the second year in a row, I had forgotten our anniversary.

The truth was that I was married to my job. Although, I wanted a relationship with my son, I didn't put much time into it. I told myself that I needed to focus on my career in order to support my family, but it also meant that I didn't have to interact with them. It was easiest for me to communicate at work and maintain my focus on the job; anything else was getting more and more difficult.

I was faced with a choice. I believed that my primary duty was to my country, the Unit, and my men. However, seeing Christine's note, I knew that if I didn't do something about my marriage, I would lose my third wife, my son, and whatever bit of "normalcy" they brought into my life.

After setting up the pre-deployment training in New Mexico, I had flown back to Fort Bragg to talk to my friend and troop sergeant major, Chris F., and told him about Christine's card. He noted that I was already well past the time when I should have left the squadron to work as an OTC instructor. The instructional period was expected of every operator who had completed two years as a team leader. "You're staying here," he said.

I was both miffed about the decision and relieved. On one hand I felt that I belonged with my team. If we were going to war, I thought I should be there. I was the only one on my team with combat experience and one of the few in the squadron.

Two years later, after instructing at OTC, I was going to get my chance to get back into combat with my men. In 1993, the "War on Terrorism," had expanded beyond the US invasion of Afghanistan to the invasion of Iraq. The Iraqi dictator Saddam Hussein was said by the US administration to be stockpiling weapons of mass destruction.

Soon after Saddam's regime fell in May 2003, I learned that I was being reassigned back to C Squadron for our next deployment to Iraq in October. This time I would be a troop sergeant major, leading three assault teams of six, along with a combat support team.

While the new position reflected the Unit's confidence in my ability to lead, I saw it as more accountability for other men's lives. Many nights I lay awake worrying that I wasn't good enough for this kind of responsibility. I hid it well by focusing on work and keeping my own physical condition at peak performance.

Welcomed back to the squadron with open arms that summer, I felt like I was home again. If I was going to war, I could not have imagined going with a better group of men. Men who prepared and trained continuously, and who believed in our mission—that we were bringing freedom to the Iraqi people.

Nor would I be the only combat veteran, as most had now seen action in Afghanistan and Iraq. But no one else in the group had been through anything near the intensity of Mogadishu—not the number of enemies, not the sustained time under attack, not the firepower thrown at them. The veterans of the Battle of Mogadishu have a special love for one another that only warriors who'd been through such a thing together could have.

On October 3, as we had every year on the anniversary of the Battle of Mogadishu, we toasted the fallen. No matter where we were in the world, someone coordinated the time and place to call, and those of us who could get to a cell phone or a computer raised a glass to the memory of those who'd given their all. Then, those who could gather at a location, would typically drink far into the night, telling stories, until passing out. The reunions were a bit of therapy for me. It kept me grounded and served as a reminder of the reality of what could happen to any of us.

Shortly before we were to deploy, I flew to Iraq to get a feel for the situation and the lay of the land. I wound up spending most of my time with my buddy Will from OTC days, who was also a troop leader. He recalled when the US military first arrived in Baghdad, they were treated as heroes. It was all about "John Wayne" and "We love you, President Bush," and US soldiers throwing candy to happy, smiling children who ran alongside the convoys or happily went on "walks" with foot patrols.

Six months later, however, attitudes were changing. There was still no reliable electricity or running water in cities whose infrastructure had been destroyed by coalition bombs and rockets. Suicide attackers and car bombs in marketplaces and improvised explosive devices (IEDs) planted alongside roads had brought a new level of violence to their lives. In some neighborhoods, children didn't dare run alongside patrols, who were walking targets.

Some of the population continued to hope that the United States would eventually bring peace, stability, and prosperity. Others, however, were growing increasingly disillusioned and saw American troops not as liberators, but as occupiers. And the worst of them were actively trying to kill American soldiers and destroy the confidence other locals had in the US forces.

Shortly after the fall of Saddam's highly centralized authoritarian regime, the US military, including the Unit, found itself dealing with an insurgency financed and directed by former members of the regime, as well as other groups under Iranian influence.

The sudden collapse of the regime had created a power vacuum resulting in weeks of looting and other criminal activity that US troops weren't prepared to handle. Not only were they dealing with insurgents, they had to battle criminal gangs who weren't part of any coordinated resistance but were in it for the money. That included kidnapping family members of government and business officials, necessitating rescue missions by Unit operators.

However, it was the insurgents who gave them the most trouble. In what may have been the biggest mistake of the war, the United States disbanded the Iraqi military. Instead of rooting out Saddam loyalists in the Iraqi command structure, while retaining other officers and troops to help provide security, the US policy resulted in the army melting back into the population, taking their weapons and skills with them. They would form the backbone of the insurgency, as well as provide military expertise for terrorist groups, for years to come.

However, these were large issues of governance that were beyond the pay grade of Unit warriors who had to follow orders and clean up issues created by others, including capturing or, if necessary, killing regime and former high-ranking military officers who'd gone into hiding and were fostering the insurgency.

This was the situation in October when I returned with my troop to Baghdad, along with Ramadi and Fallujah which were our troop's main areas of responsibility. We were based in the Green Zone, formerly the headquarters of successive Iraqi regimes, the grounds for Saddam's opulent palaces, and now the headquarters for the Coalition Provisional Authority (CPA) and interim Iraqi government.

The Green Zone was a nearly ten-square-kilometer area bordered on two sides by the Tigris River; the rest was surrounded by concrete blast walls and barbed wire fences with access through only a few entry points. In addition to government facilities, it was also a military base for coalition forces with camps for regular Army and other supporting units, helicopter squadrons, and armored vehicle units. The area was under a constant barrage of the sights and sounds of helicopters coming and going, tanks and other armored vehicles roaring like metal dinosaurs, regular Army and Marine troops drilling, and operators firing on the range, honing their skills.

Although the enemy would occasionally launch rockets and mortars from neighborhoods across the river, most of the attacks were ineffective and the area was relatively safe. The primary danger was leaving through the gates and heading into the "Red Zone," which was basically any area outside of the walls and not controlled by coalition forces.

Our troop was given a large house to live in near one of Saddam's main palaces. Each team had its own room to sleep in, and I slept in one with four other men on bunk beds we built; we all had to share two showers. It was cramped but compared to the hangar in Mogadishu, was comfortable and reasonably safe. Every so often, the air was punctuated by the sound of an explosion from an enemy rocket or mortar, usually in the distance, but sometimes close enough shake the ground and toss us from our bunks.

The troop's military vehicles, including Humvees and armored vehicles, were kept lined up outside the house. We also had access to several civilian cars, mostly BMWs, so that we could travel into the city without drawing attention to ourselves, allowing us to surprise our targets. Two Bradley fighting vehicles and two M1 tanks from an armor unit were specifically designated to be available to the troop if needed. A reassuring presence after what had happened in Somalia.

Leaving the Green Zone and entering the Red Zone was the most dangerous part of the journey. The insurgents knew where the entrances were located and focused many of their attacks there.

However, driving on the main route from the Green Zone that led to the airport, which was also the easiest way to access many of Baghdad's neighborhoods, was no walk in the park. The road was known to the US military as "the most dangerous highway in the world." The heavy military traffic and high-profile convoys made the highway a virtual gauntlet of roadside IEDs, suicide bombers, and small arms fire.

On this evening, my troop traveled several miles without incident before turning off the highway to head toward the designated neighborhood. We had pulled over to wait while the technician in the van tried to pinpoint the cell phone signal. Sitting made us all nervous; it was never a good thing to remain stationary outside of the Green Zone.

I would have preferred that the raid take place later at night when the local residents, including the target, were asleep. Then we could pounce and be out of the neighborhood with the prisoner before anyone had a chance to grab a gun or come to the target's aid. But in Baghdad that would have meant waiting until 1 a.m. or later, as the men were often out late drinking tea and talking. Sometimes the operators had to move when the opportunity presented itself.

Unfortunately, the tracking equipment in the van was a new, and unreliable, technology, particularly in a city setting with the signal bouncing off the walls of the surrounding apartment buildings. However, the technician finally radioed that the signal seemed to be coming from one of the multistory complexes, but he couldn't tell precisely which apartment.

As a result, the operators began taking down apartments, first one and, when that didn't yield who we were looking for, we moved on to another. This was dangerous for both the occupants, who would suddenly have their homes invaded by shouting, armed soldiers forcing them down to the ground, and for the operators as we waited for instructions on which apartment to try next. Each hit where we came up empty meant more time for bad guys in the neighborhood to interfere.

After the teams had already been through several apartments, the technician said that the signal now seemed to have moved to one of the houses across the street behind the apartment complex. "Did anybody see somebody run across the road?" I shouted to the Rangers who shrugged and shook their heads.

However, the technician was sure he had a fix. So, the team leaders and I quickly came up with a new plan and moved around the block to close in on the target. The house was typical for the neighborhood. A two-story, L-shaped building with sand-colored stucco-type construction and two exterior doors—one in the front and one through the carport entrance leading into a kitchen.

I split the troop into two groups, one for each door. I would enter through the garage with the team assaulting the house.

When we were set, I started the countdown over the radio: "I have control, stand by. Five, four, three, two, one...Execute! Execute! Execute!" The breachers blew the doors and the team flowed into the home's tiny kitchen.

What happened next took all of a couple of seconds. The interior of the house was dark with just the fading light of the day coming in through the windows. But looking over the shoulder of the assaulters in front of me, I saw a gunman standing on the stairs, holding an AK-47. He was pointing the weapon toward the front door where the other half of the team had just breached and was about to enter.

The operator in front of me didn't hesitate. He shot the gunman, who dropped the rifle and ran up the stairs where a door slammed. At the same time, a middle-aged woman, who was sitting in a chair next to me, began screaming.

My first reaction was relief; none of my men had been shot. But then my thoughts turned to the gunman. I'd only had a glimpse, but I thought it was possible he might even have been just a teenager.

As the rest of the team secured the house, I cautiously made my way up the stairs followed by a medic. When we reached a closed door leading to a bedroom, I kicked it in and entered with the medic right behind me.

The room looked like a typical teenaged boy's room with sports equipment and school books scattered around. Dressed in a button-down shirt and shorts, the teen was lying on his bed. He'd been shot in the chest and was gasping for air, bloody foam bubbling from his mouth. His dark brown eyes were wide open as he looked at me, and I could not ignore the fear and panic in them.

I knew the boy was dying; he was going to bleed out no matter what we did. "Do what you can for him," I told the medic before heading back down the stairs to try to console the mother, an impossible task.

In the course of a couple of minutes, an Iraqi teenager was dead and it was time for the operators to leave to continue our search for our target. We'd looked through the house, and there was nothing that indicated the target had been there, or that there was any other reason for us to be there. Even the rifle was legal; Iraqi law allowed every household to have one gun on the premises for home protection and, of course, most were AK-47s.

The boy's mother rushed up the stairs. As her wails filled the air, I knew that the men on my team were traumatized by the death of the teenager; I could see it in their faces.

In my own mind, I tried to convince myself that the teen *could* have been a bad guy. The enemy was known to use children to carry bombs or use other weapons against coalition forces. But in my heart, I knew that the boy was just protecting his home and his mother. He was probably the oldest male in the house, maybe his mother's only child. When he heard the commotion in the neighborhood and the men outside his home, not knowing who they were or what their intentions were, he'd grabbed his rifle. And now he was dead.

It wasn't the assaulter's fault. He'd done what he was trained to do and was protecting the operators coming in the front door. The teen was poised to shoot his weapon, whether he was a bad guy or simply thought he was defending his home from robbers. Sometimes horrible mistakes happened in a war zone, especially one in which the bad guys looked like everybody else, and guns were as prevalent as flies.

However, I knew that my man was going to have to live the rest of his life with the knowledge that he'd killed a teenager. No amount of being told by his Unit brothers that he'd done what he was trained to do and had saved them would erase that terrible burden. He would go over the scenario in his mind, probably for the rest of his life, wondering if there was something he could have or should have done differently. But there would be no resolute answer, nor would he be able to talk about it to the Unit's psychiatrist without concerns being raised about his fitness to continue as an operator.

I felt terrible for the boy and his mother, and for my soldier, but I had to focus on my job, which, at that moment, was to get the troop safely out of the neighborhood. The longer we stayed, the more likely the chance that the real bad guys would show up.

With the mother's screams echoing through the neighborhood, the team and I walked quickly down the road to our vehicles. I knew this night would join my memories from Mogadishu. The woman's grief. The boy's panic-stricken eyes and dying gasps. The sad looks on the faces of my own men. More ghosts to haunt me, whether I was sleeping or awake and staring at the ceiling thinking again about the boy and his mother.

As we prepared to return to the Green Zone, I notified the "battle space owner," the regular Army commander responsible for that area of town, and told him what had happened. The Army would contact the local headman and arrange for condolences and a payment to be made to the dead boy's mother. The US military regularly doled out money for such things as damaged property and injuries to noncombatants.

Getting on the radio to call in "Exfil," I wondered what the going rate for the death of a son could possibly be.

CHAPTER SIXTEEN

October 31, 2003
Ramadi, Iraq

I SHINED A FLASHLIGHT on a map laid out on the hood of a Humvee as my team leaders and troop commander gathered around in the dark. We were joined by the team leaders and drivers of several Bradley fighting vehicles from a regular Army unit that would be going with them on the hit.

When everybody was focused, I laid out the general concept of the hit and concluded with "that's the macro plan." I then stepped back to let my team leaders take over and lay out exactly what each team would be doing, as well as the responsibilities for the perimeter and armored units.

Reliable intelligence sources had tracked a Sudanese jihadi to four compounds on the outskirts of Ramadi, a small city on the Euphrates River about seventy miles west of Baghdad. The Sudanese was suspected of smuggling foreign fighters into the country to attack coalition troops, and Ramadi was the gateway to get money, guns, and men into Baghdad. The river and open desert made it easy for fighters from Syria to reach Ramadi or Fallujah undetected and then it was just a short hop from there to the capital.

What made this intelligence different was that until now there had been rumors, but not much in the way of concrete affirmation that jihadis—Islamic militants from other countries—were infiltrating Iraq in large numbers to wage holy war. Under Saddam's secular regime, most Islamic extremists were not welcome in Iraq and had been dealt with harshly. But the collapse of his regime and dissolution of his army had opened the door.

Up until this point, most of the Unit's efforts in Iraq had been concentrated on rolling up high-value targets who had been part of Saddam Hussein's regime. These included members of the Arab socialist Ba'ath Party, Saddam's Revolutionary Command Council, and former members of the military, especially the notorious Republican Guard, as well as Saddam's Fedayeen, a paramilitary group. We were rolling up leaders and their associates, money men, and scientists believed to have worked on Saddam's weapons programs, every day as the Unit climbed up the rank ladder to the next higher target.

The theory was cut the head, or heads, off the snake and the insurgency would die. To help the troops identify the most important of the fugitives if they crossed paths, the US military had created the so-called Iraqi Most Wanted Playing Cards, a deck of fifty-two cards depicting traditional suits—hearts, spades, diamonds, and clubs, as well as their value from ace to two—on one side, and a photograph and biographical information of a wanted man on the other. The higher-ranking the card, especially aces and kings, the more important the fugitive.

Saddam Hussein was the ace of spades, his sons Qusay and Uday, the aces of clubs and hearts, respectively, with the last ace reserved for Saddam's presidential secretary Abid Al-Hamid Mahmud al-Tikriti. Although the deck contained fifty-two cards, there were more on the "Black List," which was kept secret in hopes that those on it wouldn't go into hiding.

By the time our troop arrived in Iraq in October, Uday and Qusay were already dead, killed in July along with Qusay's fourteen-year-old son and a bodyguard when they resisted during a Unit raid. The ace of spades, Saddam Hussein, however, remained at large and was the primary focus for US forces, especially our Unit. Capturing or killing him would end any hopes his loyalists had of a postwar revival of his regime.

When I began my mission in Iraq, I'd imagined these former regime leaders would be surrounded by many armed men, all ready to die for their boss. However, working with intelligence, I learned that most of the men my troop hunted were on their own, or with one or two bodyguards, because a larger force would attract attention.

While the higher cards in the Most Wanted deck were encouraging and bankrolling the insurgency, they themselves were usually not fighters. They were men who liked the money and power that came with being favored members of the regime. According to intelligence threat assessment, these men were more likely to flee or surrender than fight.

Of course, that wasn't always true, and the Unit's operators had to approach each hit as if it could turn into a firefight. Sadly, through experience, I knew things could go wrong in a split second and to be ready for it or pay the price.

While there had been no sustained firefights, we had experienced plenty of harassing fire and face-to-face gun battles in close confines during hits. So far, we'd won them all, but it kept me on my toes trying to make sure there were no mistakes that might cost a man his life.

So far, the insurgency was mostly nationalist, not religious as in Afghanistan. We had come across a few of the foreign fighters, but they tended to be one or two sprinkled here and there among the Iraqi insurgents.

If this latest intelligence panned out, it could mean a significant upward shift in the threat level for US troops. Jihadis weren't fighting for money or to create a government—unless it was an Islamic caliphate. As Osama bin Laden and others had decreed, it was their duty as Muslims to kill the unbelievers and chase the infidels from the Muslim lands.

The US military was already seeing it in Afghanistan. Foreign fighters weren't hiding to avoid US troops, they were looking for strategic opportunities to go toe to toe with Americans. Their objective was simply to kill as many US soldiers, until Americans, whom they considered weak, had enough bloodshed and went home with their tails tucked between their legs. On the other hand, for jihadis, dying in such a cause was a sure ticket to heaven.

An increase in the number of enemy combatants would translate to more fighting for US troops. A month into our deployment, our troop was conducting from one to three missions per day, usually late at night, which meant that our sleep patterns never stabilized, so we adjusted chemically.

Before each mission, somebody cranked up the death metal music until it was pounding off the walls and we would work ourselves into a frenzy of anger and hatred for the enemy.

"Let's crush these motherfuckers!" someone yelled.

"KFC! Killing for Christ!"

We had to remove empathy and dehumanize the enemy. Our blood boiled. Our eyes blazed and our jaws were set. It's what kept us hypervigilant and alive.

We tossed down Rip Its, a highly caffeinated energy drink supplied to the Army like water, and, on my call, we headed for the vehicles or the helicopters, amped up and ready to fight.

As for our operators, after a night of blowing open gates, kicking down doors, hauling people out of their beds, chasing and capturing targets, and sometimes shooting it out with bad guys, we came back to the house, swallowed Ambien, and maybe a beer, and tried to sleep for a few hours. In the early afternoon, we got back up and did it all over again.

I was relieved that the first month of my deployment had passed without any of my men getting wounded or killed. I told myself that, at least outwardly, I was keeping it together. But the responsibility I felt for my men was constant and the stress of that took a toll. I was sleeping less and less, battling an increasing level of anxiety, and my Somalia nightmares started to resurface more frequently.

Lying awake, staring at the ceiling, in my bunk at night, I fretted that with each successful hit, every time I called in the All Secure, we were closer to something going wrong. It was a numbers game. I knew it and anticipated it with dread.

However, I couldn't let on to my men. This was something about which there was nobody I could talk to, so I kept it bottled up and instead I focused on the missions, meticulously planning, always checking the intelligence reports, trying not to miss even the slightest detail. I also worked out a lot on weights and the treadmill, especially before missions, heavy music blasting in my headphones, anger seething in my mind, until it was time to join them.

Ultimately, it was Halloween, of all nights, that something went very wrong.

After I informed my team leaders about the intelligence on the Sudanese terrorist, they got together and soon presented a plan to me and my troop commander, a young officer with just one previous deployment under his belt, for approval.

As I sat back and listened to my team leaders' presentation, I believed it was tactically sound. We were to be joined in the operation, code-named Operation Abalone, by a squadron from the British Special Air Service (SAS), the elite commando unit that our Unit had originally been modeled after. Then while units from the US 101st Airborne blocked roads around the four targeted compounds to prevent help from reaching the defenders, our commandos and the SAS assaulters would take down the compounds.

It was a good plan and I saw no reason to question it. However, my troop commander decided to change it. He wanted a different approach, and he also wanted to change which buildings to hit first. His modifications wouldn't have affected the mission, but I thought it wasn't the officer's job to make the call. "You're not the one going in through the door," I reminded him.

Although he obviously wasn't happy about it, the officer relented without another word.

* * *

LOADED UP IN OUR Humvees and accompanied by two Bradley fighting vehicles and two M1 tanks, along with the Brits in their armored cars, called "Pinkies" for their distinctively odd coloring, the convoy left the Green Zone and drove west toward Ramadi. As we approached the town, we pulled over into a compound in Fallujah, and were joined by additional Bradleys belonging to the 101st.

Having briefed the newcomers about the team leaders' plan, I started to move back to the vehicles to line up the convoy and get a head count of all those who would be going on to the target. Unexpectedly, out of nowhere, my troop commander interrupted. He announced again that he was changing the plan. He reiterated what he'd wanted back in Baghdad, only now he did it in front of the 101st officers and soldiers from the other units.

This was unheard of in the Unit. The officer obviously saw this as some sort of power struggle and had waited for this opportunity.

I was incensed that the man would do this for reasons that weren't tactical but instead seemed to be personal, arising from him wanting to be in command. Changing something when it wasn't necessary was a dangerous way to go into a mission.

However, I didn't want to say anything in front of the Brits or regular Army officers, so I kept my mouth shut. When I had a moment with my team leaders, who were also angry about the change, I assured them that, while the officer was out-of-bounds, his changes didn't put them or their men in increased danger. I promised them I'd deal with the troop commander after the mission was over.

Unknown to any of them, while the troop commander was busy changing the plan, the intelligence had also changed. A new report from higher up was passed down: the location of the target house had changed. While the troop commander was asserting his authority, he had potentially missed the highly critical report. It would prove to be a fatal mistake.

When the convoy reached the target area, the SAS units parked in front of a residence up the street from the four targeted compounds. Then on the "Execute! Execute! Execute!" signal from me, the operators took down their two buildings, while the Brits took down theirs.

The hits went off without a hitch, but we didn't come across any foreign fighters or intelligence that was worth a damn.

Disappointed, the SAS commandos had headed back to their vehicles. Reaching the compound where they parked, they decided to take down the house on their own volition.

As soon as they breached the gate, the occupants opened up with two machine guns and launched an RPG. Two of the SAS commandos went down, one of them killed instantly.

Although it wouldn't come out until later, they had parked their vehicles directly in front of the new location named in the missed intelligence report. The enemy had waited until the perfect moment and then sprang their ambush.

The Brits were caught in a maelstrom of automatic rifle and machine gun fire from every window, door, and the roof of the house. They were pinned down behind the low wall that surrounded the house and unable to reach the downed soldier or their vehicles.

Meanwhile, every coalition soldier returned fire. Accompanied by my medic and a US Air Force Pararescue man, I raced up to the roof of a building directly across the street from the action in order to see what was going on. I also hoped that the vantage point would allow the fire support officer and me to engage the enemy from a higher vantage point.

After what seemed like an eternity, but was probably only a couple of minutes, some of the Brits were able to reach their dead and wounded and pulled them into two of the Pinkies and drove off. Finally, the other SAS commandos were able to move the rest of the Brits' shot-up vehicles that were hindering the counterassault. With the Pinkies out of the way, the Unit's operators on the roof were able to engage the fighters inside the house.

As I took in the scene, I could smell the weapons systems engaging, the barrels getting hot, and the pungent aroma of gunpowder. A calm seemed to settle over me; this was what I'd trained for. This was who I was—a warrior in the midst of battle. I hardly noted the crack of rounds flying past or the roar of guns, as I worked to get control of the battlefield.

The fierceness of the resistance was like nothing my troop had witnessed in Iraq up until that point. The fighters in the house weren't trying to get away or surrender. They were obviously there to fight until death and take as many coalition troops down with them as possible.

I knew I needed to immediately gain superiority in firepower to slow down the enemy's shooting. I called three of the Bradley fighting vehicles and told them to knock down the walls around the front of the house. I wanted my men to be able to assault the house without anyone having to go through the gate where the Brits had been ambushed. The Bradleys made short work of the wall with TOW missiles and a 25 mm cannon capable of firing hundreds of rounds a minute.

Meanwhile the commander on the roof near me called in Little Birds to pummel the house through the roof with missiles and gunfire. I noted that the officer was so excited about calling in fire missions from the helicopters that he wasn't doing his own job, which was to keep the higher-ups informed about the situation.

I walked over and told the troop commander to do his job and let the fire support officer do his. This was met by the commander clapping his hands together excitedly and yelling, "Fire mission baby! Hell, yeah!" When I tried again to get the officer to do his job and let others do theirs, the officer ignored me.

Despite the pummeling the house took from the Bradleys, the helicopters, and the small arms fire from coalition troops, every time I thought it might be over, the occupants opened fire again. Fewer of them each time but, like vicious cornered animals, they fought savagely and refused to surrender.

Some did try to escape, but the remaining SAS commandos had set up behind the new target building. They expected that the massive gunfire being laid down by my men and coalition forces at the front of the house would cause some to flee out the back. They died as they came out of the house, except for a few who gave up fast enough to live.

At last the gunfire from the house slowed enough that I decided it was nearing the time to go into the house and finish face-to-face what we'd come to do. I briefed the troop commander on my plan and asked him to let his bosses, as well as the rest of the assault force, know so that no one would shoot any more TOW missiles at the house while my teams were assaulting the house.

However, my troop commander once again shocked me by saying he was going in with the assault teams as well. "That's my job," I told him over the sound of small arms fire, "you need to coordinate with all higher commands on target as well as our higher command in the rear and make sure they are apprised of the situation and ready to support if needed." But the troop commander wouldn't relent; he wanted in on the assault.

Once again angered by the man's dereliction but knowing there was nothing I could do about it at the moment, I decided I needed to stay outside and do the troop commander's job from the roof. I'd still have to deal with the officer later.

At last the battle was over. Nearly twenty enemy fighters had been killed, and four survivors captured. One SAS commando had been killed and another wounded, but to my relief, none of our operators had been hurt.

I entered the building and was surprised at the number of weapons, including RPGs and AK-47s, as well as a significant stockpile of ammunition, in the house and on the roof. Judging from the sleeping bags and clothing, the enemy had obviously occupied the building, waiting for a chance to fight Americans. They weren't looking to escape, they'd planned on dying, which was fine with me, at least they hadn't been able to kill innocent civilians or coalition troops somewhere else.

The next day, I learned from intelligence officers at the detention facility why the men in the house had been so determined and willing to fight to the last man. They were indeed jihadis from countries like Syria, Saudi, and Yemen. Poor, uneducated young men, they'd answered the call from Islamic extremist leaders to travel to Iraq to fight a holy war against the infidel invaders. They'd been brought in from Syria and would have had no way to go home even if they'd wanted to leave.

Hearing that, I knew that the game had changed. I wasn't sure what it would mean to me and my men, but I knew it wouldn't be for the better.

It wasn't the only change, however. Immediately following the Halloween firefight, I approached my squadron sergeant major and the squadron commander who were sitting on the porch at the troop's quarters. As I'd told my team leaders I would, I expressed my concerns about the troop commander's impulsive decisions to change plans in the middle of a mission and then insert himself into the battle when that wasn't his job. I informed them that the troop commander had been so busy trying to assert who was in charge, he'd missed the intelligence changing the location of the target house.

After hearing me out, the commander nodded. "Go send him out here," he replied.

Twenty minutes later, the troop commander had been "fired." Without a word to anyone, he packed his bags and boarded a helicopter to Balad to catch a flight back to the States. He went on to be a great Special Forces officer, but he wasn't a good fit for the Unit. The selection process was never over for any member of the Unit, even for officers.

CHAPTER SEVENTEEN

November 27, 2003
Baghdad International Airport, Iraq

THE MAN WITH the soft Texas twang turned and surprised me by asking, "Did you get him yet?"

Caught off-guard, it took me a moment to figure out who "him" was, but only a moment, as the object of the question was never far from my mind, either. Saddam Hussein. The ace of spades.

While the query was put to me in a half-joking manner, I could see in the other man's clear blue eyes that he wasn't kidding. We were standing behind camouflage netting that hung from the ceiling of the large mess hall where all the military members who worked at the airport ate, waiting for this man, President George W. Bush, to surprise the troops he'd come to visit on Thanksgiving.

Just days before the visit, Chris F., the C Squadron sergeant major, called me into the Tactical Operations Center and introduced me to "Tony," a US Secret Service agent.

Tony was tall, thin, and friendly. He was also deadly serious when he explained that Bush was coming to Iraq and that my troop would be providing security for the president. The elevated threat if the enemy learned about the visit mandated that it had to be kept top secret. I wasn't even supposed to tell my troop who was coming.

The secrecy was problematic. I needed my troop to adequately prepare for the visit but without letting them know specifically who they'd be guarding. After giving it some thought, I came up with an idea. I told them that the Dallas Cowboy cheerleaders were flying in to entertain the troops, and that we'd be watching over them. Needless to say, they were thrilled.

My men didn't need a lot of practice. As professionals in the Unit they were all well versed in providing security; we just familiarized ourselves with the area and went over the route "the cheerleaders" would take to the mess hall after their arrival. Tony was introduced to them as an employee of the Dallas Cowboys who had been sent to ensure that the women would be taken care of properly and that all details were covered.

On Thanksgiving Day, the men were in a great mood, expecting to see a dozen beautiful young women that evening. Best of all, they'd be up close to the visitors while the rest of the troops would be jealously watching from a distance.

At dusk, we were at our positions on the tarmac when I got the word over the radio that the president's plane would be landing shortly. Looking up, one of my guys noted a jet spiraling straight down from its position directly over the airport and asked, "Isn't that Air Force One?"

Smiling, I could see and sense the confusion among my men. Air Force One was the specialized blue-and-white painted Boeing 747 used exclusively for the president of the United States. It wasn't an ordinary commercial version of the aircraft and was filled with sensitive communications and other highly classified equipment, including the nuclear codes. Clearly, it didn't make sense that it was being used to transport football cheerleaders.

At this point, I decided to reveal the true identity of the VIP they'd be protecting. Any disappointment the men initially felt was replaced by the excitement of providing security for the president. They were all proud to have been selected for this duty; no matter what a man's personal political beliefs, protecting the president is an honor.

My men weren't the only ones surprised by the president's visit to Iraq. It had been pulled off with such incredible secrecy that the president's wife, Laura, his parents, former President George H. W. Bush and Barbara Bush, weren't told in advance either. In fact, like the rest of the country, they thought he'd be spending Thanksgiving with them on his ranch outside Crawford, Texas.

The ruse was carried out to such a level that White House spokesperson Claire Buchan even announced the menu to the press starting with "free-range turkey" and ending with "Prairie Chapel pecan pie made with pecans from the president's ranch."

The president's Secret Service team had sneaked him out of Crawford on Wednesday in an unmarked car, and he then flew to Andrews Air Force Base outside of Washington, where he was joined by several advisors, as well as a few selected journalists, all of them sworn to secrecy. The group then boarded Air Force One and continued on to Baghdad International Airport.

Providing security for such an entourage was no easy task. Iraq was a country at war and coalition forces faced dozens of attacks from insurgents every day. More than sixty American troops had died that month alone.

Nor was it a simple thing to secure the airport or area around it. A week before the president was due to arrive, a cargo plane had been struck by a shoulder-fired missile. The plane made an emergency landing with no loss of life, but it demonstrated the vulnerability of aircraft landing at the airport. That was part of the reason why the decision had been made to bring Air Force One in as night was falling and visibility low.

However, Bush could have been visiting Florida for all the concern he showed when he met me and my guys at the bottom of the jet's stairway. He was genuine and respectful as he personally greeted every man.

Throughout the visit, I kept within arm's length of the president, dressed in a hodgepodge of half-military, half-civilian clothes with an Iraqi *keffiyeh* scarf, my M4 rifle ready at all times. I was there when Bush sat down to dinner with L. Paul Bremer III, the chief US administrator in Iraq, and when the president served Thanksgiving dinner cafeteria-style to the stunned troops.

Bush seemed down to earth and I liked him. I just wished I could give him better news about Saddam when he asked.

As we'd worked through our daily missions taking down low-level regime loyalists, insurgents, and facilitators, my troop and I never lost sight of the main goal of capturing Saddam Hussein. In fact, the hope was that each prisoner we rolled up would help get us a little further up the food chain and eventually lead to the ousted dictator.

THERE'D BEEN VARIOUS REPORTS of Saddam being seen at different locations, but none of them had been substantiated. Capturing Saddam was more important from a psychological aspect than a military objective. Part of the reason he was so successful at hiding was that he'd gone silent; he didn't use cell phones that could be traced to him, and his whereabouts were known only to a very few people he could literally trust with his life. But it also meant he was cut off from the insurgency being fought by his followers. He'd released a few audio tapes urging the Iraqi people to "resist the invaders," but otherwise he avoided contact with the outside world.

There were so many false sightings that the troop started making up jokes about "chasing Elvis," who'd surface in some remote location but be gone when we arrived. We conducted so many hits based on unsubstantiated reports we began to wonder if he was still alive.

Eight months after the Iraqi invasion and Saddam going into hiding, there was definitely some frustration that he had not been caught. "You get him yet?" Bush had asked and despite the slight smile on the president's face, I saw in his hopeful eyes that he wasn't really joking.

Years later, I would still be wondering why I did it, but I blurted out, "We will make it your Christmas present, Mr. President."

The president grinned at that and nodded his head. "That would be real nice," he said as he stepped out from behind the curtain. "Now I need to go talk to some of the boys out here."

In all, Bush spent two hours and thirty-two minutes in Iraq. Air Force One was already headed back to the United States before his surprise visit was announced to the public back in the States at 8 p.m. Iraqi time, which was noon back where American families were gathering for the holiday.

As I watched Air Force One disappear into the night sky, I wanted to bang my head against the wall. I'd just promised the president of the United States that we'd capture Saddam Hussein by Christmas. But I had no idea how we were going to do that.

My troop returned to the routine of daily, usually multiple, hits to capture or kill high-value targets. So far, my foreboding following the Halloween firefight that the presence of foreign jihadis was going to change the nature of our mission had not yet come to pass. We were still rolling up former regime loyalists, nationalist insurgents, and scientists, as well as going after the run-of-the-mill criminals trying to take advantage of the chaos. But we weren't seeing more of the foreign fighters.

However, just because the men we were capturing weren't crazed religious extremists looking to die so that they could go to Muslim heaven, it didn't make the job safer. For one thing, we did notice an uptick in the number of roadside bombs and suicide bombers.

I learned that lesson the hard way not long after the president's visit, when we were called out on a daytime hit to take down a suspected Saddam loyalist. Based on past experiences with this sort of leader, he wasn't going to be much of a fight threat, so I wasn't worried.

The plan was to roll up to the target house in an armored vehicle fitted with a device that launched a water blast with such force that it would blow the gate open. It was quicker, quieter, and safer for the locals than breaching with explosives. I was riding in the armored vehicle while my teams were in vehicles in front and behind me. They would assault the building immediately after the water cannon launched and blow down the gate.

However, when the vehicle rolled up the driver noticed the gate was already open. Two Iraqi men were standing in the driveway smoking cigarettes. With the water cannon no longer necessary, I ordered the driver to turn out of the way. I didn't want the vehicle to accidentally launch and hurt the men in the driveway or my team who was already moving into place.

"I can't. There's a car parked in front of me," the driver pointed out.

"Push it out of the way," I replied as I opened the back of the vehicle so that I could get out and follow my men into the house.

Just as the driver nudged the car, there was a roar and the thirteen-ton vehicle was shoved backward, launching me through the air. Flipping end over end, I landed on my shoulder and neck thirty feet away, and immediately saw stars as my right arm went numb.

COMING TO MY SENSES, I realized that the car had blown up and sent me flying. I knew I was injured, but I got up and ran to join the assault teams. By the time I reached the driveway, I saw that the men who'd been smoking cigarettes weren't hurt and were being guarded by an assaulter. I immediately sent him on to continue his job and took custody of the men, so I could start questioning them.

With the hit all but over, I wondered if I'd been knocked out. Everyone was so focused on their jobs; I didn't know if anyone even saw my aerial acrobatics.

After dropping off the prisoners and getting cleaned up, I chose not to get checked out by medical personnel. My head ached and my right arm was still numb, but I hoped it would pass and didn't want to be placed on "medical break" and leave my men.

For weeks after the incident, I dreamed of being blown up and flying through the air until it wove its way into my other nightmares, but I put on a good show of being okay both psychologically and physically. I didn't want anyone thinking I was weak.

One evening, a little more than two weeks after President Bush's visit, intelligence intercepted a cell phone signal connected to Mohammed Ibrahim Omar al-Muslit. A relative of Saddam Hussein, and his personal bodyguard when Saddam was in power, we believed al-Muslit was one of the few members of the inner circle still in contact with the former dictator.

My teams had been doing so many hits that they were all running together in my mind. In that time, there'd been so many false leads and rumors about Saddam that it was getting hard to get excited about another one. However, if we could nab al-Muslit it could be the big break we'd been working toward. There was no time to lose; a target this important wasn't likely to stay put long and al-Muslit was too big a fish to miss because of a delay.

Although it reminded me uncomfortably of Somalia, I decided to roll with the standard operating procedure rather than wait for my team leaders to work up a plan. We were out of the gate ten minutes after receiving the intelligence report.

Fortunately, the target location was only ten minutes from the Green Zone, increasing the chances that the target would still be there. The teams quickly took down the house and took several prisoners but came up empty-handed as far as finding al-Muslit.

Disappointed, we were preparing to leave when the cell phone of one of our prisoners rang. The call was from the same number we'd been tracking. We traced the signal to a location just up the street.

At the same time, I heard gunfire coming from the back of the house. As I went to see what that was about, I sent one of my teams to the new location. They arrived at a small apartment building, surrounded as usual by a gated wall, with two apartments on the ground floor and two up a flight of stairs. One of the team breachers was just placing a charge on the gate when a man approached the gate from the inside. He didn't see them until it was too late, but with a gun in his face, he unlocked the gate and let them in.

The team quickly split up and took down each of the four apartments. In three of the apartments, they found no one of interest. The fourth appeared to be a dry hole as well. However, as one of my operators, Brad T., was questioning the resident, he noticed that the mattress on one of the beds looked out of place.

Pulling the mattress back, the team located a man hiding beneath it. He was clutching what turned out to be a toy AK-47 and was lucky he didn't get shot.

Brad took a close look at the man. He thought he matched the description we had of al-Muslit. The man denied it, but they rolled him up and brought him back to where I was with the rest of the troop. We took him back and he was sent on to the detention center in Balad.

While waiting for intelligence to get back to us about the new detainees, I told the troop to get some sleep. It could take some time for the prisoners to talk, and we all needed to be sharp if the news was good.

We got the good word early in the morning. The man hiding with the toy rifle was definitely al-Muslit, and he was pouring his guts out. He claimed that Saddam was hiding on a farm south of Tikrit, a small city about ninety miles northwest of Baghdad.

The location made sense. The city was Saddam's birthplace and the ancestral home of his tribe, the Tikriti, whose members had made up the majority of the regime's leaders, as well as the Republican Guard. Fugitives tend to run to places where they feel secure, and Tikrit was probably the one place in all of Iraq that Saddam would have thought he was safe and surrounded by loyal followers.

On December 13, 2003, Operation Red Dawn was launched. Because C-1, which was led by my friend, Doug C., was based in Tikrit, al-Muslit was flown there by helicopter to link up with Doug's troop. Using a map supplied by Doug, the former bodyguard indicated that Saddam was likely to be found in one of two places. He was either at a farmhouse on the property, or at a nearby home where his personal cook was living.

While this was going on, my troop and I kitted up as the heavy metal music pounded and Rip Its were again chugged. When we were ready, we boarded our five armored vehicles and started the more than two-hour drive to Tikrit.

There were still a lot of questions to be answered. Was al-Muslit lying and hoping to direct us away from his boss by steering us to the wrong location? Was it a trap? We tried to not get our hopes up too much. There'd been so many false leads. But we'd never had someone so close to Saddam's inner circle in our grasp before, and everything seemed to be lining up.

I noticed the growing excitement among my troops and had to admit I was feeling it, too. We'd been hunting for Saddam for nearly three months and, before us, B Squadron and A Squadron had also tried. Our ninety-day deployment was almost over and capturing the former dictator would be a hell of an exclamation point on the end of our tour before returning home. We did not expect any public acknowledgment for it—the Army usually credited some other unit rather than divulge that the Unit was involved in a mission—but we'd know and so would the special operations community.

Arriving in Tikrit, we linked up with Doug and C-1. The command was coordinating with the regular Army for further coverage as well as keeping the news contained. Everyone would have wanted to be part of the hit if word got out. But we managed to keep it on a need-to-know basis.

With command's input, Doug and I came up with a plan. C-1 and C-2 would be used for the raids while the 4th Infantry Division, which was the regular Army unit responsible for the area, would encircle the town, setting up checkpoints to control traffic in and out. In the meantime, we'd maintain radio silence between the two troops. We needed to keep the mission, and any capture, quiet for as long as possible for security reasons. Let the word get out in Tikrit that we'd captured Saddam and we could find ourselves in another Mogadishu.

As Tikrit was C-1's area of responsibility and they knew the layout, they were given the choice of which target to hit, the farmhouse or the cook's home. The farmhouse wasn't near any other residences, though there was a shack on the property down near a small river. The cook's house was located in a small community, like a subdivision in the United States, with a few stores on the corners.

Doug chose the farmhouse. I was disappointed because I thought that was the more likely target, but my troop would do its job at the cook's place and maybe get lucky. This cook was supposed to be a master chef when it came to fish, and we knew that Saddam loved fish. Maybe we'd catch him having dinner.

We loaded back into our vehicles and took off. C-1 was going to split off when they reached the dirt road to the farmhouse, while we went to take down the cook. The timing had to be perfect so neither one could call the other.

We didn't know what to expect. This was the former leader of his country, and he still had a lot of loyal followers. However, with newer technology such as drones, we were able to see that there was no large force of armed men near the targets. Of course, they could have been hiding in the houses near the cook's place, but there was no way of knowing that without going there.

As our convoy rolled past the 4th Infantry tanks and road blocks, I was keeping my eyes on all the locals along the roads. But they seemed just like normal civilians going about their business, unarmed and disinterested in what the Americans were doing.

We turned into the cook's place and rolled in hot and straight up to the target house. The vehicles jerked to a stop and the commandos poured out of the backs. We surrounded the house and placed breaching charges on every door, which were then detonated—all within fifteen seconds.

The teams moved into the house with me close behind. Then I felt something soft underfoot. I looked down and saw that I was practically stepping on small children who were asleep on the floor.

"How could anyone sleep through this?" I wondered. I gently picked them up and placed them on a couch.

The house was All Secure within ten seconds. But no Saddam. I made the call to the bosses, disappointed that it was another bust for my guys who'd been so excited about the possibility.

However, something wasn't right. I knew something was up when I started demanding to know where Saddam was. The cook's wife was vomiting in fear and the cook, who looked to be about 80, started clutching at his heart and gasping as if he was going to pass out. I was sure he knew where his boss was hiding, and I wanted the information and wanted it right then. I called the medic over, but I persisted in asking questions.

Frightened out of his wits, the cook denied knowing Saddam's whereabouts. He said he and his wife were just living peacefully on the property with their grandchildren.

I leaned forward so that I was in the man's face. "If it's just you and your wife, why do you have forty-five pounds of fish in your freezer?"

The other operators present knew I had him then. They'd seen the reaction to the "all-knowing American soldier" before. The cook started babbling. Yes, he could lead us to Saddam, if we'd just leave his family alone. He indicated that his boss was hiding over by the farmhouse.

I asked the medic if the cook could travel. The medic told me that he could but would need monitoring. "I don't care what you have to do, keep him alive," I said.

We were preparing to exfil and had loaded the cook up in the vehicle when we received a call from command telling us to return to base in Tikrit. I radioed back that I had a possible location for Saddam and a positive confirmation from "Jack Pot Number 2," our code name for the cook. I said I wanted to conduct a follow-on mission, meaning that I had another target I needed to investigate.

"Negative. Return to base," I was told.

I repeated my request to continue but was again denied. That was it. We had to go back. I wouldn't even get a chance to see if the cook was right.

On the return ride, I was depressed and tired. It had been a long night capturing al-Muslit, and an early morning to get ready for the raid in Tikrit. After all the planning and the long drive, I was worn out and felt like I'd been shut down so close to a real shot at catching Saddam.

When we got to the Palace in Tikrit, I went to complain to Chris F., my Squadron sergeant major. I was told that Chris was in one of the interrogation rooms, so I stormed off to find him. I burst into the room ready to unload my disappointment in having been pulled off the mission but stopped in mid-word.

Chris wasn't in the room, just a guard and there, sitting across a table from where I stood, was a bearded, shaggy-haired older man. He looked like a homeless bum from a New York subway station, so it took me a moment to realize that "bum" was Saddam Hussein.

Despite his ragged appearance, he was glaring at me with unmasked hatred. "That's him?" I asked the guard in disbelief. "This dirty old bastard looks like Uncle Fester."

At that Saddam leaned forward and spit at me, striking my cheek. I considered leaping over the table and punching him but held back. Instead I smiled and said, "That's okay. You'll be dead soon." With that I turned and walked out of the room to go tell my troop.

As I soon learned, we'd almost missed catching Saddam. There was only one man in the farmhouse when the C-1 troop went in, and he denied knowing the whereabouts of the former dictator.

However, al-Muslit took the C-1 teams across a large field to the small shack near the little river that we'd seen on the aerial maps. It too was empty. But just as the C-1 operators were about to leave, one of them noticed the end of a rope coming out from under a rug. He pulled the rug aside and revealed a trapdoor leading down.

Opening the door with their guns trained on the spider hole, the operators saw that there was a tunnel leading off from the shaft. Using an interpreter, they called out that if anyone was in the tunnel, they needed to surrender, or they were going to throw a grenade. A moment later, a disheveled old man appeared and was hauled out of the hole.

"Holy shit," one of the operators exclaimed. "It's Saddam!"

The capture of Saddam Hussein did not end as some higher-ups in the US command had hoped. They'd let it be known that the best-case scenario would have been for Saddam to die during the mission. The concern was that news of his capture would invigorate the insurgency.

However, there wasn't a man in the Unit—and certainly not present that day—who was willing to execute an unarmed man, no matter how evil. But that didn't mean Saddam got off lightly.

"I'm Saddam Hussein, the ruler of Iraq," the unkempt former dictator announced arrogantly through his translator. "I want to negotiate!"

The "negotiation" ended a moment later when one of the operators punched him in the face and stated, "George Bush says, 'Hello bitch.'" With that the search for the ace of spades came to an end.

The news of Saddam's capture spread quickly, both within the Green Zone and in Baghdad where residents celebrated by shooting their AK-47s into the air. There were certainly many happy Iraqis and coalition forces that night.

In Washington, DC, President Bush addressed the nation saying that the capture represented a turning point in the Iraq War and "a hopeful day" for the Iraqi people. "You will not have to fear the rule of Saddam Hussein ever again."

However, he had a more cautious message for Americans. "The capture of Saddam Hussein does not mean the end of violence in Iraq. We still face terrorists who would rather go on killing the innocent than accept the rise of liberty in the heart of the Middle East."

Many Americans knew of Saddam only through television reports that showed him dressed in Western suits and sitting calmly at conference tables surrounded by his regime members, or in uniform shooting an AK-47 in the air and promising the "mother of all wars." Not even that image revealed the extent of his profound wickedness.

COALITION FORCES, INCLUDING THE Unit operators who had hunted him, knew that his regime had been murderously ruthless. They'd discovered medieval torture chambers with shackles on the walls used to interrogate prisoners, and chambers used to rape the wives of the men who wouldn't cooperate. We saw how truly evil he and his loyal followers had been. It was rewarding and a relief to have sealed the end to his reign of terror.

Anyone not at the actual target site was a little bummed not to have been there at the moment he was pulled from his spider hole. But in the end, most of the men, including myself, didn't care who captured him or any of the other shitheads we were after. We had risked our lives every single night for nearly three months chasing them down. We were glad this phase was over.

The feeling among many of the operators was that our mission was accomplished. We could leave that hellhole and go home. Hopefully, never to return.

Of course, the Unit didn't get any public credit for capturing Saddam. The Army had already credited his capture to the 4th

Infantry Division. Several photographs of the captured dictator with those troops, none of them from our Unit, posing next to Saddam and the spider hole had been leaked to the press.

There would be no such "glory" photographs allowed for our Unit. However, I wanted to do something for the warriors who risked their lives to capture a brutal dictator and hopefully bring an end to the insurgency.

Hours after his capture, Saddam was to be transported to prison to await trial. I told the men in my troop to line up on either side of the hallway and that the prisoner would have to pass through us on his way out.

As Saddam reached the end of the hallway and saw all the operators lined up, he paused. Then as a videographer recorded the event, he had to walk slowly past the men who'd hunted him down.

This final humiliation of a vicious, brutal man would never be seen by anyone outside of the Unit. It would be locked away and remain a secret. But that was okay. We knew, and that was enough.

CHAPTER EIGHTEEN

May 2004
Fort Bragg, North Carolina

THE BOX JUST SHOWED up on my desk at work one day. Like a piece of junk mail somebody had tossed there as they were walking by. I opened the box and inside was a Bronze Star with Oak Leaf Cluster and a V. The oak leaf cluster was because I already had a Bronze Star from Mogadishu; the V was for "valor in combat," also my second. I glanced at the certificate that had come with the medal; there was my name and something about the award being for my valorous "persistence" in staying after Saddam Hussein. I threw it in my locker and went about my day.

We didn't do a lot of award ceremonies in the Unit. Not for something like doing our job. We were *supposed* to capture or kill high-value targets like Saddam and terrorists. It's what we signed up to do. We'd given President Bush the Christmas present he wanted. But then it was over. For the rest of the month we were on to the next big thing and the next one after that.

I DIDN'T REALLY PUT A lot of stock in medals. A whole lot of guys had done as much as I had and didn't get shit for it. Others had done more, given more; their names were on the memorial wall at Unit headquarters. Some had received a Purple Heart as their thanks for lost limbs, ruined eyes, shattered bones, damaged organs, permanent disfigurement, or physical disability.

Of course, no one gave medals for the injuries that couldn't be seen. Those weren't acknowledged: the wounds in our heads, showing up as behavioral changes. We didn't even talk about those or their consequences. Multiple divorces. Dysfunctional families. DUIs. Alcoholism. Domestic violence. Impulsive risk taking.

Most of the other guys in the Unit felt the same way I did about medals. Medals littered tables and desks all over the squadron rooms or gathered dust in a locker. I didn't even remember what I'd done with my Mogadishu medal.

Meanwhile, a lot of regular Army guys were getting medals for basically showing up, especially the Bronze Star, which the Army was handing out like candy. Sort of like participation trophies for children's sports teams.

Medals were important for one reason: they went on your record and helped with promotions and, therefore, pay. Because the Unit was so shrouded in secrecy, our operators often didn't get a lot of credit for their bravery and accomplishments, such as the capture of Saddam Hussein. But command had finally recognized that because of our unit's covert nature, we were at a disadvantage when it came to promotions, so they started putting us in for more.

On the other hand, the guys in the Unit knew going in about the lack of accolades. We weren't looking for glory or even the thanks of a grateful nation. We honorably served our country to protect its citizens, especially our families. What we lacked in the praise of others, we made up for in *esprit de corps*. We were brothers. We had each other.

There'd been a lot of tired, but proud and happy, warriors from the Unit on that plane back to the States from Iraq. We'd probably executed several hundred missions, won more gunfights than I ever wanted to be in, including the Halloween battle with the foreign fighters, and captured or killed hundreds of bad guys, including the biggest dirtbag of them all, Saddam Hussein. We'd even brought a pistol from Saddam's spider hole to present to President Bush as a late stocking stuffer.

We finished off our tour by capturing Kamis Sirhan, number fifty-four on the Black List. We'd been tracking him the entire deployment and finally caught him after he visited a brothel in Baghdad.

The only thing that really mattered, at least in my perspective, was that no one in my troop had been killed or even seriously injured. My deepest fear of leading my men into another Mogadishu had not come to pass. I still had my own inner demons to deal with, but I'd done my job, accomplished our missions, and kept my men safe.

My biggest concern as I tried to find a comfortable sitting position on the C-5 transport stemmed from being blown up. I was still experiencing numbness in my right hand, especially my trigger finger. When on missions during that last month, I'd frequently had to take my shooting hand off my weapon and shake it to get feeling back, something no operator in bad-guy territory ever wants to do. Was there something seriously wrong with my neck? I kept twisting and turning my head to get the kinks out, but it was never right. I wondered if any of the other operators had noticed—that old fear of constantly being assessed.

I was ready to go home. Although we had to spend Christmas and New Year's in Iraq, I looked forward to being back for my son's fifth birthday in March and seeing my wife. I wasn't good about calling home much when I was in Iraq. I blamed it on staying focused— "keeping my head in the game"—but I had missed her companionship and being in a safe place, even if I wasn't feeling really romantic. Our emails and the occasional letter were filled with "I miss you" and "Can't wait to see you again," and cute little stories about Thomas and what we'd do as a family when I got home. It sounded great. It sounded normal.

Mainly I looked forward to getting some rest. It seemed like it had been a long time since I'd slept well and thought that once I was out of the combat zone, my self-doubts, anxiety, and fears would dissipate. Then I could relax enough to recover mentally. I don't know why I thought that—I really hadn't slept well or "recovered mentally" since Somalia. But I guess I figured that if I lied to myself enough, it might happen.

I also hoped my physical ailments would heal, and I wouldn't have to get checked out by doctors. I didn't want to know if there was something wrong that would get me fired from the Unit. Besides, it was our way to keep moving forward, never stopping or complaining.

Of course, nothing ever turns out like you imagine it will be coming home from a war, and the first disappointment was when I walked through the front door of my house. I'd pictured my son running to me and leaping into my arms, but he saw me and burst into tears. Christine made some comment about how it must be the beard that I'd grown in Iraq. I agreed—"Yeah, that must be it"—but it hurt like hell.

It didn't take long, though, for him to warm up to me, and you'd never have guessed at the initial reception I got from him by looking at the photographs that Christine took. There he was in my arms; we were just like I'd envisioned, laughing, hugging, and loving on each other. I told myself it was all going to be okay.

The first three months after returning from Iraq were what the Unit considered downtime. You were expected to take a few weeks off, spend time with the family, decompress, get your head right. The thought was that within a couple of weeks your sleep patterns would normalize a bit. Then it would be back to work honing combat skills and traveling to different training venues. We couldn't let up; when you're the best you don't stay that way lying around the house.

I tried settling into family life. It was hard to connect to a five-year-old who had different ideas about what was fun than I did. I wanted to kick back, relax, and forget about Iraq, but he wanted to play, talk, and go places in public. I didn't like going places where there were a lot of other people around. I made a lot of excuses as to why I couldn't go right at that moment, or I suggested that we should do something else. I just wasn't good at fun anymore, and he soon turned back to his mother for what he needed.

The "honeymoon" period for Christine and me didn't last long either. Like a lot of military wives when their husbands come home from overseas, I was disrupting the pattern of their lives. She'd learned to deal with all the issues of raising a child alone and taking care of the bills and home repairs without me. Now there I was changing Thomas's routines and "the rules," demanding that the house be kept spotless, and questioning expenses or processes that didn't make sense to me. It didn't go over well, especially because I was giving a lot of orders and not helping much. She got cold and distant, and I'd just get angry.

In fact, it seemed like I was always angry. Little things, like Thomas leaving his toys out, would set me off, and I'd fly into a rage that was all out of proportion. He'd cry and run off to his mother, and Christine would let me know what a bad father I was. After I settled down, I'd feel even worse about myself. It led to a vicious cycle of anger followed by shame.

I lived with a lot of ghosts. Although my nightmares had subsided before I deployed, they were now returning, even stranger and more frequent. In one, I saw the teen we shot running up the stairs, only to be trapped at the top and turning back toward me his eyes filled with panic and fear. In another, I was at Disneyland next to the rollercoaster while angry children with weapons tried to overrun my position.

In my sleep I would hear mothers wailing over the bodies of dead sons, and the screams of wounded men, my brothers. I'd wake up in cold sweats, panicked and not knowing where I was, ready to flee, or to fight.

I tried to talk to Christine about some of the things I'd experienced and what I was going through psychologically as a result, but she didn't want to hear it. "You volunteered for this and got what you wanted," she'd snap. "Don't bring it home with you." "Quit if you don't like it."

The Unit had done a superb job of training me. But no one had trained her how to help me now, let alone how to handle me.

I realized I had no one to talk to about it. I sure couldn't say anything to my men. I couldn't let them perceive me as anything less than strong and confident; nobody wants a weak leader in combat. I couldn't tell my bosses, or the Unit psychiatrists, because I feared I might get fired. And I couldn't lay it on my family—either they wouldn't want to hear about it, like Christine, or I didn't want to worry my folks and siblings.

I didn't really have any friends who weren't in the Unit. Christine and I had become good friends with Jon Hale and his wife, Regina. They had three daughters who would babysit Thomas while the four of us got together.

Even then, my friendship with Jon had more to do with our shared experiences in Mogadishu, Israel, and Sarajevo than anything outside of the job. We would sit around his house or ours and drink and talk about work-related training while the women talked about whatever they do.

Jon never showed signs that he was hurting. He always seemed so strong and together. There were a few of the angry outbursts about something Army related, or knocking some politician, but that was just normal in our world. Had I been trained what to look for, or knew what I know now, maybe the outcome would have ended differently. But I didn't and so the die was cast.

Otherwise, I didn't stay in touch with old friends from high school, or even guys I'd known in the service before becoming part of the Unit. I thought I was alone. So, I bottled it up, screwed the lid on good and tight, and pretended that there was nothing wrong with me.

I ended up returning to work sooner than necessary. It was easier than real life. I didn't know how to relate to my family and had convinced myself that my presence was just messing up their lives. I thought that if I just focused on my job, we'd all be happier.

Pretty soon I was back to going out to the bars with my friends in the Unit, coming home late and usually drunk. My buddies and I didn't discuss what we were dealing with psychologically, because that would mean being ridiculed for "acting like a pussy," but at least we had the shared experiences.

If I did go home after work, the first thing I did was fix a drink, and then another. My sleep patterns were all messed up. I was used to getting up in the afternoon and psyching myself up for another night of caffeine-fueled fear and violence, then, maybe, a little shut-eye in the morning.

Christine liked to go to bed early, as soon as Thomas was down, but I'd stay up watching television and sucking down Captain Morgan and Sprite, playing Call of Duty on Xbox Live with a friend, until I could fall asleep, usually in my chair.

Going into work took my mind off my family problems, but it didn't really solve my problems. I never seemed to be able to relax anymore, no matter where I went. If I went to a bar or a restaurant, I wanted to sit facing the door, and the first thing I did was look for escape routes and identify potential weapons. I was hypervigilant, aware of everything going on around me, constantly doing threat assessments. I was strangely tired all the time but not in a way I could attribute to my physical fitness routine. I'd never been one to take naps in the middle of the day, but now they sounded great.

I just couldn't seem to get my shit together. So, I finally broke down and went to the "Med Shed" and talked to a doctor, a friend I had met at the regular hospital on post one day when I needed my back aligned.

After talking about my issues, he smiled. "Congratulations," he said as he handed me a bottle of Prozac. "You made it longer than most."

My friends and I weren't the only ones dealing with these issues. Two and a half years into the War on Terror, Fort Bragg and the surrounding military communities seethed with anger and pain.

It had a lot of ways of manifesting itself. There were many fights. Guys claiming combat experiences that never happened while others listened to the bullshit quietly until they'd heard enough and called out the fake commandos on their lies. Then fists, bottles, and chairs flew until the cops showed up to haul the disorderly belligerents off to jail.

A lot of risk-taking behavior seemed to be amping up. Driving drunk. Married guys chasing women. Extreme off-time hobbies, like BASE jumping, parasailing behind a car, free solo climbing. It was hard to replace the adrenaline rush of combat, but guys were trying.

As usual, the ones who suffered the most were the families. Divorce rates spiked, as did instances of domestic violence. In 2002, Fort Bragg was rocked by the murders of four military wives killed by their Special Forces husbands over a six-week period. Three of the men had returned from their deployment to Afghanistan.

In the first case, one of the Green Berets had come home and found his wife in bed with another man. He calmly took their kids to his parents' house, then returned and killed her and then himself. Another also murdered his wife before putting the gun to his own head and pulling the trigger. A third shot his wife; the fourth stabbed his to death.

An article by an Associated Press reporter noted that in response to the murders, the Department of Defense sent a sixteen-member team to Fort Bragg to examine "a broad array of behavioral health-related issues that could have led to the slayings." The Pentagon also announced that soldiers serving in Afghanistan would undergo mental screening before returning home.

That was the first I had heard about any screening of returning veterans. Maybe the regular Army did this, but I never heard of any special operations units or personnel getting checked out before or after they got home. Sounded good on paper though.

What I didn't know, because no one in the Unit talked about it, was that shortly before we were to be deployed again to Iraq, the *New England Journal of Medicine* published a study on post-traumatic stress disorder (PTSD) and US combat veterans from Iraq and Afghanistan. It found that while as many as 9 percent of soldier recruits suffered from PTSD prior to deployment, that percentage shot up to nearly 20 percent after they deployed. In human terms, that increase represented more than ten thousand additional cases of PTSD for every one hundred thousand troops who served in Iraq or Afghanistan.

Although I didn't know what to call it yet, I certainly exhibited all the signs of PTSD, defined as "a mental health condition triggered by having experienced or witnessed a terrifying, or traumatic, event." Or in the case of combat veterans, plural events.

Although I had never before heard of PTSD, what I was beginning to learn about it sounded to me like it would have been admitting weakness. And weakness equaled failure.

None of us wanted to be a broken toy. I swore I would never be one. When the time came to redeploy to Iraq, or wherever they wanted me, I was going to be ready and willing—and determined to have nothing in my medical records that might stop me.

CHAPTER NINETEEN

August 2004
Baghdad, Iraq

WE WERE ROLLING to pick up a new interpreter on the way to a hit when I saw the boy. Nine, maybe ten, years old. He was standing on the sidewalk pointing an AK-47 rifle at us. I took aim, hating what I was about to do. Then I saw the small orange tip.

"IT'S A TOY! IT'S A TOY!" I shouted into the mic. "Don't shoot. DO NOT SHOOT!" I knew that child had multiple rifles pointed at him and held my breath. No one pulled the trigger. If someone had I wouldn't have said a word—that was the nature of this war. The kid was lucky.

In the six months that we'd been gone, a lot had changed in Iraq, and not for the better. There had definitely been a transformation in everyday Iraqi attitudes toward us. Forget "I love Bush and John Wayne," they hated our asses now. It might have had something to do with the more than twelve thousand Iraqi citizens who'd been killed, and a hundred thousand or more wounded, since the invasion, the lack of progress restoring utilities and other infrastructure, and our inability to protect them from the bad guys. We weren't "saviors" anymore; fair or not, they saw us as the cause of their misery.

We were the ones who blew up the water treatment plants and the electrical power sources. They knew they weren't safe on the streets or in their marketplaces as long as we were around because we drew insurgents and jihadis like flies to shit. Basically, a lot of them believed that if we'd just leave, the insurgents wouldn't have a reason to plant IEDs or drive car bombs into their shopping areas or execute people for cooperating with coalition forces.

We were getting tired of them as well. The lies and the in-fighting. We'd deposed a brutal, repressive dictator, and the way we saw it, they were squandering the opportunity with their petty tribal politics and greed. The ungrateful bastards.

Nor were the Iraqis above using us to settle personal or inter-tribal differences. We'd once received a tip that a "high-level facilitator" was hiding out in an apartment in downtown Baghdad. We found the location and kicked in the door. Inside was a bearded middle-aged man holding a pistol. A moment later he was dead with two bullets in his skull.

Only after the fact did we learn that the "high-level facilitator" was a nobody as far as our intelligence knew. It was a setup. Some rivals had locked him in a room with a gun, and then sent us to execute him. They wanted their rivals to blame us and start attacking us, knowing we'd take them down.

Whoever was at fault for what was happening in the country—the US government, the Iraqis, the Islamic extremists—it wasn't our job to sort it out. We were just trying to do what we were told, believing that we were helping, while also trying to stay alive.

The job had changed a lot, too. When we left in 2003, we were doing one to three hits a night. In July, that was more like three to ten hits at any hour of the day.

The insurgency had not slowed down at all. After the invasion in March 2003, five hundred-plus American servicemen and service women had been killed in that year, and more than three hundred and fifty were wounded every month. It already looked like 2004 would top those statistics, both in the number of American KIA and in those wounded, which was averaging six hundred a month when we arrived.

The premonition that the Halloween firefight was just the beginning of an era of foreign fighters proved to be correct. Jihadis were flocking to Iraq from Syria for the chance to kill the American infidels and martyr themselves in the name of Allah. It was also big business for terror organizations to hire out poor foreigners to fight the Americans.

Al-Qaeda had moved into Iraq. They'd had their butts kicked in Afghanistan, though they and their Taliban allies were still holding on in parts of that country. However, they'd found fertile ground in the desert of western Iraq to set up terrorist training camps. Easy access for them from foreign countries to the West. With open desert no one was really watching at the time and highway access to Ramadi and Fallujah, it was nothing more than a hop to Baghdad.

Nor did the enemy have any compunctions about slaughtering civilians to get at us, or using them against us, sometimes in ways that just seemed to break all the norms of humanity. It only takes a ten-year-old with an AK-47 to kill a full-grown man. As a result, we took to describing potential threats as MAMs, military-aged males, which was basically teens on up.

The effect on American soldiers was devastating. If a child pointed a gun at us, he was probably going to get shot. The trauma of killing a child to defend himself or his brother soldiers would haunt a man for the rest of his life.

The nature of our missions was changing, too. In 2003, when we were mostly hunting high-value targets from the former regime, intelligence told us our targets would be inclined to flee or surrender. Now intelligence was telling us that most of the targets, especially the foreign fighters, were more likely than not to fight to the death.

The enemy had also grown more sophisticated in their attacks. When we left Iraq after our first deployment, IEDs were becoming more prevalent. However, most IEDS at that time were crude roadside bombs created by rigging old munitions to go off when a vehicle drove over a pressure plate, or by remote control, usually a cell phone rigged as a triggering device. Still, IEDs had a devastating impact if they went off close to lightly armored vehicles or troops on the ground.

Now in 2004, with the help of the Iranians, our enemies had a new weapon that was even more terrifying. They were called explosively formed penetrators (EFPs). These were metal plates with explosive charges on one side. When detonated, the explosion would shape the plate into a projectile and accelerate it into the target.

The enemy had also made improvements to their vehicle-borne improvised explosive devices (VBIEDs), otherwise known as car or truck bombs. They were bigger, better, and more reliable than in 2003. They'd also built defensive screens for the suicide drivers, which protected them from our bullets so they could get farther after crashing a gate or roadblock.

On the night I almost shot the kid with the toy gun, we'd been called out on a hit for an insurgent leader on the outer edge of east Baghdad. First, we'd picked up the interpreter, a short, skinny, excitable man whose family had been forced to flee Iraq by Saddam. He now lived in Michigan and contracted with the military for his services. We'd never worked with him before, but he supposedly knew where the bad guy lived.

Arriving in the sleeping neighborhood, the plan was for my troop to approach the target house from one end of the street with the interpreter as a guide. Meanwhile, a company of Rangers would slowly work their way toward us from the other direction. Two Bradleys and two M1 tanks waited a few blocks away in case we ran into problems.

Moving tactically single file up both sides of the dark road, we paused outside a compound on my side of the street while our interpreter-slash-informant studied the gate for a moment before shaking his head. "Not this one."

We moved on to the next residence. Reaching this gate, the interpreter got a confused look on his face then shrugged. "Not this one, either."

The half-paved, half-dirt street was typical for that part of town. A couple desultory light bulbs hanging from wires strung across the road, combined with a few weak porch lights, provided the only illumination. The lighting didn't matter to us as we viewed the world through the spectral greens and grays of our night-vision goggles. But hopefully none of the locals would look outside and notice twenty-five shadowy figures with guns creeping along the sidewalks.

The usual mangy Iraqi dogs barked nearby, but they always did that, and a generator housed in a small building on the other side of the road rattled along noisily. Otherwise the street was quiet.

I was starting to have flashbacks to Somalia with every dark window and shadowy doorway we passed on the other side of the street. It wasn't like I felt safe in armored vehicles anymore, not with all the IEDs, but a cold knot formed in my stomach, and I had to force myself to focus on the job.

"Not this one."

The interpreter continued to lead us down the street, pausing at each gate to consider and reject several more. Suddenly he pulled up short. "This is it!" he shouted and yanked a pistol he had hidden in his jacket and started blasting away at the gate.

Oh shit, I thought, *so much for the element of surprise!*

Whatever the interpreter, who I'd later nickname Wyatt Terp and never used again, thought he was accomplishing, it had an immediate and deadly consequence.

Across the street, a bearded Iraqi burst from the generator shack with an AK-47, which he began shooting into the sky. In hindsight, he was likely just guarding his generator and trying to frighten away any thieves.

The Rangers on the other end of the street, hearing the pistols shots of Wyatt Terp, then the AK-47 response from the now-dead guard, and the M4s of my guys, believed we'd walked into a firefight. The Rangers did what they do best, which was to throw themselves into the fight like a bunch of lunatic wolverines.

The once-quiet night erupted into sheer chaos. The Rangers began moving in our direction while shooting. They tossed flash-bang grenades, which don't just go off once but keep popping nine times, and contributed to the sound of a major battle erupting.

Back at the Mission Support Site (MSS), Chris F., the squadron sergeant major, was monitoring the Intelligence, Surveillance, and Reconnaissance (ISR) feed. Thanks to a drone overhead, he could see tracers flying, flashbang grenades going off, and my guys and the Rangers moving toward each other as if engaging the enemy. And he heard me radio in "Troops in Contact," meaning shots had been fired but the situation was unknown. Chris did his job and jumped into action. He launched the two tanks and Bradleys toward our position.

Worried that we'd be hit by friendly fire from the Rangers, I shouted to my guys to get the hell off the road. Operators began jumping over walls and taking down houses to get away from errant bullets. This included the target house; the teams assigned to the house weren't going to let a firefight stop them from doing their jobs. They sprinted to the wall and entered the house as planned. In the meantime, my headquarters (HQ) element, consisting of a medic and an Air Force Pararescueman (PJ), and I took down another house and met a very nice, very frightened, and sleepy, Iraqi family.

After about four minutes, the chaos stopped and we apologized for the inconvenience to our "hosts," and went back outside. The target house was under control and all of the detainees cuffed. Another team had rushed the generator building to see if there were any more armed men, but the bearded man had been alone. Meanwhile, the Rangers had set up a perimeter and were putting out concertina wire to stop any vehicle traffic.

About the same time, the tanks and Bradleys showed up. Their commander asked me what I wanted them to do. I pointed to an empty field across the street and said, "Park over there and look ominous."

As one of the Bradleys rolled forward, it inadvertently ran over the dead guard's legs, crushing them. Something about that bothered me. I didn't know for sure if the man had been sleeping in his shack, heard the shooting, and came out blasting away with his AK-47 to scare away robbers, or if he'd intended on attacking Americans. But I tended to believe that he was just a poor man doing his job and in the wrong place, at the wrong time.

Out of respect, I decided to drag him out of the street so that his body wouldn't suffer anymore indignities. I grabbed him by his arms and pulled him onto a driveway.

About the same time, a woman dressed in the traditional black hajib over her head and a long black dress came out of the house where I had dragged the body, followed by a boy who looked to about ten years old. She took one look at the bloody, mangled corpse and threw herself on top of him as she began to scream and wail at the top of her lungs.

Confused and badly frightened, the boy held on to his mother's back while he stared up at me in abject fear. It was two in the morning, he was surrounded by scary men wearing night-vision goggles who must have looked like monsters, one of them hovering over him while his mom screamed and clutched the bloody dead man lying on the driveway.

I realized in that moment that I had inadvertently dragged the man onto his own property—right to his wife and child. It shook me. I saw my own son there, hugging his mom. The woman's screams joined those of that other mother a year earlier wailing over the body of her dead teenaged son, and the shrieks of my squadron commander Gary H. lying on his back outside of a hangar in Somalia, his legs shredded by shrapnel. I didn't know what the fuck was real and what was just my private hell.

I turned away with tears in my eyes, but fortunately no one could see them behind my goggles. I couldn't break down or show weakness; I defaulted to humor. "If he wasn't an insurgent before, he is now," I joked to one of the other guys.

This was Iraq. We were at war. I'd signed up for this. On the way back to base, I let the Army battlespace owner know what happened so he could apologize to the local headman and pay the woman for her loss.

ONCE AGAIN, I WALKED away with a woman's grief echoing down a dark street and through the corridors of my mind. I knew the sound would take up residence with all the other ghosts and demons. I called in the All Secure but for the first time since I had joined the Unit, I wished I did something else for a living.

CHAPTER TWENTY

September 2004
Yusufiyah, Iraq

THE BLACK HAWK HELICOPTER HOVERED in the dark above the house on the outskirts of Baghdad while eighteen Unit operators slid down ropes forty feet to the roof. The small arms fire my troop and the helos had been taking since our arrival a few minutes earlier intensified as the last man landed and joined the others.

Directing the assault from a field thirty meters north of the target house, I watched through my night-vision goggles as the aircraft began to pull up and away. At that moment, above the fierce barking of assault rifles and machine guns, I heard the all-too-familiar whoosh and saw the red trail of an RPG as it was launched skyward.

The grenade struck the Black Hawk on its rotor blades and exploded. The elite Night Stalker pilots had been through it before and knew they wouldn't make it back to base. They aimed for a field five hundred meters from the house to put their injured bird down.

The Black Hawk hit hard but remained upright, intact, and didn't burst into flames. But the pilot and crew immediately came under heavy fire from the enemy who were running in all directions from the house.

Ah fuck, I thought, *here we go again*. Just thinking of the words I was about to radio over the command station sent a chill through me. "We have a Black Hawk down!"

The mission to take down the house in the treacherous Yusufiyah neighborhood on the outskirts of southern Baghdad started like any of hundreds of others. Walt G., the squadron's lead intelligence NCO, had been monitoring ISR—Intelligence, Surveillance, and Recognizance, a catchall for a myriad of systems the military used for gathering and processing information—and picked up a cell phone signal known to be used by al-Qaeda leader Mohammed Nuri Mutar Yassin al-Abadi. It was coming from a house next to open farmlands.

MNM, as Mohammed was known to the Unit, smuggled supplies, money, guns, and fighters on the "Rat Line," a series of back roads from the Syrian border down through Fallujah and on to Baghdad. He was the sort of high-value target we loved to go after, and we'd been looking for him since we arrived in Iraq.

We immediately launched an ISR Little Bird to locate any activity from high overheard. As Walt watched the footage pumped in to the Mission Support Site (MSS), he thought the gathering of men, some armed with AK-47s, might be a wedding party. As common as roses at a wedding in the States, the omnipresent assault rifles were fired into the air to celebrate nuptials in Iraq.

We knew, however, that these so-called wedding parties were one of the ways the enemy liked to disguise their activities. They knew we had ISR drones everywhere; it was "the unblinking eye" as we called it. I had learned to make my own decisions and assess the situations as they unfolded. Being on the edge of where the city met the open desert, and in a neighborhood where nobody would bat an eye at gunfire, it was also a good place to practice shooting at targets. And a perfect place for fighters traveling from Syria to hole up for a bit.

Wedding or not, the decision was made to take down the house and hopefully capture MNM. As my guys cranked up the music and started to get ready, my team leaders and I drew up a quick plan.

The shoddy mud-and-brick house was fairly well isolated in a palm grove; there were other houses nearby on three sides, but open farm fields and then the desert on the fourth. The ISR estimated eight bad guys in the house, but we'd also have to account for the occupants in the nearby houses. The area was notorious for housing insurgents and terrorists.

OUR PLAN WAS FOR Little Birds to drop some men quickly to provide fire support and run down any bad guys who tried to get away. A platoon of thirty Rangers would fly in on Black Hawks and set up blocking positions surrounding the target area at all the "avenues of approach" and intersections. I would land in a Black Hawk north of the house. I'd control all aspects of what was going on in the target area.

With a plan in place, as soon as it got dark and we were in battle mode, we jumped in the helicopters and took off for the twenty-minute flight, heading due south for the target to catch the enemy off guard.

When the assault force was still a couple minutes from the target, ISR reported that the occupants of the house must have heard us coming. They were rushing out into the yard where one of them had just uncovered a cache of weapons, which he was handing out. This wasn't normal for a wedding party, so I knew it was going to get interesting. It made me nervous, but I stayed focused.

We began taking fire as soon as we were in range of the defenders on the ground and it intensified as we landed and deployed. Chaos ensued as the occupants of the house scattered in all directions. Some back into the house, others into the fields and toward nearby houses.

As the Rangers and my HQ element "infilled" into our positions and began fighting, the Black Hawk carrying the Unit assault team dropped toward the roof. The operators slid down the ropes and moved to take the house as the helicopter rose and began to pull away. That's when I heard the RPG take off and saw the bird get hit.

I was relieved when the pilots were able to put the wounded bird down without further incident or damage. That meant they were probably physically okay. I ordered half the Ranger element to get to the helicopter, protect the crew, and keep the bird out of the enemy's hands.

At the same time, back at the MSS, my squadron commander told my troop commander to get someone after three men, what we called "squirters." ISR had observed them running from the house and moving away from the battle. They weren't trying to engage us, so I knew the squadron commander was worried one of them was MNM getting away.

However, I had more to worry about than chasing some al-Qaeda terrorist scumbag. My guys and the Rangers were plenty occupied defending the downed Black Hawk crew, clearing buildings around us, including the target house, and shooting at men who were shooting at us. I wasn't going to send any of them chasing after three men.

Eleven years earlier we'd been after other terrorists when a Black Hawk went down. The mission changed and because we weren't prepared, we ended up fighting eighteen hours for our lives and a bunch of us didn't make it.

So far, the situation wasn't as bad as Mogadishu.

Still, situations change and there were enough similarities to keep me worried. I had a downed helicopter that needed to be secured and its crew rescued; a night battle with heavy fire coming in from multiple directions; my force was scattered and mixed in with enemy combatants in a hostile neighborhood; and who knew if the bad guys would be getting reinforcements.

Meanwhile, it would take an hour or more for the tanks and Bradleys to get to us, and that would be after they spun up and got everybody loaded. That meant it would be at least two hours for reinforcements if needed. Two hours would be an eternity; ten seconds in combat can feel like hours, men die in seconds.

I moved with my HQ unit to the target house. It had been secured by the assault team, and all of its former occupants were either dead or captured and waiting to be interrogated by me. I was joined on the roof by my troop commander and his HQ unit.

We were trying to get a grasp on the situation when the squadron commander asked my troop commander for the fourth time to chase the three men still being tracked on ISR. This time I grabbed the mic from my troop commander and shouted into it: "This is Z22. We have a downed helo. We are taking fire from multiple directions, and we have teams clearing in multiple buildings. I do not yet have a handle on the head count and locations of all personnel on target. OUT!"

THE RADIO WENT SILENT and there were no more requests to chase squirters. The lessons learned in blood at Mogadishu were kicking in. I knew I needed to consolidate at specific locations. I put it out to all elements—Rangers and my guys—to consolidate at the target site, the downed helicopter, or one of the neighboring houses they'd taken down. I trusted the team leaders to send me an "UP" when they had accounted for their men and identified their location. Once we had that, the troop commander could pass it up the line.

In the meantime, my next job was the reason we were there: MNM. I got off the roof and went to the main room of the house where prisoners were being detained and waiting in a line. Holding up a photograph of MNM we had taken from a prisoner we'd caught earlier, I quickly established that he wasn't among them.

Whether MNM was one of the men who was picked up on ISR running away, I had no idea. But I didn't spend a lot of time worrying about it. The situation outside was still volatile. Bullets were flying and every minute that passed was another minute the bad guys had to call in their friends. I needed to get what we could from the prisoners and get the hell out of there.

I knew these prisoners were either working with the other bad guys or were too afraid to admit anything. It was my job to figure out the truth and get as much as I could before the shock of capture wore off.

We were pretty limited as to what we were allowed to do. One by one I grabbed these guys and shoved them up against a wall and got in their faces like I might rip a lung out. But it wasn't like the movies. We couldn't beat someone until he broke, or drag a car battery out and shock their nipples, or waterboard someone to get at the truth.

So, I had to get creative. The real bad guys knew what we were allowed to do or not do. They'd act all badass knowing I couldn't touch them. I didn't spend much time with them; we'd send them back to Balad for real interrogations.

However, the guys who were maybe new to all of it, or weren't so hard core, they didn't understand we couldn't torture or beat them. They frightened easily and I could see it in their eyes, if they hadn't already lost control of their bowels.

These guys were separated from the others and taken to a different room where they were offered food and water. Playing the old good cop routine while politely inquiring if they knew anything about the real bad guys in the area.

I was in the middle of questioning one of them when there was a frenetic radio call from one of my guys outside. He and his partner were chasing a fighter who had just run into a room attached to the side of the house we were in.

After a few moments of holding my breath, there was the sound of shots fired on the other side of the wall. A few heartbeats later, the house was rocked by a loud explosion. "You better hope one of my guys wasn't hurt," I snarled in Arabic at the prisoner in front of me. However, that hope was soon dashed.

The room the guy ran into didn't have a doorway into the main house where we were. With no other exit, he turned and faced them with a grenade in his hand. They shot him and he crumpled to the ground, but there was no explosion. Not until one of the operators approached and turned him over with his foot. As he died, the bad guy had removed the pin from the grenade and when his body was moved, it detonated.

The operator closest to the man, Kevin T., was critically wounded. The second assaulter, Brian S. was shielded from the blast by his partner and unharmed. Those of us in the house were lucky there was no door from that room into where we sat, or the terrorist might have been among us when he pulled the pin.

The stress was horrible. I needed to focus to make sure nothing got worse. When the medic reported back and said Kevin was in bad shape, and needed a medevac flight out of there, my answer was angry and short. "I don't give a fuck. I have sixty other people I'm responsible for." Of course, I didn't mean that. I was close to Kevin. I just couldn't let it affect me while other men's lives were on the line. So, I turned that switch to off and shut it out.

I IMMEDIATELY CALLED IN FOR the medevac, but we were going to have to make sure we were no longer taking fire before I'd let it land. The pilot would have been under fire, and I wasn't going to have another Somalia with a second helicopter going down.

The news only got worse a few minutes later, when a head count revealed that one of my operators was missing. My heart fell. Had he been shot and was lying in the dark somewhere?

The shooting had died down to the occasional potshot. But I didn't know if they were gone or regrouping somewhere, such as in the houses that surrounded us on three sides.

We still had vehicles moving toward us and away from us at high rates of speed. When my fire support officer asked what he should do about them, I said, "Kill it if it needs to be killed. If it's a threat, it dies." I also told him what I thought was close enough to be a threat. That way I could conduct my job, and he could conduct his without having to ask me each time.

It was as good a time as any to send the team back to the last known location of the missing operator. A little later, they called in that they'd found him, and he was okay.

Actually, if the situation hadn't still been dire with a critically wounded man on a helicopter who was waiting on the all clear to land, their report might have been amusing. They'd located the missing man in a field talking to cows. Yes, cows. Apparently, he was "out of it," but they didn't know the cause.

They soon got him back to the house where we sat him down and got him some water. He was speaking as if he had a severe case of dehydration, which can cause hallucinations and "confusion." He was definitely confused but I didn't have time to ask why he thought cows might appreciate his conversational skills in the middle of a firefight. I would put him on the medevac flight out with Kevin.

With everyone accounted for and the AC 130 allowed to eliminate any threats that might approach, I thought all we had to do was wait for the medevac helicopter to come in and exfil my two wounded. Then another short wait for the Black Hawks to return and give us and our prisoners a lift back to base.

Normally a downed helicopter would have been destroyed so as not to fall into enemy hands. But when I called in to the squadron commander for the Black Hawks and exfil, I was told we were going to have to wait. A DART team was being sent. I'd never heard of DART and had to ask what it was.

I was told DART stood for "Downed Aircraft Rescue Team" and was made up of test pilots who would assess the damage to the helicopter, fly back to Baghdad to get any needed parts, then return to fix it and fly it out. In the meantime, my troop and the Rangers were going to have to stay and protect the downed aircraft. I got off the radio and cursed. I understood they wanted to see if they could salvage the helicopter. They cost a lot of money. But I didn't like it.

Instead of going back to the relative safety of the Green Zone, we were going to have to spend the night in a hostile neighborhood, whose inhabitants had been trying to shoot us a few minutes earlier. I kicked myself for one of the Mogadishu lessons I'd forgotten.

Ever since Somalia, I'd never again gone on a mission without my night-vision goggles and insisted that my men take them, too. It didn't matter if it was a one-hour mission starting in the morning.

However, this time I didn't think to bring extra water. There was no water in the house, and we only had what we carried with us in our personal containers. I was already thirsty and having trouble swallowing and knew the guys who'd been running around were probably worse off. We were also going to be short on ammo if the bad guys regrouped and mounted any kind of major assault in the night.

It got worse. Headquarters radioed that two tanks and a Humvee were being dispatched but it was going to take them about three hours to reach Yusufiyah. We were in for a long night.

Sleep eluded me. My worst fear had come to pass, one of my guys was hurt badly. He needed a medevac flight as soon as possible. I kept running through my head what I could have done differently to have had a different outcome.

I smoked a lot of cigarettes standing out under the starry Iraq sky that night in the company of ghosts and voices, some of them screaming, some whispering. I thought about Mogadishu and the lives lost. Other missions and the potential for them to have gone horribly wrong. And everything that had gone on in Iraq.

Finally, our Black Hawks arrived and twenty minutes later we were back to base. I went to the Tactical Operations Center to watch the AC 130 destroy the car parked next to the home we had discovered loaded with old rockets and explosives. The explosion leveled the house and would have killed anyone inside.

We then conducted an After-Action Report and went over everything that occurred, including what happened to Kevin. What did we do right? What did we do wrong, including approaching a bad guy who had a grenade?

As for the operator who'd been out in a field talking to cows. Apparently, he'd had a breakdown caused by too much Ambien combined with too many of the energy drinks and pills we all took to stay awake. He'd be fine after a few days off.

However, after I went through his room and found all the pills, it struck me that we were all addicted—to the pills, to the energy drinks, to the lifestyle, to the cycle of rage and hatred. I'd done my best to protect my guys from the enemy without realizing that sometimes the enemy was ourselves.

CHAPTER TWENTY-ONE

October 2004
Fallujah, Iraq

WE WERE ON OUR WAY BACK from the hit when we rolled up on an unexpected roadblock composed of fifty-five-gallon drums set in the middle of a four-way intersection. Flames flickered up from the barrels only partly illuminating the eight men with AK-47s standing around them.

As we slowed, they approached with their rifles pointing at the four of us in the BMW sedan. They were dressed like typical Iraqis wearing *thawbs* and *shemaghs*, which they had wrapped around their faces. We had no way of knowing if they were Iraqi police or military, al-Qaeda terrorists, or run-of-the-mill criminals who wanted to rob us.

"Be ready to ram and go," I told the driver from my seat in the back. I didn't really need to tell him that—as a Unit operator he was already aware of what to do in this situation. But it made me feel better to say it aloud as I adjusted my rifle so that it was pointing out of the dark-tinted window at the man approaching my door. These are the moments when split-second decisions take too long. They last a lifetime and the memories do as well.

The good news was that somewhere behind us was a convoy of armored vehicles and the rest of my troop. The bad news was they weren't there yet, and if something did go wrong, they would roll in hot to save the day but with us in the crossfire.

The worse news was that Admiral M., the chief of the Joint Special Operations higher headquarters, was in one of those vehicles. He had requested to go on a hit, and his presence added an extra level of stress. Now the last thing I needed was a firefight to break out and bring the whole city down on the convoy in the confines of those narrow streets.

The BMW four-door sedan wasn't armored nor were the windows bulletproof. It was just a 321i you could buy off of any lot in America, and no matter what Hollywood tells you, a heavy 7.62×39 mm round from an AK will punch through a car door and anything inside the vehicle. In fact, the bullets' passage through glass and steel adds to the number of projectiles flying around the interior.

Rolling up on a roadblock was no joke in Fallujah. Seven months earlier, four armed American civilian contractors who worked for Blackwater were pulled from their car, beaten, and set on fire. In a horrifying scene reminiscent of Mogadishu in October 1993, their charred bodies were dragged through the streets and then hung from a bridge over the Euphrates River.

Photographs of the atrocity were distributed to news agencies, sparking outrage in the United States. When I'd heard about it, I immediately flashed back to Somalia. I knew that the barbarism of beheadings, burnings, and desecration of bodies was part of the terrorists' game plan to gain publicity and notoriety. But it also made guys like me want to retaliate by meeting violence with violence.

In April, the US military had announced a campaign to pacify the city, but it was still a hotbed of the insurgency and home to thousands of Iraqi insurgents and foreign fighters. The main roads were death traps littered with IEDs.

Now here we were, in the middle of the night, surrounded by

twice our number with a VIP coming up behind us. And there was no way for us to know if these men were friends or the enemy.

The apparent leader of the group motioned for us to roll down the windows. "Just the driver," I said. "Everybody else be ready."

It was a classic Mexican standoff. They had us outnumbered and outgunned. We were better trained, but they didn't know that, and the danger was that one of them would decide to take a chance and start shooting.

You could almost see the tension hanging in the air between us and them. I couldn't believe that with only a couple weeks left before our second deployment to that shithole known as Iraq would be over, it might end in a flurry of gunfire on a dark empty street in Fallujah.

EVERYTHING CHANGED AFTER THE Black Hawk went down and Kevin was wounded. We were two-thirds of the way through our second tour, and up until then nobody had been hurt or killed. Some of that was because we were so well trained and good at our jobs. But I like to think, and I've since been assured by some of the guys, that part of it had to do to my obsession with reading the intelligence reports, knowing what we were getting into, and having a good plan worked out with my team leaders.

Now, the streak was broken. Instead of coming back from missions grateful that no one was hurt, I was waiting—we were all waiting—for the next shoe to drop. It was just a matter of time and statistics. The more you went out, the more likely that something would go horribly wrong, only this time someone might get killed.

Like I said, we were carrying out so many missions every day that they all ran together in my mind, especially those during the last few weeks of our deployment. But a few stand out.

One was that I nearly got blown up again. We were driving on our way to a hit and had just driven under an overpass and were passing a series of dumpsters when the bomb went off next to the armored vehicle I was in. The bomb tilted the twenty-two-ton vehicle up on two wheels for a moment, knocking me to the floor and causing our heavy breaching equipment to come crashing down on top of me.

I felt an intense, electrifying jolt of pain in my lower back and saw stars. I had no idea what had happened and didn't even remember hearing the explosion. I praised the driver for not stopping after the vehicle crashed back down upright while my guys pulled the heavy gear off of me.

It was a low-level sort of incident. I brushed away the pain and knowledge that something was wrong with my back. No one else was wounded or killed. The bad guys hadn't stuck around to fight so that was good. In fact, we went ahead and finished the mission.

There was, however, something wrong with me. I kept tripping over things with my right foot and had to wave my right hand to get feeling back in my trigger finger. But I didn't go get checked out by a doctor. I didn't want to get pulled and, as a result, not be able to protect my men.

I tried to hide it, but I had to load up with so many pain pills that my squadron sergeant major, Chris F., noticed I seemed a little out of it, as well as grimacing in pain and tripping. When I tried to go to the next planning mission, he ruled me "combat ineffective" until a doctor cleared me to return.

I went to see the doc who gave me a concoction of pain pills, muscle relaxers, and sleeping pills that, he said, should knock me down "for days." However, four hours later I wandered into the planning room, loopy as hell, where the doctor happened to be present. I was told to go back to bed, or I'd be sent home. No way was I going back to the States ahead of my troop, so I followed orders.

It was four days before the doctor cleared me to return to work. Not because I was better, but I was able to mask the shooting pain in my back and numbness in my right leg through the wonders of modern pharmaceuticals.

After the mission in which the Black Hawk went down, the roller coaster wasn't slowing down any; in fact, it was picking up speed. We were doing a lot of hits around Sadr City, an enormous slum of gray housing projects and drab single-story homes on the outside of Baghdad. Sadr City was home to about a million people, a significant number of whom were the enemy.

There'd been two uprisings in Sadr City. One in April, before we arrived, that included an ambush of an American patrol that killed eight soldiers and wounded fifty-seven. The second uprising began in August, after we deployed; it was still going on.

Because of the intense hostilities, it was impossible for the United States to rebuild the infrastructure of Sadr City. That meant a million people without electricity, water, or sewage. The main roads were so riddled with IEDs that they were declared unsafe for civilian traffic and weren't much safer for our forces. Of course, the leaders of the uprisings blamed the lack of progress on Americans, a great recruiting tool for the enemy.

SADR CITY WAS A Shia enclave so there was a lot of Iranian influence. At first, due to politics, if we picked up Iranians during our hits, we had to treat them differently and pass them along to higher headquarters. But finally, at some point during the rotation, we were given the authority to detain them like any other scumbag.

We learned how to talk to them as we started encountering them more and more. At one point, my interpreter told an Iranian prisoner that I was "Ayatollah Tomala" during a questioning session on target. It seemed to give me some street credit and the detainee started talking.

As bad as things were in Sadr City, they weren't much better anywhere else. We were constantly doing hits all over our area of responsibility, concentrating on any leadership, money managers, or high-value targets passed down from higher up to kill or capture.

We knew neither we nor the US military as a whole could kill all the fighters, whether they were former regime soldiers, sectarian militia, or jihadis. One would go down and another ten pop up or sneak in from Syria or Iran. But if we could turn off the flow of money and arms, and take out the "smart ones," the planners who thought strategically, and the demagogic leaders who motivated men to die for them and their cause, we believed we could still win this fight.

We were always playing a game of cat and mouse with the bad guys. Only in this contest the winners lived and the losers didn't. The enemy might have had a Stone Age mentality when it came to human rights, but they weren't stupid or simply waiting for us to show up and kill them.

They'd sit back and watch us work, probably sometimes from just across the street, then develop a plan. They learned to place mines or IEDs along the paths they knew we would walk, or line them up along the wall leading to the front door knowing we'd gather there just before going in.

They learned to rig entire houses with explosives, and then call in a tip about a high-value target being inside. When we assaulted the building, they would blow it up. One squadron had a house blown up around them; miraculously no operators were hurt, but the bomber and his baby died. The bomber's wife was angry with our guys. My reaction when I heard about it was, "Don't live with a suicide bomber."

We countered by doing quick assessments as soon as we entered. You had to be fast and make decisions before the terrorists could. Enter, assess, continue, or exit. It had to happen within seconds, and everyone had to be looking. Anything out of place or weird, we evacuated immediately.

Several times this saved our lives. On one hit, a troop entered a house and realized it was completely empty except for a cell phone on a table. This struck someone as odd and he called for immediate evacuation. Luckily, they all got out of the house before the phone rang and the house went up.

The trick was to never get comfortable doing the same thing, the same way, at any time. Having an SOP template in Mogadishu allowed the enemy to study our habits and come up with a counter. I was constantly changing how we approached the targets.

In the summer, I used Little Birds and vehicles together on a hit in downtown Baghdad. People slept on their roofs in hot weather. The problem for us was some of them were dropping grenades and mortar rounds on teams as we were approached their doors. The challenge, therefore, was to clear the roof to protect the assaulters on the ground.

It was tricky for the Little Birds. Iraqi streets and rooftops were crisscrossed with electrical wires and television antennas. If the pilots weren't careful, their engines would suck up blankets and pillows and send the helos crashing onto the roof. Again, we had to learn this the hard way when one assaulter lost his leg during one of these crashes. But the Night Stalker pilots were the best in the business, so we made it work and hit the bad guys from the roof and the ground simultaneously.

The enemy changed his game, we adapted. Death was the alternative.

OF ALL THE PLACES we hit, however, Fallujah was the most violent. For me, Fallujah and Mogadishu were sister cities. Both were violent, devastated by war, controlled by cynical, power-hungry demagogues who manipulated ignorant, expendable young men to do their dirty work—young men who had been trained to hate Americans.

As the enemy increased his level of violence, so did we. A call would come in, the heavy metal would blast, and the Rip Its would be chugged one after the other as we worked ourselves into what I'd call a controlled frenzy, if there's any such thing. We were like sharks working ourselves into a feeding frenzy. Predators and prey with blood in the water.

It is a fact of war that to kill without hesitation you must first dehumanize the enemy. Never let yourself think that he sees himself as a patriot, or has been brainwashed by some sheik or ayatollah who, for his own power, convinces illiterate, poverty-stricken young men that by killing Americans they are carrying out the will of God. Don't even entertain the possibility that he might have a wife and child praying for him to come home from war.

When we were on hits, I didn't give a shit who we killed if they were a threat. I was as violent and ruthless as anyone. I wanted to be. I had to be. Out-killing the enemy was the only way I was going to get all my men home safe. Anything less was still my biggest nightmare. I hated that, as the troop sergeant major, I had to send other men through the door ahead of me. I would have much rather gone first than have something go wrong while I was standing behind my guys.

The fighting in Fallujah was vicious and unrelenting. We were going after hard-core foreign fighters, the smugglers who were bringing them in, and the bomb makers. The enemy was digging in and turning Fallujah into another Mogadishu with trenches. I dreaded the prospect of taking my men into that situation; there weren't enough of us and we weren't sufficiently equipped for that kind of sustained fighting.

The Unit's legacy was hostage rescue and taking down high-value targets whether terrorists, tyrants, or drug lords. We were built to take on a mission, complete it, and return home; not ten missions a day, every day. We were'nt like front-line units with more men and firepower. And it seemed like everybody was trying to do our job, too; Rangers were no longer setting up perimeters and holding ground, they were kicking in doors and going after high-value targets as well.

On that dark night of the roadblock stand-off with Admiral M. in our entourage, the good news was that the hit had gone down without a hitch. The target nearly made a fatal mistake when he heard the breacher blow the door and ran into the room with an AK-47. He dropped the weapon a moment before he would have had his brains scrambled with a couple of rounds. A minute later, he and six other detainees—men and women—were sitting on the floor with their wrists flex-cuffed behind them.

Our target was skinny, frail, and terrified. He wet his pants as I began to interrogate him. He was a former regime guy now making a living by building bombs and detonation devices for whoever had the cash to pay him for his dirty work. It was anybody's guess how many deaths of innocent people and US soldiers this guy caused. As I questioned the sniveling, sobbing, lying piece of shit, I wished he'd had the balls to resist when we came through the door.

We found bomb-making diagrams spread out on a table in the living room. Buried in the front yard was a large cache of IED materials—105 mm artillery rounds, old land mines, explosives, and blasting caps, with cell phones and garage door openers for initiating the explosions.

When we had everything we came for and had loaded up the prisoners, those of us in the BMWs took off. The rest of the convoy was told to wait three minutes and then follow.

Turning a corner in the neighborhood and heading for the highway, we came upon the fire barrel roadblock and the eight armed men. As we slowed and were surrounded, my body took over and prepared to fight.

I trained my gun on the guy who seemed to be the leader. I could only see his eyes and strands of black hair hanging below the *shemagh* he had wrapped around his head. His eyes flicked to the rifle of the driver who had rolled down his window. He had to know that no matter what the final outcome would be, he would die first.

It was one of those moments when time stands absolutely still. All of our lives—theirs and ours—hung in the balance. On that night, the bad guy blinked. He chose to live; therefore, we all did.

CHAPTER TWENTY-TWO

October 2004
Baghdad, Iraq

I WAS SO READY TO GO HOME. Beat up physically, and even more so emotionally and psychologically, I existed on Prozac, Ambien, Rip Its, adrenaline, and pain pills. My body and mind were a seething cauldron of warring chemicals that manifested in aggression, hatred, self-loathing, depression, anxiety, and suicidal ideation. What little sleep I got was haunted by the faces of the dead and the screams of the living.

In other words, I was a hot mess. The shit sandwich I'd been building for myself since Somalia was piled high and spilling out the edges with a side of mayonnaise rotting in the Iraq heat.

So how does a commando, *Sine Pari*, without equal, a man exquisitely trained to kill his country's enemies without hesitation or emotion, get so fucked up? Better yet, how did a good-hearted kid from Indiana who loved his family and just wanted to play with his friends, who'd cried watching *Terms of Endearment*, find himself such an empty, compassionless, angry shell of that former boy?

Let me try to paint a picture. Tell me what you see.

Imagine living in fear, under relentless stress and anxiety, in a constant state of adrenaline-fueled, heightened awareness for ninety-day stretches at a time. You get yourself amped up ten, maybe more, times a day on death metal rock 'n' roll and a caffeine- and pill-induced rage.

The call comes in and you strap on your Kevlar vest and helmet, check your weapons, check your buddies' weapons. Make sure you have enough grenades, extra ammo clips, night-vision goggles, water, survival gear, and medical supplies to stuff into gaping, bloody wounds and tourniquets in case you or one of your men loses an appendage.

If you're a troop or team leader you work out a plan that will hopefully accomplish the mission without getting anybody killed while songs like *Conquer All* by Behemoth rattle the house.

> *None of thy empty gods, shall ever stand above me*
> *None of thy weak brothers, shall ever share my blood**

All while the men you will put in harm's way, their jaws set, eyes burning with intensity, pound each other on the shoulders, and scream "Kill the shitheads!" and "Till Valhalla" in each other's faces.

When you've got your plan—praying that you didn't miss something, fuck something up—you give the command of execution. The door flies open and you and your men move into the blazing heat of the day or the green-tinted night. The air smells like diesel and sun-baked cement—like a truck stop on a hot day in the Midwest—and, so help me God, it also smells like death and excrement. You can't get that stench out of your nostrils.

Weighed down by eighty pounds of "light" gear plus your weapon, you run to load up on helicopters, sitting with your ass in the bay door and your feet dangling in space. You lift into the sky with the

---

* *Conquer All*, Behemoth, songwriter Adam Darski, Copyright © 2004 Sony/ATV Music Publishing LLC.

chopper blades beating the air like a war drum as over the city you go, waiting to see if the locals below will be shooting at you. Sometimes they're shooting for fun, like kids corning cars back home, only this is real and potentially fatal; sometimes they really are trying to kill you.

More likely, you pile into the armored personnel carriers sitting out front in their rows, engines growling, while tanks rumble menacingly nearby. Or it might be the BMW sedans if you're trying to mix in undetected with the locals.

Most of the time you're in ground vehicles. Rolling out of the walled fortress known as the Green Zone, you pray that a mine or suicide bomber isn't waiting outside the gate. Then you head into the Red Zone, which is any part of the city, as well as Fallujah, Ramadi, or whatever crappy little village in the desert you're headed to, that is not under control of the good guys.

You know that no matter how well trained you are, it's no protection against bombs big enough to flip an armored vehicle, or capable of punching a hole in the side with a red-hot metal rod that will zip around like a berserk hornet tearing up and burning through everyone it stings. If you get hit with a bomb, best-case scenario is the bad guys take off. Worst and most probable case, after a vehicle gets stopped by an IED, they open up with machine guns while you're trying to rescue the injured and trapped.

The enemy hides bombs everywhere. Dead donkey IEDs. In dogs. Under piles of trash. Sometimes they tunnel beneath the road and blow it up from below. There is no end to the ingenuity of a bored terrorist.

When you arrive at the hit, you strike with overwhelming intensity to overcome opposition, or else you creep up in the dark like thieves in the night, feeling like you have a thousand eyes, and maybe rifle sights, on your back. Someone breaches the door and the team pours into the building where you hope to find the residents asleep or so shocked by your sudden presence, they're barely able to function. Or you could be walking into a house full of armed men willing to go toe to toe and shoot it out with you. Maybe they're waiting for you across the street, and the apartment is rigged to blow up. The thing is, you never know.

You want to ignore the sight of what bullets do to human heads and bodies, but you can never get the visual out of your mind. Try to control your anger when you find bomb-making equipment, suicide vests, and vehicles being altered so that they can be driven into crowded marketplaces to murder innocent men, women, and children, spreading terror and sorrow like farmers sow seed.

Snarling like a raving wolf, you line up the prisoners for interrogation while the shock of capture is still fresh. Identify those who've crapped their pants or shake and sweat in fear. They'll talk. Note, too, the ones who smirk or stare at you with undisguised hatred, knowing that the rules of engagement—rules they don't follow—will protect them. You wish you could put a bullet between their eyes because they know, and you know, that if they aren't charged with crimes, they'll be released within three days to go back to plotting to kill Americans and innocent Iraqis.

When you're done, you return to the Green Zone, drop off your prisoners, and go back to your living quarters to wait for the next call. But there's never enough time to let the adrenaline, pills, and caffeine wear off before you have to go do it all again. So, you work out, practice shooting at the range, read the intel reports. Stay sharp. Don't lose that edge or you could die.

When you return after that last hit of the night and try to relax and maybe get some sleep, you know that it doesn't really matter that you're in the Green Zone. You've spent so much time in the Red that there is no such thing as feeling secure or safe anywhere. It's all Red.

You and the guys crack a beer despite General Order No. 1 that prohibits alcohol.

You swallow whatever pills the Army has given you for anxiety, depression, pain, and to help you rest. The lucky ones who can sleep are snoring all around you. You can see the torment they're living with as they lie there twitching and growling, killing someone, somewhere, or simply trying to survive the nightmares. The rest of the team—those who can't sleep—scream and shout while playing Xbox or some other game.

Outside, muffled by the walls of the house but always present, there's the drumming of helicopters coming and going, the clanking of tanks, and the diesel roar of other vehicles. You lie on your bunk and stare up at the ceiling or the bottom of the bed above you, reliving all the terrible things you've seen, heard, and done. That teenager gasping in his bed, bloody foam on his lips, eyes filled with panic. A woman and her child wailing over the bullet-ridden, crushed body of a husband and father. You're looking again into the dying eyes of a man you killed years ago. The blood and gore of your enemies and that of your friends is on your face and arms. There is no escaping the visions, the sounds, the feel, and the stench of war.

Somehow you fall asleep for a few hours, if you're exhausted enough, lucky if you don't get rolled out of bed by a nearby car bomb or rockets. The job has turned you into a nocturnal predator, hunting by night, resting by day.

You're not refreshed when you get up, just physically able enough to go on and do it all over again. Hour after hour. Mission after mission. Day after day. Week after week. Month after month.

Ninety days. One. After. The. Other. Unrelenting. So many missions that they all roll into one giant shitty memory so blended together in your head that you can't tell where they stop and start, or what day they occurred, or what year for that matter. Not even which happened first. It's living your life on a fast, violent roller coaster that won't stop to let you off, not unless you catch a bullet, or some uneducated, crazy-eyed terrorist blows you off the tracks. Or you jump and end it yourself.

Don't get me wrong. I'm not really complaining. I signed up for it. Volunteered. In fact, I volunteered four times—for the Army, for jump school, for Special Forces, and for the Unit. I pushed myself to the very edge of my physical, emotional, and psychological limits to make it through selection and OTC, when 95 percent of those who started didn't make it, because I wanted it more than anything. And every day since then I'd fought to prove I still belonged.

I did it because I love my country. I wanted to protect my family, my friends, American citizens, and other innocent people in the world from bullies and tyrants, murderers, and terrorists. I believed that I was fighting so that others wouldn't have to and could sleep easy in their beds at night. I believed that I was in Iraq to bring freedom and protect people from terrorism, a terrorism that we'd be fighting at home if we didn't stop it there. I did it so those who didn't want to, didn't have to.

To be honest, there were many things about my job that I loved. I loved being the best at something few other people in the world could match. I loved feeling useful and that what I did mattered to the world. I loved being a warrior, which isn't about killing as much as it is about protecting.

Most of all, I loved the guys I worked with in the Unit. Most of them anyway. They were my brothers, stronger than blood, my tribe.

No, I'm not complaining. I'm just trying to explain why it's not a mystery that guys were coming back fucked up and hurting to the depths of their souls. But most, including me at the time, can't admit to it. That would be weakness. Someday, many years later, those are the ones I would watch out for, the ones who needed the most help. The quiet, seemingly strong ones.

ON THE FLIGHT BACK to the States, I thought about Valhalla, the mythical Norse heaven for warriors. We used the phrase "till Valhalla" to psych up for battle, like it was supposed to make us feel better that if we didn't make it back, we'd meet again there. Then we'd battle all day, die glorious deaths, and rise again at sunset to feast and drink mead in the great hall. Sort of like when I was a child playing Army with my friends and then getting called home for dinner. Only as an adult soldier when you died, you stayed dead.

I wondered what sort of place I would go to if I died in battle. I didn't want it to be Valhalla. I didn't want to kill and be killed throughout eternity. I wanted peace, and I wanted not to hurt anymore.

CHAPTER TWENTY-THREE

November 2010
Fort Bragg, North Carolina

"PULL OVER." The limousine slowed, crunching over the gravel on the shoulder of the lonely road that cut through the Fort Bragg training area. I jerked the rear door open and staggered out.

Christine and I were on our way to dinner in Southern Pines with several couples we knew from the Unit for what was supposed to be a celebration. I'd just officially retired from the Army after a small ceremony at Unit headquarters and should have been looking forward to drinks and a steak. But I was suddenly sick to my stomach.

Stumbling into the tall grass that I had walked through for more than twenty years while training, I bent over and retched. It was nonstop and violent, as if I was trying to purge some dark poison.

Any other time, my nausea could have been attributed to having too much to drink. I was pretty much a full-on alcoholic, but I hadn't had so much as a sip all day. I suppose part of it could have been the fact that I hadn't eaten all day. The handful of pills I took for pain, anxiety, and depression could be hard on an empty stomach. But that wasn't it either.

The real reason was I was heartsick. Betrayal. Hurt to the very core of my soul, seemingly purposefully humiliated and tossed aside like trash, by the people and entity I had served for the best years of my life.

My friends and family remained sitting in the car, bewildered by my sudden bout of nausea. I'm sure they thought I'd been secretly drinking, but I explained it as "car sickness" when I climbed back in.

We continued on our way as if nothing had happened. As I looked out the window at the sun setting beyond the pine trees to the west, I had never felt so alone and lost in my life.

It HAD BEEN ALMOST exactly six years since getting home from that second deployment to Iraq, which for me was just a repeat of the first time. You fantasize about the big homecoming. Everybody's going to be happy to see you. Lots of love and "I'm so happy you're home." You play catch with your son. You kick back with a cocktail, flirt with your wife until it's time to go to bed. You think that now that you're safe, you can relax and get all that crap out of your head. Silence the ghosts. Let all the bad stuff seep out like air from a balloon.

It lasted about three days. Christine had a full-time job and her own life; I was just an annoyance. Thomas was in school and gone most of the time during the day and then off to bed early. It was just as well. I was a stranger to him, and I didn't know how to relate to a six-year-old boy. I wanted to play with him, but I didn't know how to play anymore. I knew I loved him, but I wasn't capable of showing it. I felt dead inside.

Tired of dealing with the pain, I finally went and had my back checked out. An MRI revealed that I'd suffered a massive disc blowout when the equipment fell on me. It was giving me "drop foot," which was the cause of my tripping and stumbling.

So, on top of the blown disc in my neck, I now had one in my back. My right shoulder was always in pain, but I attributed that to my neck issues and just kept going. I was concerned that my physical ailments were making it tough to keep up with the younger guys. As I was in a leadership position, it wasn't as necessary, but there was no telling me that; I hid it as best I could and trained as much as my body would let me, so that I wouldn't be relieved or replaced.

Early in 2005, I was asked to be the command sergeant major (CSM) of the combat support squadron. That meant I would be in charge of all of the Unit's "specialists" who assisted the assault squadrons in the field. These included our chemical, biological, radiological, nuclear, and explosives (CBRNE) teams who could be deployed as needed. The squadron also had heavy breachers and explosive ordnance disposal experts along with other needed specialties for combat support.

I wasn't exactly thrilled by the proposition. It would mean a lot of desk time, and I wouldn't be deploying. Like any other operator, I wanted to be in an assault squadron. I know it sounds like a contradiction. On one hand, I hated being in Iraq and was tired of the killing. But after a few weeks at home feeling like a failure as a father and husband, at least I knew I was good at war. It was what I was trained to do, and among my brothers, I knew I was loved.

However, command persisted. It was an important job, they said, and they wanted me to take it on. I didn't know how I felt about climbing the leadership ladder—the higher you went, the less action you saw and the more time you spent sitting on your ass and typing. But it was the trajectory I was on. I agreed, though reluctantly. The year 2005 was a tough one for the Unit. In coordination with SEAL Team 6 and other regular Army and Marine forces, our squadrons participated in Operation Snake Eyes, which was intended to take down local militant networks, especially al-Qaeda in Iraq. The operation targeted the "middle men"—the financial support systems, recruiters, and IED builders—all across the country.

In May, Unit operator Steven Langmack was killed during a mission near the Syrian border, the first Unit fatality since Andy Fernandez in 2003. The troops, including the Unit's assault teams, were seeing a new level of sophistication and violence in the enemy, as more foreign fighters, trained in camps abroad, slipped into Iraq, along with the Iranian influence.

Then on June 17, the Unit's assault teams stormed a house in Al Qaim, near where Steve was killed, targeting low-level al-Qaeda fighters. But the enemy had built a bunker inside the building and the operators ran into a trap. Two of them, my friends Michael McNulty and Robert Horrigan, were killed before the teams could withdraw. A precision-guided bomb was dropped on the house killing the insurgents, but losing two more guys was devastating.

Then on August 25, three more Unit operators and a Ranger were killed when an anti-tank mine destroyed their armored vehicle.

Hearing about the deaths of friends and other operators was terrible. Now I knew how helpless the other squadrons in the Unit felt when they heard about what was going on in Mogadishu. I felt like I was letting those guys down from my safe little seat behind a desk.

That many casualties were devastating to a unit as small as ours, not just in operational numbers but in its impact on our community, especially the families. Even if you weren't close friends with all of the guys, you still knew who they were, had seen them with their wives and kids. They were people with lives—and needs. Gone.

We pulled together as a community, but my anger returned. I wanted to kill terrorists, but I took it out on everybody else.

While serving as the combat support squadron sergeant major, I was called to Iraq in January 2006 to be the task force CSM. I wasn't happy when I got sent home in March. I know it sounds weird, but I didn't feel safe there. Christine didn't want to hear about Iraq or my issues.

It certainly wasn't Christine's fault that our marriage was withering on the vine. I was an asshole—easy to anger, my temper turned on a dime, emotionally distant, and I drank all the time. But I didn't have anybody to talk to about what I was experiencing; not her, not my family, who would have just worried, not the other guys in the Unit who'd think me weak, and not the Unit shrinks who might flag me to command as unfit. I certainly wish now that there had been a way to talk to someone without worrying whether it would jeopardize my career or come with the stigma that is attached to psychological issues.

In 2007, I was deployed twice to Iraq—for a month early in the year and then from April through August—as the task force CSM again.

I knew it was an honor to have been made the task force CSM and given this task, even though only in Iraq and temporarily. It was a sign of the trust from command, but it was all lost on me; I wanted to be in the fight. Oddly enough, direct combat was the only time I felt like I was in my natural element, nothing else felt as safe as when I was putting my life on the line. In combat, I needed to be the cool, calm voice on the radio, calling directions and moving men around while asking for assets to suppress enemy fires.

At home, I could be a raging beast. I tossed back pills like they were M&Ms and washed them down with Captain Morgan's rum and Sprite. I was aggressive in a lot of my interactions both at home and at work. I became someone no one wanted to talk to; I knew it but couldn't seem to get out of asshole mode. I felt I was no longer being respected at the Unit, though I was sure I could still handle the job.

THEN, IN THE FALL of 2007, I was told I was going to be given the great responsibility of squadron command sergeant major. But it wasn't going to be one of the original three; I was asked to establish a fourth assault squadron, D Squadron. The impact of the never-ending war in Iraq on the Unit was such that the three squadrons were being run ragged. The Unit had taken a real beating during the Iraq War; we'd had a 20 percent casualty rate, and 50 percent of operators had been awarded the Purple Heart.

It was an awesome responsibility and what I thought would be a feather in the cap of my career. Someone was showing a lot of faith and trust in me to give me that opportunity to work with my squadron commander, an officer I had trained while an instructor at OTC, to build an entirely new squadron.

In the spring 2008, I went in for my "over-forty" physical, sometimes called "the kiss of death physical." They did the usual checking me out, drew blood, and I went back to work thinking all was well.

We activated the squadron on June 6, 2008, the anniversary of D-day and the invasion of Normandy. It seemed the appropriate date for D Squadron. A squadron forged for war.

I'd forgotten all about the physical when I was called to the "med shed" where I was told that my cholesterol levels were "zero."

"Well, that's good isn't it?" I asked.

It turned out it's not. Zero cholesterol is not normal. The doctor asked me what I was taking as far as medications and any supplements, or any "other" drugs. I explained that other than the prescriptions they gave me, I was taking just about anything I could get my hands on at nutrition stores so I could recover from all the surgeries.

I had ordered one item off the internet without thinking and told the doc about it. It was called Nolvadex, which I was told increased testosterone and helped the body heal and build more muscle without using steroids.

The doctor didn't say much of anything, so I went home wondering what this was all about. Then late that night, I got a call from my squadron commander. We were friends and worked well together, both of us were excited about taking our new squadron into combat. Still, it was odd when he said he wanted to come over to my house to talk. He said the doctor had told him that my cholesterol reading was due to taking steroids.

"I need to talk to you," the commander said.

That meant one thing. I was in trouble. "You can just tell me whatever you need to over the phone," I said. "Just do it. I'm cool with it."

However, he insisted that we needed to talk face-to-face. He was on his way.

Waiting for him to arrive, I asked Christine for a Xanax. I felt I was spiraling down a drain and thought it might help. I hadn't taken any steroids and didn't know where this information was coming from.

When the commander arrived, we sat down so he could give me the bad news. I was being relieved by the Unit commander as squadron sergeant major due to steroid use. I was shocked, but I didn't argue. It was pointless. If the Unit commander spoke, that was it. My squadron commander was just delivering the news.

Remember when I was a kid and the bully would come up to me, call me names, hit me in the face, kick me in the balls, and I'd just stand there and cry? This was like that. I didn't cry, at least not in front of him, but I was close to it. Otherwise, I felt like I'd just been called names. Cheater. Liar. And kicked in the balls. Then when he left, I sobbed for hours.

I would later find out that Nolvadex was often taken by steroid users to counter some of the side effects, including the negative effects steroids have on testosterone. Whether the doctor read something into my taking Nolvadex, which I should have gotten a prescription for, or there was a lab error, I didn't know at the time. Some months later, however, after asking a physician friend at Womack Army Medical Center to help me investigate what happened, he told me it was definitely lab error. No one, he said, has zero cholesterol. I was the victim of quick decision making and going against the decision of the commander, whether it was based on fact or unsubstantiated reports, was not something most would do. Therefore, the decision stood, and I was removed as the CSM.

There was no other punishment, nor was I reduced in rank. But it was the end of who I was as a man. I was embarrassed to go to work, and if I did, I avoided the mess hall so I wouldn't have to deal with the thought of everybody looking at me, wondering why I'd been removed from my position. I was a failure. A loser.

At first, my friends defended me. Yet, while they were supportive to my face, I don't remember anyone going to bat for me. Who would want to risk their job or get ostracized for backing me up?

Eventually even the support faded away. My friends went on with their lives in the Unit, and I disappeared. I cannot to this day describe the pain of that.

I didn't know what to do with myself. I didn't have a job, but with only two more years to go to retirement, I needed to stay in. I took what the Unit offered, a special mission to Iraq. It's still not one I'm allowed to talk about except to say that it was a "reconnaissance mission." It didn't last anyway.

Before I left for Iraq, I'd had an MRI on my shoulder. Then about a month after I deployed, I got a call from a Unit doctor. He said I had to come home; my shoulder was a bigger mess than I imagined. He said not to pick up so much as my rucksack or anything else heavy. My labrum was torn and almost totally gone. I needed surgery immediately.

AFTER I RECOVERED FROM surgery for a bit, no one knew what to do with me. So, I was assigned as a liaison officer to a school just down the road for Special Forces soldiers to teach shooting and CQB. The guys I worked with were top notch Special Forces operators. I still loved teaching and that was probably my saving grace.

After work, I was a recluse. I drank myself to sleep every night. I quit answering personal phone calls. I didn't even have a homelife to speak of; I was just someone who lived in the same house with Christine and Thomas, sleeping in the spare bedroom.

Finally, in 2010, it was time to retire. In all honesty, I was fine with getting my papers and never stepping foot on Fort Bragg again. I had decided not to have a retirement ceremony and just disappear into my new life. However, the commander of C Squadron, who'd also been one of my OTC students, asked me to have a ceremony in my old squadron classroom.

I argued against it. I was bitter and just wanted to be done. But he thought I needed that closure and wouldn't stop pressing me on it. Finally, I relented.

On the big day I arrived in the Unit parking lot with my family in tow.

The thing is, I already knew something was up. A last knife in the back. I'd been to the personnel office the day before to sign some paperwork and noticed I would be receiving an award during the ceremony. I had been put in for, and thought I deserved, the Legion of Merit, given for "exceptionally meritorious conduct in the performance of outstanding services and achievements." Apparently, I wasn't going to get it and would instead receive a lesser award that I already had five of.

So, when I saw the command sergeant major standing in the parking lot, I asked him about it. "We didn't want to go to bat for you for such a high award after what happened," he responded.

"Really? Want to clarify that?" I asked. This was a guy I'd been on the same team with for years. We'd fought together in Somalia. I'd laid mattresses up along the walls and one of them had stopped shrapnel and debris from hitting him when an RPG hit the house. We'd bled together.

His response was that he didn't know what to tell me. He just stood there, looking uncomfortable.

"That's what I thought," I said and went inside for a ceremony I didn't want. But they weren't done kicking me in the balls.

The room was full of people. Mainly Unit staff, a few old friends, and my family. I was told that Gen. Austin "Scott" M., the ground force commander during the Battle of Mogadishu and now a deputy director of Special Operations in Afghanistan, would be calling in.

It didn't take me long to figure out where the next blow would be coming from. They'd laid out my awards and certificates, and the plaque I'd receive on a table. But there was one very conspicuous absence, the one that meant the most to me. My unit's colors.

A unit's colors are the small flag that is carried on a staff along with other flags when a unit is marching. It is traditional upon the retirement for the colors to be framed in a glass-covered case and presented. It is treasured by those who served as much as any medal, but apparently, I wasn't going to receive them.

Again, I asked the CSM what was going on. "The last two years, Tom," he replied under his breath.

"I did what you asked me to do for the past two years," I said, "not to mention the eighteen before that." But he just stood there, again silent.

I couldn't believe what was happening. This was a direct assault on my life, everything I'd done for the Unit, my dedication. This humiliation was my reward for twenty-five years in the Army, Soldier of the Year, Airborne, Special Forces, and twenty years in the Unit.

This is what I earned with five Bronze Stars, two of them with Valor—one of those won during the longest firefight in the US military since Vietnam, the other for my part in capturing Saddam Hussein. And for all the other awards and commendations I'd received over the years. I'd never paid much attention to them, I guess the Unit didn't either.

Apparently, my unit's colors were too much to ask after multiple deployments to Iraq as a team leader and a troop sergeant major and hundreds of missions hunting down terrorists and insurgents, going through doors, any of which could have had death standing on the other side. Then again as a squadron sergeant major and finally as the command sergeant major, the highest-ranking non-com in this nation's most elite military unit.

Maybe it would have been better if I had been shot entering a door. I would have assuredly gotten the unit colors, along with a folded flag handed to my widow.

I'd taken on other dangerous and clandestine missions to places in the world that most Americans have never heard of, much less knew that people there were plotting to kill them. And stopped them.

My life had been laid on the line more times than I could count. My body was broken, my mind a mess. My dedication to the job had cost me two marriages with a third on the rocks. I was estranged from my son, and hardly spoke to my parents, siblings, or friends. I grieved for those who didn't make it home from the battlefield, as well as for those who did but were as messed up as I was. And this was my thanks? This was my punishment really. Selection really is ongoing. Until the day you walk away. Then you are left to judge yourself with all your mishaps and blunders remembered and none of the good.

When I was relieved from my job standing up D Squadron, I'd tried to continue being a good soldier. I told myself it was just the Unit protecting itself. That finally, after twenty years, command had decided I wasn't good enough anymore. I'd expected that to happen someday, but not like this.

I had to hold back tears that afternoon as I listened to General Miller talk about my heroism in Somalia, Iraq, and other places, along with personal stories of us all training and having fun around the States. It was a very nice and personal dedication, but, ultimately, just meaningless words to me. I know he meant them, and they were a nice testament to how he viewed me, but I was devastated.

After the general's soliloquy, Christine was given flowers and my son, Thomas, was given the bullshit ribbon to pin on my uniform. I was handed the traditional simple triangular wooden plaque with the Unit emblem and a single word, "Thanks."

When it was all over, I plastered a smile on my face and shook hands. Then left as soon as I could.

Christine had rented a limo to take us and our friends to dinner. As we passed through the Unit's gates, I was quiet as I tried to deal with all the emotions rolling around in my head, crushing my heart, and clawing at my gut. Someone had made a conscious decision not to tell me about the Legion of Merit, and especially the Unit's colors, so that I would still go to the ceremony and be humiliated. Suddenly, I was sick to my stomach.

"Pull over."

Standing there in the dark, wiping bitter spittle from my mouth. I felt like the Unit had used me, and now, when I was a broken soldier, had wadded me up and thrown me away like a piece of trash. I would always love my brothers from the Unit, and I was proud of my service to my country. But the Unit, and those in it who didn't want to ruffle feathers and stand up for me, cut me the deepest.

If I'd died at that moment, laid down in the grass where I worked so hard to be the best of the best, I would have preferred it to living.

CHAPTER TWENTY-FOUR

May 2013
Seymour, Indiana

I HARDLY NOTICED the pretty blonde woman the first time we met. I don't think I said two words to her.

All I knew was that she and her company had been contracted to shoot an advertisement to run in movie theaters for a company owned by a former Unit operator. The company promised civilians the chance to be "operators," enter buildings CQB-style, and "kill" role-players pretending to be zombies with paintball guns.

I was in charge of "training" the civilians in how to wear their kit, load and use their weapons, plan a mission, assault a building, and save the world from the zombie apocalypse. I also led the missions to kill the zombies, most of them former special operations soldiers in need of a job. It was all very fake, but the civilians loved playing Army as much as I did as a child.

The afternoon the blonde and I were introduced, I resented even having to be there talking to her and her crew. They'd been fed a line by my boss about what a "legend" I was in special operations, and I felt like a fraud. I also hated having someone else exploit my past to make money. But it was a job and I needed the income.

That didn't mean I wanted to fraternize with those in the "art world." To me they all went to bullshit colleges, made macaroni art, complained about having it so tough, and told soldiers how wrong we were for killing people—as if we actually liked doing it. These people had no clue what I, or any of the other guys, had been through.

It turned out that I was as clueless about them as I thought they were about me. But that would take some time.

In the meantime, I was being trotted around like a trick pony. They even gave me a stage name, "Baller," and made up a fictional biography for advertising purposes. That's how low I'd sunk since 2010.

TEN DAYS AFTER MY "retirement party" three years earlier, I was in Amman, Jordan, working for a company that had been contracted to run shooting ranges and training at King Abdullah II Special Operations Training Center. It was perfect for me. I would be working with foreign and US military units, the latter either on their way to a war zone, or coming from one and needing to train away from the day-to-day missions. I set up the ranges and the CQB house, instructed when needed, and ensured that they had everything necessary to get better at the job.

I was like a lot of other combat vets after they get out of the service, more comfortable overseas than at home. That's where the jobs and money were, and where the pressures of living a "normal" life weren't. A perpetual TDY trip (temporary duty), the length of a deployment, in a city with bars and hotels and an apartment. How awesome this was going to be.

After nine years of war, a thriving cottage industry had sprung up around supplying "contractors," especially former special operations veterans, to provide counterterrorism protection and VIP security for private industry, as well as training other countries' militaries. It was either that or work for the US government pulling security for the State Department, or working in black ops for the CIA or the National Security Agency.

Unfortunately, for special operations combat veterans, almost all their training goes into learning how to kill other human beings. Very little time or effort is spent teaching that soldier how to come back to the "real" world. So, when guys get out and go looking for work, many of them fall right into contract work which, in effect, puts them right back where they were.

If you were smart, you took advantage of the educational opportunities, such as college classes. Those who enlisted and worked in the intelligence or computer specializations, personnel, or explosive ordnance disposal have skill sets that translate to the civilian world. But not so much the guy who laid his life on the line in combat. There's not much call for shooting people in the civilian world outside of maybe police work, where it's a last resort, or contracting.

Using the GI Bill for education is one thing, but there isn't much done to teach life skills for coping in the civilian world. Many of the young guys who go into the service right out of high school and then get out after a few years have not learned the skills they'll need to live autonomously. They're still in the same place in life as they were when they entered the service. They may be able to drive a tank, but they can't balance a checkbook or create an effective résumé. And when it comes to applying for positions in the civilian workforce, they also lag behind their counterparts who attended college during the time they served.

It doesn't have to be that way. With a little imagination and applied resources, the lessons taught by the military should be considered assets in a civilian context. These include leadership skills, accountability, dependability, loyalty, teamwork, and an enhanced emphasis on getting the task done even in stressful and adverse situations.

But it isn't just about who is the most educationally prepared to adapt to civilian life, or convincing employers that veterans have so many desirable skills and traits. There's a reason why combat veterans gravitate to overseas contractor jobs beyond the pay or using what they've been trained to do.

For those dealing with PTSD, the troubles are magnified at home. When you're cranking out missions in Iraq, no one pays much attention if you're angry, depressed, aggressive, hypervigilant, or violent. But take it back to the States with you and you're ostracized as too bad, or too broken, and unable to cope with life and assimilate into societal norms.

I was capable of putting two rounds into the head of a terrorist while running. But no one taught me how to go home, lock all the violence and brutality away in some safe in my head, and then relate to my son or help my wife decide what color to paint a bedroom wall. Nor had anyone taught them how to cope with a father and husband who was always angry, short-tempered, and demanding, yet emotionally unavailable.

Small wonder PTSD manifests itself in alcoholism, substance abuse, domestic violence, impulsivity, and poor decision making that turns into DUIs, extramarital affairs, and run-ins with the law. What civilian boss wants to deal with that sort of personality, one with an explosive temper or addiction to alcohol and/or pain pills? I'm not even touching on secondary PTSD that affects the spouses and children at home.

I understood now what those homeless Vietnam veterans begging on street corners in Indianapolis were going through. They'd gone away to war and when they came home, as many as 30 percent of them were suffering psychological issues due to "combat exposure," according to the Department of Defense. There was nothing for them here. The community wasn't accepting of their role in an unpopular war, nor appreciative of their service. No one, outside of a few social workers, cared if they were hurting and needed help readjusting.

PTSD just isn't a popular topic of discussion for the military. I never heard it brought up in the Unit. I'd hardly heard of the term and had no idea I might be suffering from it. I just thought I was an angry, hypervigilant loser who couldn't sleep or have fun without getting drunk. I didn't give a lot of thought as to why I might be that way; I just knew that I was. And tended to blame myself.

The truth of the matter is that even for combat veterans who recognize that they have been adversely affected by PTSD stemming from their combat tours, they're more comfortable in a military setting or war zone than trying to be "normal" back home. I know I was and that's how I ended up in Jordan. The phrase "I miss it" is thrown around repeatedly by veterans suffering.

I took the position out of an obligation to support my family. I could not have cared less about it myself. My whole persona had been wrapped up in being an operator in the Unit, where I felt that I was doing something good in the world. But the way I'd been humiliated and tossed aside like garbage when I retired made me wonder if it was all an illusion. At least when I was overseas training soldiers to fight, I knew what I was doing and who I was.

I was happy enough in Jordan and would have stayed, but after about a year, the program funding stopped and I found myself heading back to the States again. Without a job and without a plan, I felt more like a loser than ever. I couldn't even support my family, not on a sergeant major's retirement pay.

It's fair to say I really tanked after Jordan. Without the structure of the military, which was the only life I'd known since I was a teenager, I was lost and in pain both physically and mentally.

A half dozen back, neck, and shoulder surgeries had done little to alleviate the pain; pills for depression and anxiety did nothing to dispel ghosts or chase off the nightmares. My service was a sham. I couldn't maintain a relationship with a woman, or my son. I didn't feel comfortable in my own skin or even my own country.

My moral compass was also askew. While in Jordan I was having an affair. I blamed Christine, of course, telling myself that she was incapable of giving me what I needed. Later I learned from one of her former friends that Christine told her that she wished I'd find a girlfriend so that I'd leave her alone. I obliged her halfway around the world and convinced myself it was because she made me feel unloved and had chased me into the arms of another woman.

Of course, I didn't consider that maybe I was the unlovable one—that living with me and my issues wasn't what she'd signed the marriage certificate for. After returning to the States from Jordan, I basically laid around for months, miserable, drinking, sleeping all day, and watching TV all night. Looking back, I see that I was giving up on life, dying a little bit every day.

I was finally desperate for any help I could find. The Army, however, said I didn't have PTSD. The way they, or I should say a Veterans Administration psychiatrist, determined that was pretty odd and not in the least scientific.

During one of my trips home from Jordan, I went in for a physical at the VA. A previous physical had only given me a 10 percent disability for arthritis in my knees. I was certainly more disabled than that, including alcoholism, and went in for another physical.

This time the psychiatrist told me I had traumatic brain injury caused by repeated exposure to explosions as a breacher. That, she said, was the cause of my alcoholism, and she determined I had a 50 percent disability.

However, the "good" news was that my myriad troubles were not caused by PTSD. She explained that she knew this because of the way I had answered a question on a PTSD survey. There were the usual questions: "Do you have nightmares?" "Do you see things in the day?" But the one that tripped me up was this: "Would you go back?" As in would I go back to the war.

I replied that I didn't want to go back, but I would. Of course, I would—out of loyalty, for my brothers, to help others. It was what I'd spent my life training to do. But I would have dreaded it and hated every moment.

Yet because I had answered that I *would* go back, according to the shrink, I didn't have PTSD. She said those with PTSD would refuse to go back no matter what. It was an assessment that seemed a parody of the popular concept of the bureaucratic Army mentality.

After a few months of lying around, I received a call about a job from a former Unit guy. He had some contracts with the government to train Rangers and wanted me to be an instructor, as well as help him with a new "entertainment" venture—teaching civilians to be "special operators" and shoot zombies. He wasn't one of my favorite people in the Unit—in fact, he'd been kicked out—nor was I real excited about teaching civilians to shoot zombies, but like I said, I needed the money.

I was even less enthusiastic when he came up with the idea of filming an advertisement for the zombie company that would be shown to movie audiences before the start of a film. He sort of sprang the introduction to the film crew on me while we were in Seymour, the town where I was born, scouting for good locations to film. I may have nodded to the blonde, but I got out of there as fast as I could.

It wasn't until my longtime friend Jake, who'd been with me in Somalia, Iraq, and at the meeting, asked if I noticed the "hot chick" who was going to be doing the filming. He went on and on about her so much that I looked up her LinkedIn profile. Her name was Jen Halski. She was pretty, blond with freckles and hazel eyes. More than that she looked kind, caring, and intelligent; I felt drawn to her without knowing why.

How I'd missed noticing her the first time, I have no idea. Too wrapped up in my own misery, I guess. At that point, I had no way of knowing I had just met the person who would save my life . . . in more ways than one.

CHAPTER TWENTY-FIVE

August 2013
Akron, Ohio

SITTING IN THE DRIVER'S SEAT OF THE RENTAL CAR, I pulled the Glock 22 pistol from under the seat. The heft of the gun was so familiar, as much a part of my hand as my numb trigger finger. Tears welled in my eyes as I contemplated what I was about to do.

I was hot and sweaty and still dressed in my camos after a long day shooting videos that the company I worked for used to promote its special operations training programs that we sold to the US military.

I'd driven back to the hotel where I was staying with my "actors," all former special ops and Rangers, plus Jen Halski, the director of filming. Pulling into a spot in the hotel parking garage, I'd told the passengers—my friend Teddy L., a former Special Forces veteran, and Jen to go ahead without me.

"I'm gonna wrap this up," I said, holding up my phone like I had a call to make. "I'll meet you in the lobby in a few."

Jen gave me a quizzical look, and I wondered for a moment if she sensed something was wrong. I knew I'd been quieter than normal that day, especially on the ride back to the hotel. And usually I'd walk with her to the lobby; we'd go to our rooms, stash our gear, and then all meet in the bar for another night of pounding down cocktails. But she got out of the car, grabbing her camera gear and looking back at me one more time.

"See you in there, buddy," Teddy said with his soft North Carolina drawl. The self-proclaimed "redneck" Green Beret climbed out. He and Jen walked away, leaving me alone with my thoughts.

And the gun.

I watched Jen walk away, regretting that things couldn't be different. *Goodbye*, I thought.

When we were shooting those initial zombie advertising videos, I quickly learned that Jen was a consummate professional in her own right. Like my old drill instructor, she knew what she wanted for each scene and had her film crew and the rest of us jumping.

Jen also began shooting videos of the training we were doing with the Rangers, which the Army loved. It meant that she had to get right in close to the action.

A self-described tomboy, Jen fit right in with the military guys and wasn't fazed in the least by explosions, gunfire, or standing beneath helicopters hovering over her head as guys were fast-roping to the ground. Later I learned she'd wanted to be a *National Geographic* photographer and anthropologist, so when the opportunity presented itself that she could study another culture and shoot it at the same time, she fell right into the role and owned it. It attracted me to her even more.

Jen was also fun to be around. She gave as good as she took from our sometimes-dark military humor, and despite being all of a hundred fifteen pounds, could toss back cocktails at the end of the day with the best of us.

Little by little, as I got to know her talking during the day and after hours, we started sharing things about our personal lives. She was a good listener and I began opening up about some of what I was going through, the issues my wife didn't want to hear about. Nothing specific yet—not the horrors of Mogadishu or Iraq—but the disappointment of a relationship that had long gone cold, a son I was losing a connection to, and some of the pain my body was putting me through day and night.

By this time, I was separated from Christine and all that was left for divorce number three was filling out the paperwork. Even though I worked out of Fayetteville, I stayed in a hotel while she and Thomas remained in our house. I wasn't home much anyway so living out of a suitcase was easier.

Jen was struggling with her own marriage. Her husband, who was her creative partner in their design, film, and photography studio, was a nice guy, her best friend. But while there was nothing wrong on the surface—no big fights, no dramatics—she hadn't felt connected to him as a husband in a long time. She was staying with him for the sake of their two young children, Luke and Claudia, but they were talking about separating.

Talking about our marriages and loneliness was probably what initially brought us together as friends. But as I got to know her— whether talking face to face after a video shoot or through numerous texts and phone calls—I grew more attracted. Every time the phone buzzed I grabbed it, immediately hoping it was a message from her. I found myself acting silly, like a middle-schooler trying to impress a girl, to get her to laugh. She had a great laugh.

She seemed to like me, too, though I couldn't figure out what she saw in me. I believed that everything good I'd been in the Unit was pretty much gone. I was overweight, checking in at two hundred sixty pounds, and looked like I probably drank myself to sleep every night and swallowed pills by the handful. Which was pretty much true.

The wear and tear of PTSD, anger, and depression had etched lines in my face that refused to smooth out even when I was relaxing. My back ached constantly, my neck was perpetually stiff, my shoulder was still a mess, and I just hurt physically in a way that I couldn't explain. But above all, the psychological issues should have sent up the "Warning! Do Not Approach!" red flags to Jen. She'd already seen the temper flare-ups and drastic mood swings, but she kept talking to me.

In most every way we were complete opposites. She was a self-described hippy chick; although not political in the least, she leaned toward a more liberal mindset, she spent her life in the creative arts with other artist types, was a serial optimist, and looked at the world and the people who occupied it as generally "good."

I was the stereotypical military guy—conservative, skeptical, closed off to my emotions and to the world. I talked the way I thought I was supposed to as an operator, loud and crude, especially my remarks about women. I referred to the people I fought, like the Somalis, Iraqis, and foreign fighters, by the derogatory nicknames we'd picked up, like "skinnies," "towel heads," "camel jockeys," and "muj."

However, Jen was more than capable of putting me or one of the other guys in our places if we made remarks she thought were really out of line.

Instead of heavy confrontation, she would listen and wait until she had the chance to talk. Then she'd make her point.

Other guys commented on this, and I noticed a softening of their tone, demeanor, and posturing—at least in front of her. I know how she did it because she did it to me too.

Gradually, she began to change how I talked about and saw the world. Maybe it wasn't such a bad place. Maybe other people and cultures had value.

Don't get me wrong. I have no sympathy for terrorists and tyrants who kill innocent people, especially women and children. But talking to Jen helped me see others—even the enemy—as human beings instead of just targets. That maybe they saw themselves as patriots, or obeying God's will. Maybe they thought of themselves as the good guys, and that we were the bad guys. Maybe they dreamed of going home to their wives and children, too.

We grew closer every month. When shooting on location, she would always ride with me and wait for me to walk her back to the hotel. Even surrounded by other people involved in the videos, we spent most of the time together. Hardly an hour went by that there weren't texts and phone calls between us.

I should have been happy about that and in a way, I was, but it also worried me. I was afraid I would just screw up her life, like I'd screwed up my own marriages. Still prone to fits of rage and self-contempt. Still in spiritual and physical pain. I didn't want to pull Jen down with me.

As I sat there in the parking garage, the gun in my hand, tears in my eyes, I thought about all the things that were wrong with me. I thought of the times I had considered suicide but never pulled the trigger. Clearly, now, it would be better for everybody if I was gone. I'd experienced suicidal ideation since Mogadishu, but I don't think I really wanted to die. I just didn't know how to live anymore, and I had made up my mind that this was the best solution.

I turned the gun over, studying how it fit so naturally in my hand. How many times had I fired it, or one like it, in training and in combat over the years? How many lives had I taken with it? What was one more—my own—in the scheme of things?

I wondered how best to accomplish the deed. Should I put the barrel in my mouth? Maybe between the eyes? Or what about the side of my head?

Don't fuck it up, I told myself. I'd heard all sorts of horror stories. The guy who tried to kill himself with a shotgun, but the gas escaping the barrel ahead of the 00 buckshot had pushed his head back, blowing off his face, but he'd survived. Other stories debating gun in the mouth versus to the side of the head noted the instances when a poorly placed bullet left the shooter in a vegetative state. I didn't want to become even more of a burden if I didn't get it done right.

I wasn't going to leave a note. My last act of selfishness. I figured no one cared anyway. If I felt bad about something, it was making a mess for the rental car company to have to clean up.

I sat with my hand shaking, yet my mind was now still. Blank. It was time to get it over with. But just then there was a buzzing on my cell phone letting me know I had a text message. I glanced at the phone. It was from Jen.

Where are you?

Ignoring it. I lifted the gun.

Another buzz.

Hey! Why aren't you in the lobby? Are you okay?

FUCK! *No, I'm not okay. I want to die.* But I didn't respond.

BUZZ. We're waiting for you.

Man, that girl understood how to get me to react. In the short time we'd known each other, she grasped that I had a thing about showing up where I was supposed to be, when I was supposed to be there. Twenty years in the Unit will do that to you.

Looking back on that moment, I realize that I probably wanted to be saved. And if there was anyone in my life at that time who could have pulled me back from the brink, it was Jen. I was drowning and while part of me wanted to let go and end the suffering; another part of me reached for the lifeline she tossed.

I texted back. On my way. And placed the gun back under the seat.

Sitting there for a moment, I found myself shaking, cold and covered in sweat. I'd almost done it. A few more seconds and I would have. My pain would have stopped and, I thought, everybody else would be relieved.

As if in a fog, I got out of the car and walked to the hotel, heading straight for the lobby bar. Everybody was there, and already well into the night's debauchery.

When I walked over to Jen, she gave me a concerned look. "Are you okay?" she asked.

"Yeah, yeah…just, uh, smoked from a long day," I replied. I could tell she didn't believe that was all there was to it, but she dropped it.

I wasn't in much of a party mood, coming that close to killing yourself does that, and we ended up sitting off to ourselves at the bar, just talking. I didn't explain about what I'd been doing in the car or that were it not for her well-timed text, I'd have been dead. If I'd done it right. Brains splattered all over the inside of a rental car, but my pain gone. I don't even remember what we talked about, but I was grateful she was there.

*   *   *

I DIDN'T TELL HER ABOUT the suicidal ideation for several months, not until after we'd spent the weekend together in St. Louis right before the twentieth anniversary reunion for the Battle of Mogadishu veterans.

By the time we met in St. Louis, we were in love. I still wrestled with whether that was a good idea for her sake. And, in fact, she said she had tried to avoid falling for me too but saw something in me that she wanted. She and her husband were splitting and going through hell as they untangled the business, as well as emotional web of their lives. But he already had a new girlfriend and they eventually managed to stay friends and good co-parents.

Up to this point, I hadn't gone into much detail about Mogadishu or Iraq, but Jen knew that I wrestled with a lot of demons. She'd heard me cry out in my sleep, fighting unseen enemies, and dealing with guilt and ghosts. One night she'd tried to wake me from a nightmare and narrowly missed getting punched by quickly rolling out of bed and onto the floor. After that, if she wanted to wake me from a nightmare, she did it by yelling or throwing a pillow.

When she first brought up Somalia at the outdoor table in the Clayton District, I was okay with it. As long as I stuck to the usual lines of "it was chaotic and long," I was okay. But it hit me like an IED when she asked me, "What was it like?"

It instantly took me back to October 1993 when I walked into my house after returning from Somalia and my first wife asked me the same question. Back then I'd broken down and sobbed, only to see the look of shock and confusion on her face. I'd quickly pulled myself together and never talked about it again, except with other veterans of the battle, and a few cursory replies to questions from curious younger operators.

I didn't bring it up with Brandy, who wouldn't have cared, and I stopped trying with Christine, who would have told me to leave my job at work. But when Jen asked, it was as if the dam holding back the waters of that silence began to crack.

I was embarrassed when my eyes teared and I choked up. But instead of shock, or confusion, or telling me she didn't want to hear about it, Jen listened. Then when I wiped at the tears and apologized for being weak, she grabbed my hand and assured me, "It's not weak to cry."

With that the dam burst, and I couldn't have held back the flood-waters of my misery if I'd tried. Tough guy. Elite warrior. Best of the best. *Sine Pari.* I sobbed like a child at an outdoor table in a tony area of St. Louis's financial district, with other patrons surrounding us and people walking by on the street.

Over the next two hours, I poured my heart out. I wasn't looking around for escape routes or using a salad fork to take out a bad guy. I was talking about my feelings for maybe the first time since before I joined the Army. It flowed out of me, and if I tried to stop, she encouraged me to keep going. Get it all out.

Not once during that time did Jen act like she had heard enough, or that she thought I was demented or weak. She assured me that anyone who had been through what I had seen, and done, would have also responded like I did. That it was completely normal. She stood in the torrent of what came out like a boulder in a stream as the waters of my PTSD dashed against her, sweeping off to either side. From that point forward, I would always think of her as my rock.

Finally, I ran out of words. We returned to the hotel and got ready for the evening. She was taking me to a jazz club, something I'd never experienced. She had a love and appreciation for music, she was an old soul with a young heart. Wild and free yet wise and deep. She was taking me into her world more and more, and I liked it.

As she fell asleep in my arms that night, I was so grateful that this woman had listened to me and allowed me to cry without judging me. I was in love, but with that realization came guilt for what I was sure would follow. I'd just knew I would wreck her life. I was an angry, aggressive, alcoholic loser. Some sort of monster who had mutated out of a sweet kid from Indiana.

Still, when I left for the reunion in Fayetteville, I had hopes that Jen and I would somehow find a way. I didn't think I deserved her, but I wanted to try.

Spilling my heart out to Jen in St. Louis was not a cure for PTSD. It was like lancing a wound and draining an evil black fluid from my soul. But the infection was still there and would continue to fester.

Maybe part of what made Jen so understanding was that she had her own PTSD to deal with. She'd been raised by a mother who was raised by a father who passed down unresolved anger and issues to their families. She was relentlessly bullied in middle school and was raped when she was eighteen years old. That was the straw that broke her and sent her into a self-destructive cycle that rivaled my own.

It doesn't matter how you get PTSD, when you've got it, you've got it. I always tell people that, if you broke your arm in Iraq or Iowa what does it matter? It's still a broken arm that needs to heal. She didn't know the hell of war, and I could never understand the trauma of rape. But we understood some of where each of us was coming from.

A month after the St. Louis weekend, we were talking on the phone when I told Jen about that evening in the parking garage when I'd contemplated suicide. I sort of just blurted it out.

At first, she didn't believe me. It was so out of left field and off the topic we'd been discussing, but I suddenly felt the need to unload that burden.

"You saved me when you texted me that day. I was sitting in the car about to pull the trigger and your text stopped me."

Jen still couldn't wrap her head around it. She thought I was making some dark joke and kept asking if I was serious. She probably didn't want to believe how truly messed up I was, and I know it was hard for her to think of me sitting in the car, so miserable and lost that I was psyching up to kill myself.

In a perfect world, I would have been happy with my relationship with Jen. But PTSD is a thief. In addition to the depression and anger, it robs you of your sense of security and self-worth. It even steals your ability to feel like you deserve good things to happen in your life.

So, you push back. You sabotage anything good. You tell yourself that this can't last so I'm going to end it now, before it ends some other way and I get hurt. Or before I hurt someone else. You unleash the beast of self-fulfilling prophecy.

As I dreaded, the beast did return to nearly tear us apart when, two years later, Jen and I got married. In January 2014, we'd started our own military training company with former Task Force 160 pilot; the guys ran the training, Jen was in charge of filming and production.

We'd both worked our way through our divorces and were in the throes of a new, exciting love affair. We didn't live together. She was still in St. Louis and busy shooting and editing the missions we went on together, and I was based in Savannah though traveling a lot for my job, most of the time with Jen.

I was grateful we worked together which made the contracting work fun again, since I could see it through her eyes. A fresh perspective.

The problem was I was pulling her into my world, not the other way around. When we got together, especially around my friends, we partied like college students on spring break. I liked having this smart, beautiful blonde girlfriend on my arm, and she liked being with a "bad boy."

It was fun. Too much at times. We worked hard, we played harder. But PTSD was always lurking around every corner waiting for the opportunity to fuck up what I had with this woman who was becoming the most important person I'd ever had in my life.

We would drink. Fight. Wake up. I'd say sorry. She'd say, *"It was the booze. Maybe we shouldn't drink so much?"* But we did. And it would happen again and again. I didn't know it at the time, but I was self-sabotaging this relationship that felt too good to be real, because deep inside, I kept waiting for her to leave.

However, Jen accepted my proposal, and we started to plan out our lives together. I would move to St. Louis, so Jen began searching for the house we would share with Luke, Claudia, and, hopefully, Thomas. She knew city living wouldn't be good for my PTSD and started looking in the hilly suburban area that she grew up in.

The next time I visited St. Louis we looked at a few houses and fell for one of them. We put in a lowball offer and the couple accepted. We started the loan process but found out on a Friday that we couldn't get a VA loan unless we were married. It had to be done by the Monday of the following week, just a little more than a week away.

Jen immediately got to work ordering a dress and making plans. It wasn't what we wanted. We'd planned on tying that knot in Bora Bora or Tahiti at the end of the year. But we didn't want to lose the house either.

When Jen arrived in Savannah the next Thursday, I was in a bad mood and treated her coldly. Even though she'd handled all the planning, including finding a justice of the peace to marry us on Tybee Island beach, and a photographer to record it all, I acted like I was the one who was being inconvenienced. I didn't know why, but stress and anxiety took over.

Was I making a mistake? Worse, was she? Would I fuck it up again? Could I survive the pain of losing her? I compensated by hiding in my shell and pushing her away.

On Friday, we left my apartment and went to a hotel near the river downtown. It was a warm sunny day, so after we checked in, we went for a walk. I was quiet and she didn't push. Then it was time to get ready and head for Tybee Island.

We were trying to time the ceremony for the sunset so with a little time to spare, we stopped at Jen's favorite beach restaurant and had a drink. We then headed for the beach where it had just rained, which cleared the beach. So, when we arrived, and the rain had stopped, we had it all to ourselves.

It was a beautiful ceremony. We'd both written our own vows and then posed for photographs after. If you saw the pictures now, you'd see a happy, good-looking couple obviously very into each other and looking forward to living happily ever after. It was all very romantic, except it was also an illusion.

After we were done at the beach, we'd arranged to meet some friends at a downtown restaurant near the hotel. When we got there, I started drinking like I was afraid the bar would run out of liquor before I was ready to stop.

I don't know why I was so intent on getting blasted. Some people can't handle pain, I couldn't handle joy. As a result, I have only the fuzziest recollection of what happened that night, burying it, perhaps, in shame. Jen, on the other hand, remembers it all.

Apparently, I spent the whole evening sitting at a table talking to someone else's wife—a person I didn't have any interest in—and paid no attention to my own bride. I didn't talk to her. I didn't dance with her. And when she'd finally had enough of being ignored and wanted to go back to our hotel room, I got angry.

We were only a short distance from the hotel, just a block or two. Jen let me know what she thought of being ignored. It embarrassed me and made me feel ashamed, both triggers for my anger response. I flew off the handle during our walk, ranting and yelling.

Reaching the lobby of the hotel, I told her I was going to the room. "You can do whatever the fuck you want," I yelled.

I caused enough of a scene that the front desk manager motioned to her to see if she was okay. Embarrassed, she nodded and quickly moved us to the elevator.

As soon as we reached the room, I pushed her out of my way, causing her to fall onto the bed. When she got up, I was in her face. Knowing how I look when interrogating prisoners, it must have been terrifying, especially when I punctuated my words by jabbing her shoulder hard with my fingertips.

At some point, I threw a glass makeup container, shattering it against the wall. Only then did she escape to the bathroom and lock the door, while I raved outside like a lunatic.

Curled up in a ball on the bathroom floor in her wedding dress, Jen wondered if she should try to leave and stay the night at my apartment. But she decided that if I woke up and she was gone, I might kill myself. So instead she cried herself to sleep, only coming out of the bathroom once to check on me after the room fell silent.

Emerging from the bathroom in the morning, she found me passed out on the bed and woke me up. She said she was leaving.

I didn't remember the fight or what I'd done, but I could see by the look on her face that it was something horrible. When she told me what had happened, I collapsed onto my knees and begged forgiveness.

Jen stood there with tears streaming down her face; a face that was normally bright and happy was now hurt and scared. She said she didn't trust me anymore and that I'd frightened her. She'd realized she had married a man whose mood could turn on a dime from "happy Tom" to "Unit Tom," a man who could kill her in an instant if he lost it.

She wanted to spend the day thinking about it but told me she was considering going to the courthouse on Monday and having the marriage annulled. It wasn't a threat to make me feel bad, but she was afraid that the next fight might result in something worse than bruises.

I told her that I was a complete piece of shit, "a devil" who didn't deserve an angel like her. I said the only good thing that could come of my life would be to end it, which just made her angry. Now, she said, I was trying to hold suicide over her head. I tried to take it back; I wanted desperately to take it all back.

We packed up the hotel room, picking up eyeshadow and makeup that had been thrown around the night before. As we got in the car to leave, I asked her if we could go to the beach where we'd just married. She didn't want to at first but agreed after I kept begging.

On the way over, she was so quiet. Normally, she would have been talking a mile a minute and cracking jokes. There was none of that, and I just felt doomed. Not even a day and I'd already fucked up marriage number four.

Arriving at the beach, we walked to a swing that we always sat on. I asked if I could hold her hand, but she told me, "No. I'm not ready for that yet."

We sat quietly for some time, and then she said that she wasn't going to leave me. She wanted to go home and sort out what had happened and then we would talk about next steps.

After she got back to St. Louis, we spoke on the phone. She said she could forgive me, but she wouldn't go through that again. She would only stay if I got help.

I eagerly accepted her conditions. I knew that I needed to change. If I couldn't defeat PTSD, I was going to lose the one person in the world who I not only loved but whose love might be able to save me.

Prior to our marriage, I'd agreed that I should seek counseling for anger management, but I'd kept putting it off. I didn't want to put in the work to get better. But now, with everything on the line, I called first thing Monday morning and was seeing a therapist that afternoon.

It was a small step, and alone would have meant nothing. PTSD wasn't something that you cured by a few sessions on a couch with a shrink. It wasn't a puppy you smack with a rolled-up newspaper and it behaves. I was a ravening monster that would consume everything it got near and would not be easily or quickly defeated.

I was going to be fighting the biggest battle of my life and wondered if I was up to the task. I'd been through a lot of brutal selection processes in my military career with Special Forces and the Unit. Yet I knew that neither of those was going to compare to the selection process in front of me if I wanted to preserve my marriage to Jen.

Once again, the odds were against me. All I could do was start by putting one foot in front of the other and, hopefully with her by my side, get to other side of the mountain.

CHAPTER TWENTY-SIX

November 9, 2017
US Capitol Building, Washington, DC

STANDING AT THE FRONT OF THE HEARING ROOM off the Capitol Visitor Center I scanned the faces of the crowd gathering to hear me speak. As usual, I was assessing the situation by trying to make eye contact with every person who entered the room, gauging their level of interest.

Seven years removed from the Unit, discerning the intentions of people in rooms and crowds, or for that matter crossing a street toward me, was still second nature.

Old habits die hard. They and superior training had kept me alive through hundreds of operations in some of the most dangerous environments in the world. Nor would the habits of a lifetime let me go now that my mission was trying to get the word out about post-traumatic stress (PTS) and the growing epidemic of suicide among combat veterans.

Even walking up to the US Capitol building entrance that morning, I'd noted with professional detachment a security officer standing with his back to me facing the building, instead of watching for danger approaching from outside. The butt of the young man's

283

sidearm was exposed, just waiting for someone to take it and start shooting.

It was chilly that morning and I saw another guard with his hands in his pockets. *"And that's where they'd still be when he died,"* I'd growled under my breath to Jen as we walked past the security detail while they chatted among themselves.

Once inside, I relaxed as much as I'm ever able, though the hyper-vigilance that is part of my internal struggle never sleeps. Probably better than most, I knew that the guards and the metal detectors were all only an illusion of safety. Just like security at airports and ballgames and shopping malls—mere props to ward off the specter of terrorism and make people feel protected, or in the Unit's parlance, "All Secure."

In my experience, "all secure" is a relative term, and fleeting, in a dangerous world. I'd spent nearly half of my fifty years "guarding the walls," and beyond the walls, protecting the people back home from men so evil that they couldn't conjure them up in their worst nightmares.

I'd been proud to shoulder that responsibility, but the killing, the danger, the stress, the loss of my friends, and fear had taken their toll. I could see it in the deep lines etched in my forehead; it racked my body with constant pain; and the more insidious enemy waged war on my brain with nightmares, flashbacks, paranoia, rage, sleeplessness, and violent responses to stress.

The psychological guerilla warfare going on internally had cost me three marriages, and almost a fourth, as well as my relationship with my son. It was an enemy that for years I'd tried to neutralize with alcohol and the handfuls of pills the military and then the Veterans Administration prescribed for my pain and my demons. The battle had nearly ended four years earlier in a parking garage with a gun on my lap as I considered how best to finish it. *Side of my head, or in my mouth. I don't want to fuck this up.*

Only an innocent text from Jen, who was now seated to my left at the table in front of the rows of seats, my "force of nature," had saved me. And she'd kept saving me, sticking with me when she had every reason to leave. She'd even changed careers to learn everything she could about PTS and how to help me with lifestyle changes and getting me off the pills and into counseling.

She was as committed as I was to this last mission to save as many of my brothers and sisters in arms as possible. That's why we were in the nation's capital, hoping someone who mattered would listen.

This morning's audience comprised mostly young staffers from congressional and senate offices, sent to take notes and report back. As I studied their faces, I wondered if they even cared about our cause, this last mission, to push for better diagnosis and treatment for PTS and other mental health issues that were driving more than twenty veterans a day to commit suicide. *Nearly eight thousand a year, more in that period of time than died in the wars in Afghanistan and Iraq combined over the past fifteen years.*

Could Jen and I get them to understand how many lives—not just soldiers, but their families, and their communities—were damaged and destroyed by an enemy more deadly to our troops than all the terrorists we'd faced over the past two decades?

Or would they get bored and go back to texting their friends about things that mattered in their safe, normal lives? Would they look up and see weakness or strength when my voice inevitably cracked, and when the tears sprang unstoppable to my eyes while I fought for control?

Would they smile politely and then return to work uninspired by my message? Or would they go back to more senior staff members, and the policy wonks, and from there would what I had to say reach the desks and ears of the politicians?

This is an epidemic, but does anybody care?

It was time to begin, a young woman, Emily Blair, a lobbyist for the National Alliance for Mental Illness specializing in veterans' issues, walked over to the podium to introduce us—"retired Command Sergeant Major Tom Satterly, and his wife Jen." I squeezed

Jen's hand for strength and stepped to the podium. I looked down at the papers on which I'd typed my speech, rehearsing it over and over again, even when pressing my pants that morning. I could already feel the tears gathering as I looked back up and began.

A lot of water had passed under the bridge in the three years since I'd nearly torpedoed my marriage to Jen. It was a testament to Jen's toughness, as well as her love, that she didn't walk away completely, or simply stay on the sidelines while I worked my way through my issues. Strength comes in many forms, hers was compassion and empathy. I would be the beneficiary of this as she became my greatest advocate and champion, but so would thousands of other combat veterans and their families.

Starting with the special operators she met when we were working for the "zombie company," but especially after we started our new company in January 2014, Jen got to know a lot of special operations veterans with the same kind of issues, both physical and psychological, I had. She has a knack for getting people, including elite warfighters, to open up in ways that they won't around other people, even their own spouses.

What might have begun as just joking and drinking after hours with these vets, would often end with her talking to them in some quiet corner of a bar. Or they'd ask for her number so that they could talk to her in private after they got home.

It wasn't easy on her listening to a tough guy break down talking about a friend's suicide, or going through yet another divorce and shattered family, or the black hopelessness of never being happy again.

I would tell her she was taking on too much, sometimes talking to five or six combat veterans a day from the time she woke up until late into the night. I know that sounds like a low number considering how many there are out there who need help, but each guy had his own story and she wouldn't put a time limit on them pouring their hearts out. It didn't matter what I said, she wouldn't let one go by without talking to them. If they asked for help, she was there. Period.

The more she got involved, the more a voice in her head started telling her, *"You have GOT to help. You HAVE to do something."* She began researching PTS and other combat-related health issues and was surprised at how little information was available.

In September 2015, Jen secured a scholarship from the David Lynch Foundation for both of us to take transcendental meditation classes. We were both dealing with PTS from our own experiences and she thought that she could be of more help to me, if she could also deal with her own issues. Although it took some time to get used to sitting quietly, with my instructor's help, I noticed a reduction in my stress levels and anxiety within the first week or two.

As much as transcendental meditation helped, it became clear to us that PTS was a complex and multifaceted affliction and that no one technique, program, or treatment was sufficient to deal with all the issues. But even the counselors, and psychiatrists, and other "experts" couldn't agree on how to treat it. And unless they were located near a large military facility, their only exposure was the sort of PTS seen by the general public—such as violent crime or vehicle accidents—not the particular sort of combination of trauma, fear, stress, and duration experienced by combat veterans.

In July 2016, Jen quit her job as the director of film and photography at the company we had co-founded two years earlier to go to school to become a certified health coach. From her research, Jen had become increasingly convinced about the role good nutrition and a healthy lifestyle could play in the healing process.

I continued on with the company I co-founded, which require a lot of traveling to training areas. Sometimes I would be gone for weeks at a time. But I was tired of it and worried that if I kept that pace up, I'd lose Jen and the family we were building. But like so many other veterans, I didn't know what else to do.

It all came tragically together for me one night in January 2017 when I got a call from a friend who'd also been in the Unit. "Jon Hale's dead. He killed himself."

"What the fuck!" At first, I didn't believe it.

I'd lost contact with Jon after he retired and moved back to Ohio with his wife and three daughters. In the years that followed, I'd heard rumors about drug use. Some of his friends from the Unit, concerned about the reports, drove to visit him but were turned away by Regina. *"He's fine,"* she told them. *"I'm helping him."* So, they'd left without seeing him, unaware that his demons were also hers and that they both needed help.

Then came the strange news that Jon had faked his own suicide by pretending to hang himself. Apparently, he wanted more drugs than were being prescribed and that's how he thought he could get them.

In early January, there'd been another call. Regina had died from a drug overdose. Three weeks later, I got another call. Jon had really gone through with it.

Devastated by the news, I struggled to comprehend how such a strong man, a supreme warrior, brave and indefatigable in combat, had been brought so low. But in the end, it wasn't so hard for me to understand. The details might have been different, but I knew what he was dealing with. I didn't do other drugs, but I'd tried to mask the pain with alcohol. It wasn't the drugs that killed him, though, it was the PTS. The same enemy who almost got me that evening in the parking garage.

I'd been saved then by Jen, and as I reeled from the news about Jon, I couldn't help but think if only he'd had someone like her to text or call him in that moment of truth. Back then I wasn't connecting the dots to PTSD.

In fact, I didn't think I had it. I'd actually been told by an Army psychiatrist that I didn't because I'd been willing to go back to war and stand beside my brothers. My thought process was that I was a fuck-up—worthless to my family, my friends, and the Unit. I was hurting so much mentally and physically that I just wanted it to stop. But I didn't consider that maybe there was a reason I was in such pain, except that I was weak.

Jon's obituary in a local newspaper gave no hint that he'd been struggling. It said only that he was born January 18, 1961, in Bellefontaine, Ohio. That he graduated Xenia High School in the spring of 1979 and joined the Army that October. That he married his high school sweetheart, Regina, in June 1980. And that he was survived by his parents, his siblings, and three daughters, Mackenzie, Katie, and Allison.

As for his military career, it noted that he'd been a Ranger—with no mention of the Unit—and that he'd received the Legion of Merit and the Bronze Star with Valor. Missing were the ghosts that haunted his dreams, the screams he heard in the night, the images that played over and over in his mind. There was no discussion of the fear and stress and the loss of his friends, or his need to blunt the edges of his pain with drugs.

Jon's suicide dredged up a lot of memories for me. I thought about how he, Earl, and Robin were so close, closer than brothers.

Now all three of them were gone far too early in life. The first two in their thirties, and Jon was only fifty-five.

PTSD had done what the Somalis, the Iraqis, the terrorists, tyrants, and drug lords had not been able to accomplish—killed that great American hero. I was lost in the tragedy of it and spilled my guts, and a lot of tears, to Jen who held me as I sobbed like a child.

Jon Hale's suicide roiled the Unit. I knew because I talked to guys who were still in the Unit or in contact with his other friends. No one wanted to believe it. He'd been one of the Mogadishu vets, a legend in the Unit known for his courage and dependability. But still no one talked about the enemy that killed him, no one said anything about PTSD.

I realized how close I came to being Jon. Lifeless and gone, with family and friends left to deal with the aftermath. I knew that something had to be done. I wanted to stop this and help those who felt there was no hope. But I also had to face my own demons and pain, and at least start on the road to complete health, before I could help anyone else.

It was certainly clear that something had to be done. According to the VA, more than twenty-two veterans were killing themselves *a day*! That was more than double the national average among civilians. Terrorists had not been as effective at killing American soldiers as PTSD; in fact, just the yearly suicide rate for combat veterans was higher than all the casualties of the Iraq and Afghanistan wars over the past eighteen years combined.

The statistics on the number of veteran suicides in a day might have even been low. Not all suicides are reported as such, if they're reported to any national databank at all. There's also the difficulty of determining how many of those suicides are tied to combat-related PTSD. Because a lot of the underlying symptoms can also be present without PTSD—such as depression, chronic pain, addiction, or negative life events, such as divorce—it is difficult to separate what suicidal ideation is combat stress related.

Whatever the number, it was an epidemic. Jen and I realized that we had to be part of the solution, in some way; we had to help. In April 2017, Jen started looking into creating a nonprofit organization to be a resource guide for those lost in looking for ways to heal from combat trauma. Initially, we saw this as a clearinghouse for information that was out there on PTSD.

In May 2017, Jen got her certification as a certified health coach and started me on a program of taking pharmaceutical-grade natural supplements and regular exercise. The concept was like choosing what fuel to put in a nice car; what goes in the tank, runs the machine. Bad fuel equals bad performance. It all starts in the gut and, as she pointed out, I had been neglecting mine for far too long.

Almost immediately, I began noticing a difference in mood and joint pain. I was sleeping better, had more energy, and lost thirty-five pounds in five weeks.

I began telling others about my results, starting with close friends, but then posting on social media. Before I started the program, I was taking twelve different pills prescribed by the VA for everything from high cholesterol and blood pressure, to depression, sleeplessness, and acid reflux. Within weeks I was off all of them when my blood tests came back and said I didn't need the cholesterol or blood pressure medication.

Other veterans started coming out of the woodwork, contacting Jen to learn how they could help themselves. Hundreds reported back that they'd tried the supplements along with diet and exercise and got similar or better results.

Jen wasn't just passing on nutritional advice. She was literally spending ten hours a day, seven days a week on the telephone talking to vets. It would usually start with a conversation about their physical health but almost always ended up talking about what was going on in their heads and in their personal lives.

Tough guys, battle-hardened killers every one of them—Special Forces, Rangers, SEALs, Marines, the Unit—men who would have never admitted weakness to each other, or even their own spouses, discovered Jen's den-mother nature. "Taking care of her boys," she was nonjudgmental and empathetic; they could, and did, tell her everything, including their affairs and the things that haunted their sleep. She'd laugh with them and cry with them, and when that call was over, she'd pick up the phone and move on to the next.

In some ways it was like listening to her husband a thousand times over. *I'm angry. I can't sleep. I fly off the handle over the smallest issues. I drink too much. I fuck around on my wife. My kids hate me. I got a DUI. I can't hold down a civilian job. I'm ashamed. . . . I want to kill myself.*

Some calls were tougher than others. Daryl S. was a kind soul. Everyone in the Unit talked about how he was the nicest guy to ever walk the hallways. It took him a few calls to Jen, though, before he got around to telling her about the darkest time in his life.

Daryl's son, a combat medic, had committed suicide on the front lawn of his parents' home shortly after returning from a deployment to Afghanistan. Daryl had been home at the time and was administering CPR on his twenty-one-year-old boy when the ambulance arrived.

The paramedics, he told Jen, were confused because he was so unemotional as he futilely worked to save his son's life. He'd explained that he'd done triage many times, on many others he loved. And like so many of those others, he had not been able to save his son.

Daryl was lucky. He had a strong, loving wife, and they took turns falling apart. But after a few years of trying, the stress and trauma came crashing down on him. He was lost in a thick fog of hopelessness. His nightmares were becoming more frequent, and he couldn't shake the things he saw and did when he was in service. He told Jen he kept seeing the faces of the people whose lives he took. There was no escape.

Despite all that, he said that he wanted to be happy, he just didn't know how to go about it anymore. Like most of the people she talked to, he called because he saw our posts on Facebook and wanted to know how he, too, could get his life back.

Whatever she told him to do—whether nutrition, exercise, meditation, sleep practices, books to read—he did it. And slowly he began coming back to a happier and healthier self. He could think more clearly, and sleep better. "You changed me," he told her in a call. "You're the foundation for my change." She laughed and said, "Hey I think you just created our new slogan." The best part of hearing her on calls is the laughter. They both need it, everyone needs it.

As she had done for me, Jen was creating a safe space that existed nowhere else in their lives. The volume of calls grew exponentially. One guy would tell his buddy, who would tell two more.

All that outpouring of emotion was taking a toll on Jen, too. She cried a lot along with her boys. I'd find her perched on the edge of the bed, or strangely—so I thought—in the bedroom closet, in tears. After finding her in the closet a few times, I asked her why she went there to talk and cry.

At first, she said she didn't know, and hadn't thought about it. It's just where she happened to go during some of the calls to find some quiet time and so the kids wouldn't hear her talking to the guys about the dark stuff they were going through; and she definitely didn't want them to see her in tears. But then she remembered that when her mother would fly into one of her rages, "I would hide in my closet. I guess I find it comforting when confronting something difficult."

Jen wasn't all about just a sympathetic ear and gentle advice sometimes. She gave these guys the tough love they needed to hear. As she'd write blogs, messages on social media, and during phone calls, her message was clear:

> You can't just face your demons; you have to expel them. Not all of them will want to go. And you won't always feel like going to battle with the shit buried deep down. It's hard work. It's exhausting work. It's dark work. It's fucking miserable at times. But staying where you are isn't an option if you want any kind of a life.
>
> The pain of your past won't go away in the future unless you deal with what's making you miserable today. The stuff you're carrying around is a heavy load on others who love you, too.
>
> At the end of the day, and the end of the week or month, every ounce of progress, every step in the right direction will add up to something significant. You're in the driver seat, your foot is either on the gas or the brake.

In August 2017, we filed the paperwork to create the All Secure Foundation. The "foundation" part we'd got from Daryl's comment to Jen. The thinking was that any strong structure started with a strong foundation and went up from there.

When we were thinking of what to call this foundation, Jen asked me for different military terms. She had named several companies and come up with hundreds of logos and slogans in her advertising career, but she couldn't come up with a name that would mean something to what we were trying to accomplish.

One day, she came charging into my office and asked if there was some call over the radio we'd use to indicate that "everything is okay."

"Yeah, 'All Secure.'"

"*That's it!*" she said. We both knew at that moment it was perfect.

With that settled, she started working on a logo for the foundation and ended up using the tattoo we both got on a warm day in October on her thirty-ninth birthday.

Jen wanted something to represent the strength it took for both of us to deal with the trauma we'd suffered in our lives. It was an old symbol she found of an arrow and infinity symbol. It meant that even when an arrow was drawn back in a bow, like being drawn back by life, in truth the arrow is gaining the strength to go forward to the target.

We envisioned All Secure as a resource library for PTSD, addiction, relationships, health, nutrition and wellness, and even jobs. Jen had such a difficult time trying to find help dealing with me, now she decided to put it all up on a website for others. But the initial vision we had continued to evolve, including the way we looked at and labeled this insidious illness.

In the fall of 2017, we like many other mental health groups, as well as organizations devoted to helping veterans, dropped the "D" from the term post-traumatic stress disorder. The word "disorder" implied that this issue was strictly a "mental illness" problem. And there were two difficulties with that. One was the stigma attached to mental illness; no one, especially a tough-minded warrior, wants to own that.

More importantly, however, the latest research indicated that while there are mental health issues associated with PTS, it is a physiological and biological reaction to stress that produces high levels of cortisol, the body's main stress hormone, as well as adrenal fatigue.

Cortisol helps trigger the body's fight-or-flight instinct during a crisis. But it also plays a role in managing how the body uses carbohydrates, fats, and proteins; keeping inflammation down; regulating the blood pressure; increasing blood sugar; controlling the sleep/wake cycle; boosting energy in order to handle stress; and then restoring a balance after a crisis has passed.

Normally, cortisol is important for self-preservation. However, too much of it—such as under conditions of constant stress—can lead to anxiety and depression, headaches, heart disease, memory and concentration problems, digestive issues; trouble sleeping; and weight gain.

The effects of cortisol on the body are pretty well established and can be measured. My cortisol levels were off the charts, I had adrenal fatigue, I was extremely deficient in minerals and vitamins. Just like most combat veterans, my body was completely out of whack.

Adrenal fatigue, on the other hand, is less understood and less accepted by the medical community. According to the Mayo Clinic, adrenal fatigue is "a term applied to a collection of nonspecific symptoms, such as body aches, fatigue, nervousness, sleep disturbances, and digestive problems."

Adrenal glands produce a variety of hormones essential to life. The medical term "adrenal insufficiency," or Addison's disease, refers to inadequate production of one or more of these hormones. It can be measured with blood and stimulation tests.

Taken together, the research indicates that these are the physiological and biological reasons behind PTS. And that the mental health issues associated with it—such as anger, depression, and anxiety—as well as some of the physical manifestations like sleeplessness and fatigue, are caused by these biological imbalances caused by stress.

Imagine how much cortisol and adrenaline courses through the body of a soldier in combat, especially one engaged in several missions every day for weeks and months at a time. On a personal level, cortisol and adrenaline kept me going during the Battle of Mogadishu. But in Iraq every time we got a call for another mission, every time we rolled out of the Green Zone, every door we kicked, every gunfight we got involved in, my guys and I were running on not just Rip Its and pills, but cortisol and adrenaline.

Understanding the physiological and biological causes of PTS removes the stigma of mental illness. Also, if the presence of high levels of these hormones can be identified by testing, it could lead to earlier and more accurate diagnoses of PTS. That in turn could lead to earlier and more effective treatment prior to it ruining lives, as well as maintain the combat readiness and health of our troops.

WHEN WE STARTED ALL Secure there were already a number of great organizations that helped special operations veterans, such as Warriors Heart, which provides in-house substance abuse rehabilitation for special operations veterans and first responders, and Task Force Dagger Foundation, which helps wounded, ill, and injured special operations veterans. There were groups that organized hunting and fishing trips to get veterans outside, and others that encouraged healing through artistic expression.

Each served a purpose, and the best part is it's a tight group with one goal in mind: helping special operations veterans. We didn't want to replicate what they were doing but believed there were other needs that we could meet. One of those was supporting the spouse, significant others, and families of veterans with PTS.

When Jen talked to the spouses and significant others of special operations combat veterans, she recognized stories that were so familiar to her own—the isolation and fear of loving someone and being afraid of them. Of sharing their warrior's anxiety and depression. Or the confusion of what happened to the person they married who went off to war and came back a totally different person. The frustration of not being able to help or to calm the storm down before it raged out of control again. The overwhelming sadness of watching the person you love most in the world going through such torment and pain. The fear that someday they'll decide it's too much.

Jen knew how to respond because she'd been through it all with me. As she continued taking calls from veterans, and veterans' wives

and girlfriends, she realized that for all of the groups out there helping the warfighters, there wasn't much in the way of resources or
support for the women. Yet, in many ways, they were the ones who
got the brunt of PTS. They're the ones who had to put up with the
anger, the remoteness, the drinking, the womanizing, and, far too
often, the violence.

It was great that a group existed to take veterans with PTS on
hunting trips. But who was paying for the wife to get away and take
a break from the trauma of living with PTS?

Who was going to help a woman like Regina sort out her husband's demons without succumbing to her own demons? Who's
helping her and her kids when he's raging at the top of his lungs and
breaking things?

A PERFECT EXAMPLE OF THE need to do something for the families of warfighters was our friend Teddy L., the former Special Forces
operator who was with us in the car that day when I contemplated
killing myself. A big loveable country boy, he'd been my drinking
buddy in the dark days before I met Jen, and they'd become close,
too. But he was also an alcoholic, like me.

I knew Teddy had his own demons, but we didn't talk about them
back in the day. We buried them in a flood of booze and partying.

After I got married and moved to St. Louis, Teddy took a job in
Fayetteville and we didn't see each other much anymore. I'd call
him sometimes, and he seemed off, but I couldn't quite put my finger
on what was wrong.

Jen and Teddy were close, too. But when we visited Fayetteville
over the years, he always had an excuse not to see us, which just
wasn't like him.

Then one day, he called Jen. He was crying. His issues were far
worse than either of us knew; he was using every drug imaginable—
heroin, cocaine, meth, you name it. He'd also been cheating on his

wife and was ashamed. He said he wanted to kill himself. Jen stood there heartbroken for him and his family and shocked that we didn't know any of this until now.

I was away conducting training when Jen phoned to tell me about the call. We knew we needed to get him into the Warrior's Heart twelve-week program. But it cost a lot of money, thirty thousand dollars, and Teddy didn't have that kind of money.

Then I had an idea. I told Jen about a wealthy investor in our company who had told me just days earlier that he would like to help veterans in financial need. Jeff K. had come up to me after a motivational talk I gave for his company and thanked me for all I was doing for veterans. He'd said that if I ever needed anything to just ask.

Jen told me to pick up the phone and call him. "Maybe he'll chip in some money to help Teddy."

I did that and Jeff K. not only said he'd help, he picked up the entire tab. He only had one question, "Where do I send the check?"

Jen and I were both thrilled on behalf of our friend. She pointed out, however, that while it was great that Teddy would be getting help, he would be gone for twelve weeks leaving Suzie to take care of the kids and keep the household running. He might as well have been deployed again.

Jen asked who was going to help her? "No one," she replied to her own question. "I can't stomach this, *She* needs help. *She* needs healing."

Jen can be quite a force of nature when she gets angry, and she was riled up about this. "Well, Goddammit, that's not okay. She isn't military. She didn't sign up. She sacrificed for decades and went through hell over and over again and look where it got her."

Thinking about it for a moment, Jen made an executive decision. "We will heal the warrior *and* the family."

War and PTS affected everybody, she said. America owed it to its veterans to get them the help they need to heal, but somebody needed to look out for the "collateral damage" of PTS as well. It wasn't a political or military issue alone; it was a humanitarian crisis affecting millions of American military spouses and family members. "It's not okay to look away."

When they called to talk to her, Jen began asking the guys if they would be interested in the All Secure Foundation helping with their relationships, such as marital retreats or a retreat on PTS wellness and health. Every single one of them responded with some variation of "God yes, please. Help me with my home life."

We knew then what our primary mission would be. Rebuild the foundation at home.

Jen got to work researching therapies for families dealing with PTS in a loved one. During this time, we hired a licensed therapist who teaches in the method emotionally focused therapy (EFT). She and Jen immediately set to work creating workshop programs for warriors and their partners.

In the meantime, we were working another front to get the word out that PTS isn't a mental illness, it's a biological response to stress, and the implications of that. We were trying to navigate the difficult path to reaching a large number of people using social media but also getting out in front of people to talk about the issue.

One day, we got a call from Emily Blair, a lobbyist for the National Alliance for Mental Illness. Matt Kuntz from NAMI Montana had originally reached out to see if I would speak at an event in Montana, but he passed along my story to Emily. She told us that she specialized in veterans' issues and wanted to know if Jen and I would come to Washington, DC, to help her lobby politicians to identify PTS in veterans with biomarkers that identify inflammation in the brain to help veterans get the assistance they need immediately.

She hoped we'd also be willing to talk about our personal experiences in front of congressional staffers who, she pointed out, were the ones who worked behind the scenes on legislation for their bosses. It would mean me talking about my issues as a combat veteran suffering from PTS and Jen as the spouse caught up in the nightmare of dealing with it.

At first, I hesitated. Was I ready to talk about my failings? And what did I have to offer except being a broken soldier with issues myself. How could my story help?

While we'd been talking about me hitting the lecture circuit to raise awareness about PTS, we didn't know how or where to start. The thinking was that if I was willing to admit to needing help—a former Tier One operator with the Unit—other veterans suffering from PTS would see it was okay to seek help. But I'd hoped to start with a middle school or something where if I fucked up it would be no big deal.

Going face-to-face with politicians and their staff members and asking them to support the NAMI bill for biomarkers was intimidating. What if I let everybody down? Was I ready to talk publicly about my issues and at this level?

In spite of my fears and reservations, I said I'd do it. It was just too good of an opportunity on too big a stage to pass up. I would just have to suck it up and do my best.

As the day approached, I grew increasingly nervous, especially after meeting a former congressman from Kansas at a fundraiser. I told him about our upcoming visit to Washington DC, but he warned me not to "expect a warm welcome or anything to come of it." He said they would be cordial, but nothing would come of it. "Everything moves too slow in DC."

Fortunately, our reception was anything but chilly. The first day was a whirlwind of running from congressional office to senate office with Emily and Matt Kuntz, who was working with Senator Jon Tester, a Montana Democrat and strong supporter of veterans' issues.

We mostly met with staff members from congressional and senatorial offices who, Emily assured us, were the ones we needed to convince to get the ball rolling. They'd be putting together any recommendations for budgets and legislation to put on the desks of their bosses. Several of the politicians shook our hands upon leaving their office with a "We will do everything we can to make changes here." Some even with "We've never met with a spouse before." Which was shocking to Jen and me.

I was impressed by these bright young people and discovered that many of them were former military. When I talked about my experiences, there was a lot of head nodding that I knew came from a place of true understanding. I was proud of them for taking their leadership skills and continuing to serve their country in DC.

Our warmest reception was with Senator Patty Murray, a Democrat from Washington state. She was extraordinarily attentive when I laid out what we were trying to accomplish, but she was also very empathetic. I didn't expect that from her.

When I got to my suicide attempt and started to break down, she realized I needed a break to pull myself together. She turned to Jen and reached across the table to grab her hand.

"Now, tell me YOUR story," she said as she and Jen held hands.

Jen told her "our" story and talked about the needs of families and spouses. When she was finished, Senator Murray had a look of determination on her face. "Something will be done," she said.

By the time we finished running from office to office, we were exhausted but pleasantly surprised by the amount of interest and time each person gave us. But these were the politicians that NAMI had already identified as being receptive to veterans' issues. We were going to need to convince others if we were going to get anywhere, and our chance to do that would be our talks Emily scheduled in a briefing room in the Capitol building.

Now that the moment was almost upon me, I didn't know if I was ready. Jen and I had practiced our speeches over and over for weeks leading up to this, but that night as we walked down the street from our hotel to a little wine bar to grab something to eat and relax, I could hardly talk. I was nervous, but doing nothing was exactly what was killing veterans at a rate of more than twenty a day. We'd do it for them.

As we talked about the importance of the next morning's event, Jen gripped my arm. "This is a major moment in our lives," she said, "not because this has anything to do with us; we're just speaking for everyone out there suffering. Tomorrow isn't our day. Tomorrow is the day we say what desperately needs to be said to wake up these politicians, to wake up Americans."

As usual, she knew just what to say to inspire me. Yes, tomorrow was the day I'd speak up for my brothers and sisters in arms, and for their spouses and families.

As I stood at the front of the room, assessing the interest of those showing up, I thought about my friends who'd sacrificed their lives for this country—Earl, Matt, Jon—and so many others who were gone or suffering silently. I thought about the epidemic of suicides and the shattered families. I was afraid, afraid of messing this up, but I knew I owed it to them to try.

As a leader of men, it had always been my most important goal to bring my guys safely back from war. Now I had one more mission. I needed to do what I could, with Jen's love and support, to bring them all back home "all secure" and that's how I found the courage to step up to the podium when Emily introduced me.

I cleared my throat and looked out over the crowd. The room was packed and for the moment, I had their attention.

"We thank you for taking the time to hear our words today. It's an honor to be invited to address you on behalf of NAMI, the National Alliance for Mental Illness, and to share the unique challenges veterans face in their reintegration into civilian life. This, after sustaining mental, physical, and emotional trauma that is often misdiagnosed and untreated."

As I looked up from my notes into those expectant faces, I could already feel the emotions building up inside of me. Somewhere in the recesses of my mind, Earl was being dragged off a street in Mogadishu, a boy sat on a stairwell with an AK-47 in Iraq. Mothers wailed in grief. The wounded screamed in agony. Flags were presented to widows under bright blue Iowa skies. A daughter or son missing a parent whether by suicide or deployment or just lost in themselves.

"I can tell you from personal experience that it is true that 'there are wounds that never show on the body that are deeper and more hurtful than anything that bleeds.'"

I nearly choked on that one but cleared my throat and went on. "We all volunteered to serve our country and I hold a great reverence for it, and pride in knowing I gave the very best of myself in those twenty-five years, twenty of them in the Unit. Please hear me when I say to you that we are not done. We want more than to come home; we want to heal. We want to rebuild our lives, our relationships, and offer the leadership we've shouldered over the years to the homes and communities we live in now.

"I have a deep love and gratitude for the opportunity I was given to serve this country and provide for myself and my family. I value beyond words the friends who became family..."

The tears were starting to blur my vision and I had to blink to see the words on the paper in front of me. I hoped I wasn't making a fool of myself, crying again, this time in front of staffers with their pens and paper out. I could feel my chest and face getting hot.

"I am not the same man I was before my friends fell around me, lost to the viciousness of combat, and for years that was not a good thing. My sense of guilt, sorrow, and rage for still breathing when my brothers had died, made me someone that you are fortunate not to have known.

"You may wonder, depending on your personal experiences, why there is such difficulty in walking away from what was, and making a new life with what is. Why is it not a simple thing to retire from service and just pick up the threads of the life we left behind.

"Let me tell you my story..."

Spring 2019
St. Louis, Missouri

IT'S BEEN A LITTLE MORE than a year since I gave my talk in that congressional hearing room. I was gratified by the reception Jen and I received by the staff members, many of whom came up to us to say how moved they were and that they would relay my message and their support to their bosses.

One former Ranger who'd served in Afghanistan and was now working for a congressman thanked me for speaking out on behalf of all veterans who need help. He later told my co-author Steve Jackson that he, too, was dealing with PTS issues and that if a Special Forces guy could admit he was broken and needed help, so could he and the brothers he served with.

Since that first nerve-wracking speech, I've talked to thousands of people with dozens of organizations ranging from Congress to veteran groups, first responders, nonprofit organizations, universities, and corporations. My message: "The greatest failure is the failure to try."

As a result, we've received thousands of responses on our social media sites, as well as texts and phone calls.

Of course, we have a few favorites, like Teddy, who not only completed the program at Warriors Heart, but has also been clean and sober with the support of his lovely wife, Suzie. What's more, he did and has done so well, the program gave him a position as an ambassador spreading the word.

MEANWHILE, JEN'S WORK WITH spouses and families has been so well received that she started a new social media platform under the All Secure Foundation umbrella called Virago, which means a "female warrior spirit." She saw a need for women to support other women who are going through the same thing—loving a warfighter who is battling the demons of PTS. Just as veterans lean on each other, so should spouses.

From the early days of having Virago up on social media, the responses were so very encouraging.

"I need this in my life so much," wrote one wife.

"Thank you!!! I wish we'd found you sooner. My husband and I are coming through to the other side of hell and can finally see the light. We are stronger, closer, and more transparent with one another than we have ever been in our twelve years of marriage. Our blessings are abundant. I am so grateful. I want to help. I don't know how, but my heart yearns to help others going through it."

From another:

"I just wanted to say thank you. My husband is a Ranger. We have had four combat deployments in four years, and I have been so frustrated with the military not providing any information for care to families. We are just left to navigate it on our own, and you are offering us the support I have been searching for. We recently lost a former team leader to suicide after his wife left him. It was devastating. The lack of support is terrifying and what you are doing is appreciated more than words could ever say."

Messages like these have brought us to tears because they mean we're having a positive effect on the lives of veterans and their families.

In the meantime, our hope is the Department of Defense adopts the idea that it's okay for warriors to admit they need help and still be trusted to do their jobs.

How the military deals with these issues affects this country's wartime readiness, especially as it pertains to fighting terrorism. While our traditional adversaries, including Russia, China, North Korea, and Iran, remain a potent threat that must be countered, most of today's and tomorrow's wars are being fought against non-nation enemies and terrorists. In those cases, it will be special operations troops doing the fighting. It is in our best national interest that we look after the health of our best warriors.

In 2016, US Special Operations Forces were deployed to 138 countries—that's 70 percent of the world—and not just to the battlefields of Iraq, Afghanistan, Syria, and Africa but to counternarcotics efforts in South America and in the Far East. Though it is but a small fraction of the total conventional military, Special Operations Forces are doing the lion's share of the fighting, which means they're also experiencing the greatest impact from PTS-related issues.

Special Operations command has recognized that the pace of deployment—known as "operational tempo"—is wearing out our best warriors. As I've described, for an elite operation like the Unit, to perform at required levels, they have to spend most of their time training. Constant deployment and being stretched thin to meet global obligations reduce the Unit's readiness. And it is impossible to mass-produce special operations groups whether they are the Unit, Special Forces, Airforce PJ's, Rangers, SEALs, or Marine Raiders .

Also troubling, reliable studies suggest that the pool of possible war fighters is small, and getting smaller.

Beyond that, military recruiters polled have said that more than 70 percent of the "targeted recruiting age range" would not be eligible to serve due to health reasons, including obesity, education, criminal backgrounds, and physical appearance preferences that don't adhere to military standards.

This makes it even more imperative to take care of those we have.

On a personal level, I am far from "cured" of my PTS issues. Sometimes the whole process feels like two steps forward and one, or more, steps back.

There are good days when PTS leaves me alone. During those times, I'm happy, relaxed, calm, and motivated. I feel better physically and healthier psychologically. In spirit, I'm a little closer to that kid from Indiana and quite a bit farther from the monster who shook his wife on their wedding night.

There are bad days when I don't want to get out of bed. Those are days no one wants to be around me, though Jen is here—thick and thin.

I still deal with depression, anxiety, rapid mood swings, and fits of anger. Sleep can be elusive. I am still haunted in my nightmares by ghosts, those of my friends and those of my enemies. Jen sometimes has to wake me as I shout in my sleep, though she knows to keep her distance until I'm awake. I know I will never be free of some of what I've seen and done. We both understand it better now and realize that it will be a constant struggle. Armed with knowledge, love, and persistence, we know that we will defeat the demon that is PTS.

When I met Jen, I was taking thirteen types of pills, all of them prescribed by my former Unit doctors, Army doctors, and civilian doctors after service, for everything from depression and anxiety to pills to counteract the side effects of the other pills. I now take zero pills minus the occasional allergy medicine and keep up on the quality supplements we found that work. I have never felt better in my life.

In April 2018, we both started emotionally focused therapy (EFT) with therapist Stacey Stone to help with how we communicate with each other.

EFT has worked wonders for me on how I view my behavior and responses to stress and family events that used to send me into angry rages. We communicate more clearly now, and I can understand when I am starting to feel overwhelmed with emotions that are not properly related to the events unfolding in front of me.

In February of this year, I began transcranial magnetic stimulation (TMS) at the recommendation of another former Unit operator Scot S., who said it helped him. TMS is a noninvasive form of brain stimulation in which a changing magnetic field is used to cause electric current at a specific area of the brain through electromagnetic induction.

The treatment, which is generally accepted by Tricare, the veterans' health plan through the VA, is used to treat depression and obsessive-compulsive disorder. I have already noticed many changes, such as a reduction in anger and depression. My mid-range emotions have started to return, I sleep better, and suicidal ideation is gone.

I'm willing to try whatever works. I just know that if you do nothing, nothing will change.

It's not a comfortable process. Then again, neither is talking about my personal issues in front of crowds, or writing a book laying out my life with all its warts and shadows. But as the Ranger told Steve, if a Unit command sergeant major can open up, discuss these issues, let his "tough guy" guard down and be vulnerable—cry for God's sake—hopefully others will seek help, too. Asking for help, is not a weakness, it's a strength.

The road home to All Secure is going to be a long one for many of us. Some won't make it, but just like we've been taught since boot camp, and learned the hard way in Mogadishu, no one gets left behind. Not if we the living can help it.

We can do this. Our souls and our hearts, as well as our bodies, have blisters on them; we're wounded and exhausted, sometimes beyond human endurance. But just keep moving forward, always forward, until we are All Secure.

FROM TOM SATTERLY

I am honored to be able to acknowledge the following for being there and trusting me to get this book out. A lot of time and energy came together through dedication and hard work to make this happen.

Thank you to our editor, Kate Hartson, and the team at Hachette, especially Jaime Coyne and Sean McGowan; my literary agent, Chip MacGregor; my co-author, Steve Jackson; the Unit in which I spent more than twenty years, working with me to ensure the security of its people and missions; and, of course, all the heroic men and women with whom I have ever worked or shed blood. I also want to acknowledge those who have gone too soon in the defense of this great nation, and all the spouses who spend years alone raising families and putting up with our emotional distress when we return home for those short visits, as well as the children of the warriors, and the widows and widowers who continue on in life without their soulmates. I want to acknowledge the freedoms afforded by this great nation to allow me the ability to write this, and my family for always supporting me in my life's endeavors and more specifically my sister

Shelly Aspenson for helping with my speech to Congress and being an Ambassador to the All Secure Foundation. I want to thank my brother Steve Satterly for always lending a supportive shoulder to cry on and helping me through humor and my mother, Martha Satterly, for her strength and the toughness she gave me growing up.

I want to thank my very determined son, Thomas, for being strong and loving me through all of my absences, and understanding when I wasn't always a good father. And most of all I would like to thank my wife, Jen Satterly, for always supporting me, understanding me, and pushing me out of my security zone into a world that allows us to help so many more with our experiences. I love you, Jen.

FROM STEVE JACKSON

I would like to thank my co-author, Tom Satterly, for choosing me to write his story. It was an honor to work with him. His courage on the battlefield is legendary, but the courage he's shown battling his personal demons and then sharing that story so that others can be helped might be greater. And heartfelt thanks to Jen Satterly, who knows her husband's story better than anyone and whose insights, and efforts to keep the ship sailing forward, were invaluable.

I'd like to thank my agent, Chip MacGregor, of the MacGregor Literary Agency, who is simply the best in the business, especially at calming overwrought authors and finding homes for their work. Thanks, Chip, for believing in me. I'd also like to thank Jacqueline Burch, a friend and editor whose work on the manuscript prior to turning it in to Center Street made all the difference. And thanks to Kate Hartson at Center Street for her patience and for seeing the value in Tom's story.

Last, I'd like to thank my family and friends whose love and support keep me typing, especially Laura, who lights up my life. The dedication for this book belongs to Tom, but I'd like to dedicate my part in it to my father, Donald C. Jackson Jr. (September 1919–April 2018), Cdr. USN (Ret), another American hero. I miss you, Dad.